STUDIES IN
MODERN HEBREW LITERATURE

GENERAL EDITOR
DAVID PATTERSON

ISAAC DOV BERKOWITZ

I. D. Berkowitz. Photograph taken in 1934. By courtesy of Mrs. T. Kahana.

ISAAC DOV BERKOWITZ

Voice of the Uprooted

BY AVRAHAM HOLTZ

EAST AND WEST LIBRARY

———

CORNELL UNIVERSITY PRESS
ITHACA · NEW YORK

Published in co-operation with
the Institute for the Translation of Hebrew Literature Ltd
Tel-Aviv

First published 1973 by Cornell University Press

International Standard Book Number 0–8014–0722–2

Library of Congress Catalog Card Number: 72–3591

AT BRITAIN

Contents

Preface

THE works of Isaac Dov Berkowitz are essential reading for any student of modern Hebrew literature. His writings describe a crucial phase of modern Jewish history, and depict life in the three most important areas of Jewish settlement at the beginning of this century—Eastern Europe, the United States and Palestine. Berkowitz was an impassioned and involved observer, and through his eyes the reader is made aware of the decline of the *shtetl* in Europe, the superficiality of Jewish life in America, the aspirations entertained by the Jewish pioneers in Eretz Yisrael and the difficulties which they encountered.

Part One of this volume begins with a sketch of Berkowitz's life and times to allow the reader to set the author's work in context. The following chapters contain a critical appraisal of his achievements as a short-story writer, novelist, playwright and translator.

Part Two includes new translations of five substantial short stories, and a chapter from one of his most popular works, *Menahem Mendel in Eretz Yisrael*. It is hoped that the translations will enable the interested reader to appreciate, at least in part, the characteristic features of Berkowitz's writings. The extended bibliographical note should prove of value for serious students of modern Hebrew literature.

In Memory of my Grandfather,
Shalom ben Avraham Nadel,
and my Grandmother, aunt, uncle and cousins,
nine of six million

Acknowledgements

PERHAPS the most pleasant aspect of publishing a book is the author's privilege of expressing his indebtedness to all who have helped him during the various stages of preparing the volume and contributed towards its final shape.

Some three years ago Dr David Patterson, editor of the series *Studies in Modern Hebrew Literature*, commissioned me to write this study. Despite his manifold academic involvements, he has counselled and buttressed me through the chafing and, often, dispiriting chores of major and minor revisions. I am grateful and beholden to him.

I owe acknowledgement to my sister, Mrs Helene Kalkstein, my colleague, Dr Shoshanah Shechter, my former students, Mrs Shelley Buxbaum, Mr Simcha Kruger and Mrs Gila Landman, and particularly to Mr T. V. Parfitt of Oxford, England. Their generous assistance lightened the burden in many ways. I am grateful, too, for the valuable suggestions made by Mrs Tamara Kahana, the daughter of I. D. Berkowitz.

I am much obliged to the dedicated staffs at the Jewish Division of the New York Public Library, the Jewish Theological Seminary of America, the Hebrew University-National Library in Jerusalem and the Genazim Archives in Tel Aviv.

I appreciate the patience of Mrs B. Horovitz of the East and West Library and Mr B. Kendler of Cornell University Press.

Jewish Theological Seminary of America   A.H.
New York City
October, 1972

PART ONE

BERKOWITZ AND HIS WRITINGS

Chapter 1

A CATACLYSMIC CENTURY

THE WRITINGS of I. D. Berkowitz[1] reflect Jewish life in Russia from the end of the nineteenth century until the early years of the Russian Revolution, when Berkowitz left Europe never to return. In addition, many of his works portray Jewish life in America and Palestine during the second and third decades of the present century.[2]

The years 1885–1967, the span of Berkowitz's life, were among the most fateful in Jewish history. This period was one of great political, social, and economic upheaval in Europe, and witnessed the decline and ultimate decimation of the Jewish communities of Eastern Europe, which at the beginning of this period had been the most populous centres of Jewish life.[3]

1. Except where otherwise indicated, the citations are quoted from *I. D. Berkowitz—Writings*. Vol. 1, *Sippurim u-Maḥazot* (Tel-Aviv, 1959) includes *Menahem Mendel be-Eretz Yisrael, Maḥazot* and *Yemot ha-Mashiaḥ*; Volume 2, *Sippurei Zikhronot* (Tel-Aviv, 1963) includes *Ha-Rishonim Kivnei Adam* (originally published in 1959) and *Yom Etmol* (originally published in 1963). Hereafter volume one is cited just as *Writing*, vol. 1, and volume two or as *Writings*, by the titles included therein, i.e. *Ha-Rishonim* and *Yom Etmol*.

2. Curiously, neither Berkowitz's short stories nor his fictional letters and memoirs contain any reference to historical events after 1940—that is, no mention is made of the European holocaust, the Second World War or the establishment of the State of Israel.

3. For comprehensive studies see: S. W. Baron, *The Russian Jew Under Tsars and Soviets* (New York, 1964) particularly chapter 4; *idem*, 'The Modern Age' in L. W. Schwarz, ed. *Great Ages and Ideas of the Jewish People* (New York, 1956), pp. 315–484; *idem*, *The Jewish Community* (Philadelphia, 1942), especially chapter 3; S. M. Dubnow, *History of the Jews in Russia and Poland From the Earliest Times Until the Present Day*.

The growth of nationalism in Eastern Europe had been accompanied by a process of industrialization and urbanization which bred a plethora of revolutionary movements.[4] Many Jews participated in these new revolutionary movements, but a large part of the Jewish population left Eastern Europe and migrated in increasing numbers to the United States, England, and Palestine, which by the end of the Second World War had become major centres of Jewish life and culture. It has been estimated that in 1880 there were over seven million Jews in the world; of these some seventy-five per cent lived in Eastern Europe. Fifty years later, the same areas contained only forty per cent of a much expanded Jewry. Other parts of Europe now contained about twenty per cent and the Americas thirty per cent.[5]

A radical change in both ideology and opportunity attended the demographic shift of Jews from the confined *shtetl* to urban centres. Afforded a wider range of subjects, Jewish authors focused upon the young Jew who, caught in the maelstrom of events, contended with his environment in an effort to retain his individuality as a Jew while pursuing the charms of Western civilization.[6]

The nineteenth century also witnessed a phenomenal growth in the Jewish population of Russia. With the annexation of

trans. I. Friedlander (Philadelphia, 1916–20), vols. 2 and 3; I. Elbogen, *A Century of Jewish Life*, trans. by M. Hadas (Philadelphia, 1944); L. Greenberg, *The Jews in Russia* (New Haven, 1944 and 1951), especially volume 2; and H. M. Sachar, *The Course of Modern Jewish History* (New York, 1958).

4. A discussion of this subject is available in S. W. Baron, *Modern Nationalism and Religion* (New York, 1960); especially relevant to the present study are chapters 1 and 7.

5. Detailed statistics for this period can be found in A. Ruppin, *The Jews in the Modern World* (London, 1934), and Baron, *The Russian Jew, op. cit.*

6. A critical assessment of Hebrew literature as a mirror of the socio-historical forces that shaped modern Jewish life is provided in S. Halkin, *Modern Hebrew Literature: From the Enlightenment to the Birth of the State of Israel: Trends and Values* (New York: Schocken, new edition, 1970).

Polish territories, a widespread tendency towards early marriage and large families, and a decreasing mortality rate, the number of Jews in Russia increased from approximately 800,000 at the beginning of the century to about five and a half million by 1900. This growth in population, coupled with economic and social hardships, aggravated by governmental restrictions and the competition of new industries, led to the widespread pauperization of the Jewish community, which had relied on crafts and methods of commerce which by now had become obsolete. Berkowitz's European-based narratives reflect the fact that, by the turn of the century, as many as fifty per cent of some Jewish communities were considered indigent and in need of local charity.

The tendency towards large families and its consequences provided the social background to several of Berkowitz's works. *Ben Zakhar* (A Male Child) is entirely concerned with the birth of a ninth child and the disastrous way in which this affects the other members of the family. The shadow of extreme poverty hangs over almost every one of Berkowitz's Eastern European Jewish settings. Need and destitution figure as antagonists that inspired defiance yet frustrated all hopes.

The accession of Alexander III in 1881, and his appointment of the infamous Pobedonostsev as chief adviser, marked the beginning of a period of oppressive reaction, which continued through the reign of Nicholas II and culminated in the events of the pre-revolutionary years. Pogroms, which had once been no more than local uprisings, came to be openly tolerated and even supported by governmental bureaux and officials. The pogroms left the affected communities ravaged. Moreover, they disillusioned all those who had placed their confidence in the government and had pinned their hopes for a brighter future upon co-operation between Jews and Gentiles. Incidents of armed attacks against the Jews grew in number throughout the final decades of the nineteenth century and reached their peak in the massacres of 1903–5, the most famous of which, the Kishinev pogrom, affected some fifty thousand Jews and evoked the protest of both liberal Russians and foreign

dignitaries.[7] The first Russian Revolution, preceded by the establishment of the 'Black Hundreds',[8] brought in its trail a wave of
pogroms that spread to some 660 communities.

A crucial economic development during this period was the
steady decline of Jewish participation in petty commerce,
industry, and agriculture. This trend was accompanied by a
parallel increase in the number of Jews engaged in the liberal
professions and the civil service. Jewish shopkeepers and artisans
often became the victims of technological change. These socio-
economic developments are reflected in Berkowitz's works.
There are frequent references to grain merchants who, like the
author's father, stood at the crossroads waiting for farmers from
whom they would purchase produce for immediate resale at a
meagre profit in the highly competitive market. Also mentioned
in these works are leather tradesmen, oven-makers, smiths,
shoemakers, and tailors. The children of these merchants and
artisans, however, aspired to the more elevated positions of
skilled craftsmen and professionals. Almost every narrative
includes at least one child from the lower stratum of Jewish
society determined, despite formidable odds, to become a
doctor, lawyer, pharmacist, or, at worst, a *gymnasium* graduate.
There are, too, several examples of wealthy, middle-class
farmers and merchants who are presented by Berkowitz as
ostentatious *nouveaux-riches*.

Alexander III's programme of enforced urbanization forbade
Jews to acquire rural properties. The growing Jewish population could no longer be supported in the *shtetl*, while advancing
industrialization helped to effect a radical shift in Jewish demo-

7. Bialik immortalized these events in his poetry. See Hayyim Nahman
   Bialik, *Kol Kitvei H. N. Bialik* (Tel-Aviv, 1953), *Al ha-Shehitah*, pp.
   35–6 and *Be-ir ha-Haregah* pp. 82–5. For English renditions see I. Efros,
   Chaim Nachman Bialik, Complete Poetic Works (New York, 1948).
8. The Black Hundreds was the name given to the activist group of the
   Union of the Russian People founded in 1904 in St Petersburg. It was
   responsible for the systematic assassination of hundreds of Jewish and
   non-Jewish liberals. By 1906 the Union had 3,000 cells all over
   Russia.

graphic distribution. There was a continuous influx of Jews to urban areas such as Odessa, Kiev, Ekaterinoslav, and Vilna which became the chief centres of Hebrew and Yiddish cultural activities. Odessa's Jewish population grew almost ninefold from 17,000 to 150,000, Kiev's increased from approximately 3,000 to over 50,000, and the Jewish community of Vilna, 'The Jerusalem of Lithuania' rose from 23,000 to 72,000. By the end of the century over half the urban population of Lithuania and White Russia was Jewish.

Consequently, the *shtetl* forfeited its hold upon the younger generation. Some abandoned it with contempt, others with regret and even grief.[9] Several of Berkowitz's heroes with unabashed nostalgia contrast the now decadent *shtetl* with the *shtetl* of former times. At the same time, the image of the *shtetl* as an idealized symbol of a once tranquil society continued to beckon, aided by the nostalgia that obscured the reason for its decline. Berkowitz's essays and stories reflect both antipathy and affection towards the *shtetl*.[10]

9. An anthology of translated literary sources and records that cover a wide range of topics about East European Jewry between 1772 and 1934 is available in L. S. Dawidowicz, *The Golden Tradition: Jewish Life and Thought in Eastern Europe* (London, 1967).

10. Unfortunately Berkowitz's essays on literary, social, and political issues still remain scattered in the newspapers and journals in which they were originally published. These ambivalent attitudes are reflected in *Betokh ha-Tehumin* (Within the Pale), a series of articles by Berkowitz written under the pseudonym B. Ernst. Examples may be found in *Ha-Olam*, vol. 4, no. 44, Nov. 17, 1910, pp. 13–15; no. 46, Nov. 24, 1910, pp. 13–15, or in the author's series entitled *Pinkas Patuah* (Open Book), for example, *Ha-Zeman*, Vol. 2, no. 75, April 17, 1905, p. 4. The latter series was published under the pseudonym BRK (Barak). See also *Ha-Toren*, vol. 3, nos. 7–8, April 14, 1916, p. 2. In *Ha-Olam*, for instance, he writes, 'The *shtetl* is no longer the peaceful, blessed nest for which the city-dwellers yearn with covert passion. The Jewish *shtetl* is devoid of all meaning . . . God's mercy has abandoned it.' (vol. 5, no. 26, July 30, 1911, p. 9.) However, a contradictory mood is expressed in an unpublished letter of Dec 12, 1929 (available in the Genazim Archives, Tel-Aviv), in which he voices his disgust with Europe and nostalgia for the *shtetl*.

A growing desire for secular education was another disintegrating factor. Despite the *numerus clausus*, which had been more strictly enforced under Nicholas II, and the restrictions initiated against Jewish lawyers and doctors, the desire among younger Jews for a general education in the secondary schools and universities became more widespread. The study of Russian language, literature, and other subjects was undertaken by middle-class children and frequently attracted the more gifted children of the lower classes. By the turn of the century, over two thousand Jewish students were attending secondary schools. The legal restrictions that limited their number created a class of Jewish externs, who, although not officially classified as students, pursued their studies privately.

Several of the author's short stories and essays are devoted to the difficulties of these Jewish externs, who would often suffer extremes of privation and frustration in order to enter a university. Berkowitz described the student's suffering with considerable empathy in one of his many essays devoted to the subject.

> Only a year or so ago, these boys would have been sitting contentedly in their father's house in some small town, with Jews milling to and fro in the central square, the doors of the *Beit-Midrash* still wide open, the entire day spent in sacred studies. God was still kind and merciful, their mothers still cared for their needs, the world was simple, cloistered, warm and affectionate . . . then came the stormy winds that tore them from their moorings, and roughly tossed them into the great, teeming, perplexing city with its crowds of strange confused people; where every man is concerned with himself, skies are for ever hidden from sight, God seems to have vanished, sacred things are trampled underfoot. The new studies are difficult, impenetrable . . . the universe seems cold, remote and enormous . . . chaos reigns over the cosmos . . .[11]

In an earlier article written in 1905 in Vilna, the great centre of Jewish student life during this period, Berkowitz reproached the local Jewish community for its lack of support for these

11. *Ha-Olam*, vol. 5, no. 9, Mar. 16, 1911, p. 11.

young men who had trusted that the intelligentsia would welcome and encourage them, only to find themselves abandoned and unwanted in this, one of the largest Jewish communities in Europe.[12]

Throughout this period, slow but very definite changes were being wrought in the traditional religious education of Jewish children.[13] In most communities the *melammed*, often a ne'er-do-well turned teacher, continued to instruct his young charges in the rudiments of Hebrew reading and writing. The *Talmud Torah*, a free, charity-supported school for the poor, also retained some of its more unpleasant features. However, efforts were continually being made by enlightened instructors to remedy the ills of these traditional systems by introducing graded curricula, classifying the students according to age and achievement, writing and distributing new textbooks for the study of the Hebrew language, replacing the untrained and untutored *melammedim* with qualified teachers and substituting sound pedagogic methods for the *melammed*'s stick.

One such dislodged *melammed* is described in *Malkot* (Lashes). Gedaliah, a sadistic old *melammed*, being deprived of the opportunities to satisfy his perverted appetite by flogging his young pupils, berates all manifestations of the new 'wave of impiety'.

> By the 'vague' term, 'Holy Tongue' Gedaliah refers to all those new books and thin, illustrated booklets containing pictures of birds and animals, commonly dubbed 'text books', which have recently inundated every village. No home is immune. About their content and value, Gedaliah knows nothing nor does he care to learn. Of one thing he is certain— that they undermine and abuse the study of the Hebrew

12. *Ha-Zeman*, vol. 2, No. 92, May 14, 1905, p. 3.
13. On the *melammed* and *Talmud Torah*, see M. Zborowski and E. Herzog, *Life is With People* (New York, 1952), pp. 88–96; D. Patterson, *The Hebrew Novel in Czarist Russia* (Edinburgh, 1964), pp. 168–9 in which a realistic description of this unique educational phenomenon is translated from Peretz Smolenskin's *The Wanderer in the Paths of Life*, see also pp. 140–1. Within this context see Berkowitz's tale, *A Barbarian*.

language . . . Just imagine the profound wisdom that one acquires in learning that a horse is a horse, or that a dog is a dog. Above all, these fools with clipped beards have outlawed beatings. These days no one is permitted to raise the whip or stick, anyone who strikes a child's backside is doomed. Instead, kind words, coddling and persuasion are preferred, the cat-of-nine-tails is replaced by an ultra-modern device—the ruler which is tapped upon their charges' fingers. What can come of such training? Indeed, the young urchins strut unashamed about the streets carrying satchels on their shoulders and following the birds in flight. . . .[14]

Several other tales reflect this conflict between the die-hard advocates of the established educational order and iconoclastic, idealistic innovators who, like Berkowitz, accepted the new practices in defiance of adamant communal opposition and, at times, at considerable personal risk.[15]

In addition, new ideologies captivated the mind and imagination of despondent young Jews, drawing them away from traditional practices. This was an epoch of organizations, movements and parties based upon new political and nationalistic ideas and socio-economic theories. The various socialist movements attracted large numbers of idealistic Jewish intellectuals. Some rose to positions of leadership and influence. But the cause that won the allegiance of the majority of Russian Jewish radicals was that of the *Narodniki* (Populists)—that is, the call to rehabilitate the Russian peasant by education, special technical training, and guidance. Berkowitz's writings refer to these historical movements, but at the same time reflect his own disillusionment with them and a firm conviction that Jewish participation in them was futile.[16]

Contemporaneous with these political and social currents

14. *Writings*, vol. 1, p. 14. Unless otherwise indicated all translations are by the author of this volume.
15. See *A Barbarian* and section 2 of Dawidowicz, *op. cit.*, pp. 145–68.
16. See *Severed*. The entire narratives *Viddui* (Confession) and *Banekhar* (In A Foreign Place) deal exclusively with these movements. Cf. Dawidowicz, *op. cit.*, sect. 10, pp. 405–57, and below, pp. 52–3, 57.

was the birth of the Zionist movement, which quickly gained the support of large sections of the Jewish population. Influenced by the powerful movement of Pan-Slavism, and spurred on by the deteriorating plight of their communities, Jews in several countries banded together to plan for the establishment of a national homeland in Palestine. But with the exception of one trifling short story, *Nedavot* (Contributions), included only in the earliest edition of his collected stories,[17] Berkowitz never wrote about the dilemmas of young Zionists in their confrontation with Jews who regarded them as bearers of false messianism, and as sinners, who wished to hasten the Messiah's coming by 'devious' human means. His novellas and shorter narratives make only tangential reference to Zionism and the rebuilding of *Eretz Yisrael*.[18] On the other hand, after his emigration to Palestine, these subjects become paramount concerns in his novel, and matters of exclusive interest in the fictional memoirs.

Jewish life was in flux. The various changes led to the breakdown of strong family ties—a basic theme in many of Berkowitz's stories. This disintegration of the traditionally cohesive Jewish family, the extreme impulse towards social and economic advancement, and the unprecedented opportunities for open contact between Jews and Gentiles all helped to loosen religious and national ties. For differing reasons large numbers of Jews converted to Christianity, an issue which provided a recurring topic in Berkowitz's essays. However, the incidence of conversion remained small and never affected the main body of Eastern European Jewry. Nevertheless, as the number of converts increased during these years, conversion

17. *Nedavot* was published in I. D. Berkowitz, *Sippurim* (Crakow, 1910), pp. 165–8. This is available in an English translation. It is listed on p. 235.
18. Berkowitz's essays, articles, and feuilletons do, however, reflect an abundant affection for *Eretz Yisrael*. He frequently expresses the thought that he, too, would like to settle there. He once took the liberty of criticizing the *Yishuv* for what he considered to be an offensive Purim play which he learned had been performed in Jaffa. See *Ha-Olam*, vol. 6, nos. 49–50, Jan. 12. 1912, p. 3. Cf. Dawidowicz, *op. cit.*, pp. 367–401.

became a cause of serious concern to some members of the community, and in 1911 Berkowitz devoted five articles to the subject. Since the more learned defectors deprived the Jewish people of their talents, Berkowitz tended to lament the possible effects upon the unity and cultural development of Jewish society, rather than analyse the causes underlying conversion.

Above all, this period can be called the age of mass Jewish migration. Prompted by economic depression, famine, and political upheavals, the Jews of Russia and Poland began to migrate from townlets to cities, but more significantly, perhaps, they migrated in increasing numbers to Germany and England and particularly to the United States. In the four decades between 1870 and 1910 nearly two million Jews migrated from Eastern European countries to the United States, which by 1929 had absorbed almost three million Jews.[19] Several of Berkowitz's short stories mirror these events. Many future doctors and lawyers, the author points out, displayed their aptitude as child prodigies by being able to address envelopes in Latin characters for the uninitiated with relatives abroad. There are many references that indicate the preconceived notions and formidable fears that European Jews had of America. It was reported, for example, that the United States was a country which 'consumed its inhabitants in a mire of plenty', and was a haven for unwed mothers, rebellious sons, and the numerous unlucky husbands who, unable to earn their livelihood in the 'old country', ventured into the new world in search of capital.[20] On the more favourable side, there were

19. On this subject see, for instance, Zoza Szajkowski, 'How The Mass Migration to America Began,' *Jewish Social Studies*, vol. 4, no. 4, Oct. 1942, pp. 291–310. In Berkowitz's works references are also made to migration to England. On this migration see, L. P. Gartner, *The Jewish Immigrant in England, 1870–1914* (London 1960). An interesting study could be made by comparing Berkowitz's fictional characters in America with the description provided in O. I. Janowsky, *The American Jew: A Composite Portrait* (New York-London, 1942).

20. See *Severed, In a Foreign Place, The Letter, Twilight.*

reports stressing the unrivalled freedom and equality that pre-
vailed. Yet were one to judge solely from Berkowitz's accounts,
one would have to conclude that America played havoc with
Jewish culture and literature. Berkowitz viewed the American
Jew as a coarse, luxury-seeking figure, unmoved by ideals and
motivated solely by the dollar.

In contrast, Berkowitz's writings about Palestine describe the
vitality and dedication of the Jewish pioneers at the turn of the
century and throughout the period under consideration. The
halutzim (pioneers), convinced of the justice and feasibility of
the Zionist cause, were determined to restore the national
Jewish homeland in *Eretz Yisrael*. But they were also resolved
to change Jewish society and the Jewish ethos. Driven by
recurrent outbreaks of anti-Semitism, the largest wave of
aliyah occurred in 1925 when over thirty thousand Jews,
mainly drawn from the middle classes, arrived from Poland
where they had been victims of boycott and restrictions. In
Palestine this was an era of land speculation during which land
prices boomed. This brief period provided the scenario for
Berkowitz's comic, and at times satiric, caricatures of current
life as chronicled in the letters of Menahem Mendel, a roguish
character through whom Berkowitz projected contemporary
events. Menahem Mendel himself partakes in the latest fad of
land speculation only to taste, along with hundreds of others,
the bitterness of the depression which followed close on its
heels.

Menahem Mendel's letters and Berkowitz's novel about
American immigrants to Palestine also acquaint the reader
with the problems and progress of revived Hebrew cultural
activities, then in their infancy. The young community in
Palestine, founded by the same individuals who had borne the
message of the Hebraic national movement in their European
homelands, undertook to revive the Hebrew language as their
vernacular and to foster Hebrew literature, drama, and
journalism. Hebrew newspapers, literary and scholarly journals, theatrical groups and theatres were established, which
guaranteed that Hebrew would be the dominant language and

its literature the authentic expression of the revived Jewish homeland. As will be seen in the ensuing chapters on his life and works, Berkowitz played a significant role in determining the shape which this emergent literature was to take.[21]

21. For a study of the socio-historical and ideological forces that motivated *ḥalutziut* (pioneering) and its impact on modern Hebrew *belles lettres* see Halkin, *op. cit.*, chap. 5, 'Ḥalutziut in Palestinian Literature,' pp. 100–10. Much information on the condition of the Jews in Palestine during these years is available in A. Revusky, *Jews in Palestine* (New York, 1945).

Chapter 2

LIFE AND WORKS

ISAAC DOV BEN ZELIG BERKOWITZ, the second of seven children, was born on the seventh day of Heshvan, October 16th, 1885 in Slutzk, White Russia.[1] His devout, lower-middle-class family resided on the all-Jewish Wigoda Street along with other traders in flax, wool, and wheat. On one corner of this street was the 'merchant's' synagogue, where his respected and learned father frequently served as cantor.[2]

In accordance with traditional practice, Isaac Dov, at the age of three, was admitted into the elementary *heder* where he received his basic Hebrew training under the tutelage of the traditional *melammed*. Other tutors later taught him Bible and introduced him to the study of Talmud and Hebrew grammar. By his thirteenth year he was enrolled in the local *yeshivah* and had gained a reputation as an extraordinarily alert student. He had a taste for solitude and rarely participated in his friends' youthful pranks.

Disappointed with the conventional curriculum, the young Berkowitz sought solace in the renascent prose and poetry of the Hebrew enlightenment. Like many modern Hebrew writers and *illuminati* of this period, he was compelled to

1. The details mentioned in this chapter are drawn from I. D. Berkowitz, *Pirkei Yaldut* (Tel-Aviv, 1965), *Ha-Rishonim*, the journals on whose staff Berkowitz served, and E. E. Lisitzky, *Eleh Toledot Adam* (Jerusalem, 1949), pp. 18–22.
2. Descriptions and photographs of Slutzk and Wigoda Street are available in Berkowitz, *Pirkei Yaldut*, pp. 172–83, and in N. Chinitz and Sh. Nachman, *Pinkas Slutzk u-Venoteihal* (Slutzk and Vicinity) (New York, Tel-Aviv, 1962). Berkowitz wrote an article for this memorial volume entitled *Slutzk Shel Maalah* (The Celestial Slutzk). A photograph of the Berkowitz family in 1908 appears on pp. 417–18.

conceal the current Hebrew volumes behind the large tomes of the *Gemara* lest, suspected of heresy, he be expelled from the *yeshivah*. He soon discovered the local Hebrew library, from which, for a nominal charge each month, he borrowed thirty to forty items—journals (i.e. *ha-Shaḥar, ha-Melitz*), novels, and volumes of poetry. Having read and re-read the modern Hebrew classics by Mapu, Smolenskin, Braudes, Brandstädter, and Shomer he began borrowing Yiddish books, but apparently remained unexcited by them. Once, however, the librarian, Mr Pesaḥ Koren, a good friend of his, offered the avid young student a special book on the condition that he should not complete it at one sitting. Rather, he was to read it slowly and thoroughly in order to appreciate its finer points because, Koren stressed, its Yiddish was masterly. Through this volume in the *Yiddishe Folksbibliotek* series, Berkowitz was introduced to Sholom Aleichem. The ensuing nights that were spent reading Sholom Aleichem for the first time were described by the author as the most decisive in his literary career. He later wrote, 'for the first time in my life I really felt the beauty and artistry of the written word.'[3]

After his father had left for America in 1902, Isaac Dov persuaded his mother to engage a private tutor to instruct him in Russian grammar, history, and literature. Though no longer a regular student in the *yeshivah*, Berkowitz continued to study Talmud on his own in the desolate local synagogue where he also prepared his Russian lessons. He later recorded: 'At the sight of the Holy Ark, shrouded in gloom and abandoned, my heart reproached me. The Holy Ark, however, remained sorrowful, and mute. The dreary walls of the *Beit-*

---

3. *Ha-Rishonim*, p. 15. Among the modern Hebrew novels he read while in the *yeshivah* were: P. Smolenskin, *Ha-Toeh be-Darkhei ha-Ḥayyim* (*Wanderer in the Paths of Life*) and R. A. Braudes' *Ha-Dat ve-ha-Ḥayyim* (*Religion and Life*). On these works see: D. Patterson, *The Hebrew Novel in Czarist Russia*, on *Wanderer*, pp. 84–6, 167–8, 173–5, 228–9; on *Religion*, 160–2, 196–7, 225–6. Berkowitz expressed particular disgust with the novels by Shomer (Nahum Meir Sheikowitz (1847–1905)). On Sheikowitz see Patterson, *op. cit.*, pp. 26–8, 226–7, 235–6.

Midrash heard for the first time the odd sounds of Russian verbs and the strange foreign names of Russian heroes.'[4] Having mastered the rudiments of the Russian language, he undertook a systematic and intensive course of study in the masterpieces of Russian literature. He came under the spell of Dostoyevsky and Turgenev, but was influenced profoundly, as a short-story writer, by Anton Chekhov. While commanding his deep admiration, these Russian classics never deflected Berkowitz from his early allegiance to Hebrew *belles-lettres*.[5]

By the turn of the century, Zionist ideology had penetrated Slutzk. Among its most ardent adherents was the young Isaac Dov who, along with several friends, formed 'The Committee of the Builders of Zion' which sponsored a meeting hall and a public reading-room.[6] With youthful enthusiasm they issued a mimeographed literary sheet called *Hatzair* (The Young) which was distributed among the library's readers. The first issue included the earliest version of Berkowitz's tale *Baal Simḥah* (A Proud Father) which draws directly on Chekhov's narrative, *The Lament*.[7] At this time, too, although only a lad

4. *Ha-Rishonim*, p. 17.
5. On these influences see below:
    The following authors are specifically enumerated in his memoirs: Pushkin, Lermontov, Gogol, Turgenev, Dostoyevsky, and Tolstoy. *Ibid.*, p. 18. Berkowitz translated one of Tolstoy's biographical narratives *yaldut* (Childhood) published in *Kitvei L. N. Tolstoy*, vol. 1 (Vilna, 1911), pp. 105–7. He also translated one of Arthur Schnitzler's one-act plays into Yiddish: *Letzte Masken* (Final Masks) which appeared in *Die Zukunft*, Oct. 1908. pp. 617–25.
6. Among Berkowitz's friends in these undertakings were Meyer Waxman, author of the five-volume *History of Jewish Literature*, and Abraham Epstein, a Hebrew literary critic. A photograph of the first page of *Hatzair* is available in *Slutzk and Vicinity*, p. 48. The first issue was published in a single copy. Two subsequent issues were published in mimeograph form. The copies of these numbers were burned when Slutzk police raided the printer's home.
7. Chekhov's *The Lament* is available in English translation in C. Brooks and R. P. Warren, *Understanding Fiction* (New York, 1959), pp. 203–10. In *Ha-Rishonim*, Berkowitz mentioned Sholom Aleichem's admiration for

of sixteen, he began to teach Hebrew and was instrumental in establishing a progressive *ḥeder*, a Hebrew-speaking circle, and a dramatics group, for which he composed several satirical parodies that lampooned contemporary Jewish communal life and the deluge of 'isms'.

Through the efforts of Yitzhak Katznelson whom Berkowitz had befriended in Lodz, several of his earlier short stories (*On Yom Kippur Eve, Mishael,* and *Lashes*) were published in *Ha-Tzofeh*, a leading Hebrew journal. On March 16, 1903, this weekly announced the first literary contest in the history of modern Hebrew literature. The noted authors and critics, I. L. Peretz, Dr J. Klausner, and A. L. Levinsky, were to act as judges. Eight months later, of the thirty-two short stories submitted, Berkowitz's entry *Moshkele Ḥazir* (Moshkele Pig), was awarded the first prize by a unanimous decision. The judges concluded that Berkowitz 'possesses extraordinary talent and we foresee a brilliant future for him. Moreover, in the present state of the Hebrew short story, we do not anticipate a work that will outrank this one in content, coherence and form.'[8] The sudden fame that brought the young author, then only seventeen years old, to the attention of older writers and into the forefront of the Hebrew literary stage, might easily have jeopardized his native talents but for the intelligent criticism and encouragement of I. L. Peretz, and other members of the Warsaw literary circle.

In 1905 Berkowitz left for Vilna where he served as editor of the literary section of the widely circulated monthly *Ha-Zeman*, and he continued to write short stories and feuilletons (under the pseudonym Barak) for the daily edition. His Vilna colleagues immediately welcomed their talented young associate. H. N. Bialik, who by this time was generally regarded

Chekhov and the latter's literary influence on Sholom Aleichem's style and humour (p. 240).

8. See *Ha-Tzofeh*, Nov. 8, 1903, no. 255, p. 1094 for the full texts of the announcement and the citation. Cf. G. Kressel, *Shetei Teudot* in *Moznayim*, vol. 25, June 1967, pp. 20–2, in which document Berkowitz discussed the prize and the people involved.

as the Jewish poet laureate and who was in effect a national spokesman, often praised Berkowitz and his close friend, the poet Zalman Schneour. Berkowitz particularly cherished Bialik's comments because he had been a zealous reader of the latter's poetry and had frequently committed entire works to memory.

In a letter to Bialik one can see that Berkowitz was a prey to the same gnawing depression that dominated his fiction.

'At times, in this atmosphere,' Berkowitz confessed, 'I forgot that literature must be different and that writers must be unique. In addition to their desire for fame and their passion for talent and controversy, authors must really love literature; it must be love for love's sake . . . but for some reason which I do not understand, I am often terribly depressed. At this season, although it is springtime, I sense our indigence everywhere . . . How can we write? How can we rejoice in our achievements? We are severed from the universe and do not realize that we stand alone in this world with no one to care for us . . . We have created an illusion but it is being atomized before our eyes, our world is tottering . . .'[9]

This intolerable sense of isolation is the dominant mood throughout most of his representative writing.

This depression was dispelled, if only temporarily, during a meeting in 1905 between Berkowitz and Sholom Aleichem (the most popular Yiddish literary figure of the day) who had come to Vilna in order to give a number of public readings.[10] This meeting was to have far-reaching consequences. Berkowitz paid a visit to Sholom Aleichem and together they discussed Berkowitz's professional achievements and especially his prize-winning story which Sholom Aleichem had read with much

9. This letter was published by M. Ungerfeld, *Bein H. N. Bialik le-vein I. D. Berkowitz, Moznayim,* vol. 25, June 1967, p. 18.

10. On Sholom Aleichem (Sholom Jacob Rabinowitz, 1859–1916) see Waxman, vol. 4, pp. 508ff.; L. Falstein, *The Man Who Loved to Laugh: The Story of Sholom Aleichem* (Philadelphia, 1968) and M. Samuel, *The World of Sholom Aleichem* (New York, 1943). Several of his works are available in English translation.

interest. At the first of his recitals, Berkowitz was introduced to Sholom Aleichem's daughter Ernestina, whom he married at the end of that year.[11] Upon reading Berkowitz's review (signed B. Litvak) of this performance, Sholom Aleichem invited Berkowitz to translate some of his Yiddish compositions into Hebrew. Although Berkowitz produced an exquisite translation that elicited Sholom Aleichem's warm approval, he refused at that time to become his official translator.

Hereafter, Berkowitz's personal life and literary career became inextricably linked with the Rabinowitz household in general and most particularly with its head, Sholom Aleichem. Despite his almost legendary fame and popularity Sholom Aleichem never achieved any degree of financial security; and so it was not long before Berkowitz became involved in his father-in-law's many unsuccessful business ventures, and his speaking engagements. Moreover, the political situation in Russia and Sholom Aleichem's deteriorating health required the family to move about from country to country. For a year and a half, until Sholom Aleichem's first trip to the United States, the family lived in Geneva close to Mendele Mokher Seforim, with whom Berkowitz would frequently discuss contemporary literary developments. Berkowitz also maintained close contacts with Ben-Ami whose heartrending Russian stories on the impoverished children of the *shtetl* had for some decades influenced a wide audience. Ignoring his father-in-law's advice to enrol in medical school, Berkowitz continued to write for Hebrew and Yiddish journals. In 1906 his wife gave birth to their only daughter, Tamara, who was to be one of his chief translators into English.

In 1907, while en route for New York to visit his parents,

11. Sholom Aleichem's daughter writes in a recent biography of her father, 'My first impresssion [of I. D. Berkowitz] was of a very handsome young man who spoke only when absolutely necessary and when he had something important to say . . . My father at once accepted him as an older son with whom he could discuss all official matters.' Marie Waife-Goldberg, *My Father Sholom Aleichem* (New York, 1968), p. 166. On Berkowitz's associations with Sholom Aleichem, see p. 12 and ch. 3.

Berkowitz stayed in London and called upon J. H. Brenner who
told him, 'You have a fine mind and a perfect body, whereas I
was born mangled and misshapen.' For his part, Berkowitz
found that, despite his poverty, Brenner embodied 'a radiance
and vitality that could only emanate from the recesses of an
unsullied soul and a pure mind.'[12] Although different in many
ways, the two men remained firm friends for a number of years.

In New York, Berkowitz lived with his parents in Brownsville, a new and predominantly Jewish residential quarter of
Brooklyn, which provided the background for a number of his
short stories about American-Jewish life. He published several
short stories and essays in the local Yiddish press and literary
journals.[13] At the same time he came into conflict with Jacob
Saperstein, the editor of the New York *Morgen-Journal*, a leading Yiddish daily newspaper. This dispute ultimately led to his
withdrawal from its staff, and deserves special mention since it
reveals something of the strength of Berkowitz's personality.
The paper's editor had advised him to expunge all instances of
'Russian psychology' from his prose in order to render it more
palatable to the average American-Yiddish reader. This Berkowitz adamantly refused to do. On the contrary, as he later recorded, he felt impelled to express his own restlessness through
fictional portraits of lonely figures whose plight mirrored that
of so many recently-arrived immigrants.

While in America, Berkowitz joined Dr Yitzhak Wernikov-
sky (1876–1940) in the publication of a literary journal *Ha-Am*
of which only a single issue appeared (in 1908) and which contained *Yarok* (The Greenhorn), Berkowitz's first realistic Hebrew sketch of American Jewish life.[14] Berkowitz seems to have
felt a very real concern for the welfare of other Hebrew writers.
Indicative of this is an appeal he sent out, on the death of the
popular Hebrew writer Judah Steinberg, on behalf of his widow

12. *Ha-Rishonim*, p. 133.
13. Berkowitz published his works in *Tageblatt, Der Yiddisher Kempfer, Der
    Amerikaner*, and the *Morgen-Journal*.
14. Berkowitz's abortive attempts with regard to *Ha-Am* are described in D.
    Persky, *Kedabber Ish el Reieihu, in Hadoar*, vol. 15, Dec. 27, 1935, p. 140.

and family. At this time Berkowitz accepted a position as a teacher in an afternoon Hebrew school. Unable to endure what he described as 'this hell', he left after two months.

Having failed through lack of financial support to establish a Hebrew literary journal, Berkowitz joined the staff of the light Yiddish journal *Der Groyser Kundes*. During this period he was responsible for the publication of Sholom Aleichem's works in Europe and America, and was simultaneously engaged in adapting Sholom Aleichem's plays for the American-Jewish stage. However, his relationship with the American-Jewish theatre seems to have been rather less than cordial, and he had frequent recourse to criticism of its directors, producers, and writers.

In August 1908 Sholom Aleichem, who had been compelled to travel extensively, despite ill health, collapsed on stage with a tubercular attack. Thereafter he became increasingly dependent upon his dedicated son-in-law. In 1909 Berkowitz felt sufficiently confident of Sholom Aleichem's physical progress to return to St Petersburg, five years after his last visit, in order to resume his career as journalist and fiction writer. He soon discovered, however, that there had been radical changes. The once famous Hebrew journals had either lost circulation, ceased publication, or transferred offices to Odessa. Only the popular Yiddish press had maintained its position and even increased its sales. Angered by what he found, Berkowitz published a highly charged criticism of Yiddish journalism in *Die Neie Velt*. In 1910 unable to tolerate such conditions and disappointed by the state of Jewish affairs in Russia, he rejoined his family. During the same year, his first volume of collected stories (*Sippurim*) was printed and received wide acclaim. During this period Berkowitz started the arduous task of translating Sholom Aleichem's works into Hebrew. In order that the Hebrew-reading public should think that Sholom Aleichem had translated them himself, these early translations were published anonymously in *Hed ha-Zeman*. They were eagerly welcomed.

While in Warsaw, Berkowitz composed *Haggadah of the Press*. This parody of the traditional Passover Haggadah ruthlessly satirized the abject quality of the Yiddish press and theatre. Within a few days its entire first edition of over seven thousand copies was sold out.[15]

Invited to join the staff of the leading newspaper, *Ha-Olam*, and serve as its literary editor, Berkowitz moved to Vilna. There, under the pseudonyms Barak and B. Ernst, he wrote a weekly column in which he commented upon local and world affairs and reviewed the current literary scene. Vilna's Hebrew and Yiddish literary circles provided a cultural environment in which Berkowitz was happily able to devote his full time to writing and translating. In 1911 three volumes of Sholom Aleichem were published in Hebrew as well as a translation of a short story by Tolstoy (*Childhood*).

A number of his friends had expressed the feeling that by spending so much time on Sholom Aleichem's works he was necessarily limiting his own literary development. These comments, it would seem, had some effect on Berkowitz. In his memoirs he quotes S. Anski's (S. Rapoport) remarks on the subject, adding that his relationship with Sholom Aleichem outweighed any misgivings about its ultimate value for his literary career.

In 1912 *Ha-Olam* moved its offices to Odessa which by now had become the greatest centre of Jewish nationalist activities in Russia. Once again Berkowitz came under the direct influence of Bialik who, as co-partner in the Moriah Publishing House, offered Berkowitz a monthly honorarium in return for the exclusive rights to publish his Hebrew renditions of Sholom Aleichem. Those familiar with both languages marvelled at Berkowitz's linguistic virtuosity. The year and a half spent in Odessa was Berkowitz's most fruitful period; it was there he reached the zenith of his literary career.

This idyllic interlude was short-lived. In order to avoid military conscription Berkowitz had managed to obtain false documents. He was consequently under constant fear of arrest and deportation. In 1913, unwilling to endure the strain any longer,

15. Details are recorded in *Ha-Rishonim*, p. 244. To my regret, I have been unable to find a copy of this work.

he joined Sholom Aleichem in Berlin. With the outbreak of war they were expelled from Germany and made their way to Copenhagen. Shortly afterwards they left for the United States, where Berkowitz remained from 1914 to 1927.

Until Sholom Aleichem's death in 1916, Berkowitz acted as his personal secretary and impresario. He arranged his public engagements, prepared his works for publication and adapted his plays for Maurice Schwartz's Yiddish Art Theatre in New York. Yet, despite this demanding schedule Berkowitz found time to engage in his own literary work. He became the co-editor of *Ha-Toren* and published many critical essays, short stories and brief notes, using the pseudonyms I. D. Barka and Y. Avi-Tamar (Tamar's father). He joined with Dr Shemarya Levin and Dr S. M. Melamed in organizing 'The Society of the friends of *Ha-Toren*' in order to ensure the financial stability of the journal. This enabled the editors to enlarge its circulation, convert it into a weekly and raise its standards. From 1919 to 1921 he also served as editor of the Hebrew monthly *Ha-Miklat*, and as executive manager of the Shtybl Company under whose auspices he published a series of pointed Hebrew readers for children (*Mikraot Ketanot*) in addition to a children's magazine (*Eden*).[16] Daniel Persky, co-worker with Berkowitz in several of these enterprises, recognized the calibre of this assiduous new editor and described Berkowitz's editorial policies and practices as follows: 'When Berkowitz examined a manuscript he read it, re-read it, studied it, and emended everything. . . . In many instances he would recopy and recast the entire article or story to such a degree that its author no longer recognized it. When the latter complained, Berkowitz would devote hours defending his corrections. . . . There is no other Hebrew writer whose manuscripts can compete in clarity and aesthetic perfection with those of Berkowitz. I do not believe there is another editor who would check every reference and footnote . . . he spurred us on to efficiency, precision, and honesty . . . he abhorred unfounded abstractions and casuistry . . . above all else

16. For this series, for example, Berkowitz abridged and translated two short stories by Chekhov, *Mikraot Ketanot*, pp. 3–14.

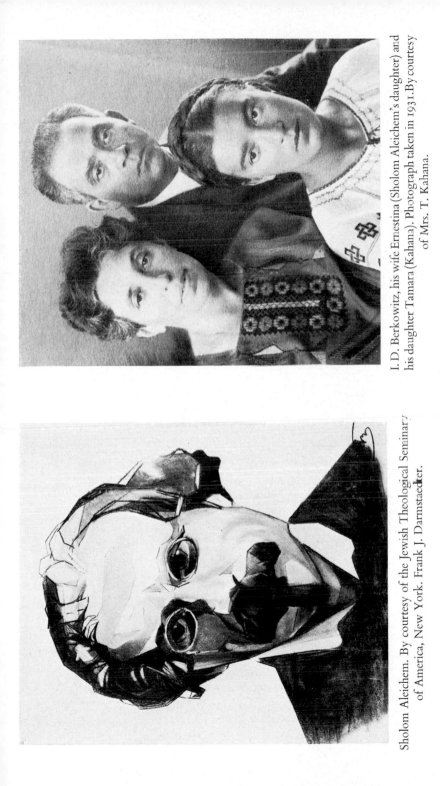

Sholom Aleichem. By courtesy of the Jewish Theological Seminary of America, New York. Frank J. Darmstaedter.

I. D. Berkowitz, his wife Ernestina (Sholom Aleichem's daughter) and his daughter Tamara (Kahana). Photograph taken in 1931. By courtesy of Mrs. T. Kahana.

A Family Portrait. I. D. Berkowitz is standing second from the right.

From Nachmani, Samson (ed.), Pinkas Slutsk (Slutsk and Vicinity Memorial Book), New York 1962. By courtesy of the Jewish Division, The New York Public Library. Astor, Lenox and Tilden Foundation.

he sought accurate and authentic Hebrew usage. . . .'[17] The standards which he required of others he demanded with greater severity of himself. His consummate classical style has become the hallmark of modern Hebrew prose.

In 1923, a dramatic rendition in Yiddish of his prize-winning tale, *Moshkele Ḥazir*, was presented simultaneously in New York and Warsaw. The script and production were praised by reviewers and audiences on both sides of the Atlantic. Three years later, Berkowitz published a Yiddish volume on the life and works of Sholom Aleichem. The following year he and his family took up permanent residence in Tel-Aviv. In a weekly series in *Moznayim*, on whose staff he served as co-editor, he recorded his impressions of Palestine and its people. Other numbers included memoirs of his association with Sholom Aleichem, and the early versions of several novellas about the young Jewish community of Palestine. Subsequently these were collected to form the volumes entitled *Menahem Mendel be-Eretz Yisrael* (Menahem Mendel in Eretz Yisrael) and *Ha-Rishonim Kivnei Adam* (The Elders as People). During the year 1924 a serialized form of the Yiddish novel *Meshiah's Zeiten* (Messianic Days) appeared in the literary supplement of the *Daily Forward* published in New York. This was later translated by the author into Hebrew and, with minor revisions, became the Hebrew novel, *Yemot ha-Mashiaḥ*.

At the request of the producers and directors of the newly founded *Habimah* National Theatre in Tel Aviv, Berkowitz adapted his own plays and those of Sholom Aleichem for the revived Hebrew stage. The resulting productions were widely praised. *Oto ve-et Beno* (Him and His Son), a play based on the character Moshkele Ḥazir, met with a particularly favourable reception. Among its admirers was the poet Bialik, who had settled in Tel-Aviv in 1924. Berkowitz's outstanding virtuosity

17. Persky, *op. cit.* See, too, Michael G. Brown, 'All, All Alone: the Hebrew Press in America: 1914–1924,' *American Jewish Historical Quarterly*, 59, 2 Dec. 1969, pp. 139–78, especially pp. 154–5, 160. On Berkowitz's mastery of the Hebrew language see A. Bendavid, *Leshon Mikra u-Leshon Ḥakhamim* (Tel-Aviv, 1967), pp. 253–4.

in the field of Hebrew letters led to his being invited to join the Hebrew Language Academy, the authoritative body in matters related to Hebrew language and usage. He served on its council as an active member from 1928 until his death on March 29, 1967. In 1944 Berkowitz was awarded the Tcherni-khovsky prize for his fifteen-volume Hebrew version of Sholom Aleichem's works. For his own collected works he received the much coveted Bialik prize and the Israel Government Prize for *belles-lettres*.

During the last years of his life he translated *Ha-Rishonim Kivnei Adam* into Yiddish and published it in serial form in the Israeli Yiddish literary journal *Die Goldene Keyt*. Concurrently in *Moznayim* he published a series of childhood reminiscences which were later collected into two volumes: *Pirkei Yaldut* (Chapters on Childhood) appeared in 1965 and a second volume which he was preparing at the time of his death has not yet been published.[18]

Before he died, Berkowitz had expressed a desire that *Kaddish* at his funeral should be recited by Ka-Tzetnik (Yehiel Denur), a survivor of the Holocaust and witness at the Eichmann trial. Among those who spoke in praise of Berkowitz at his funeral were Zalman Shazar, President of the State of Israel, Zalman Aran, Minister of Education, and Golda Meir. He was buried with full honours in the Old Cemetery in Tel-Aviv alongside the most famous modern Hebrew authors, his revered masters and cherished colleagues.[19]

18. A photographic reproduction of a page of this unfinished volume was published in *Moznayim*, vol. 24, 1967, p. 357. Among his last recorded conversations were those with N. Chinitz. See N. Chinitz, *Misiḥotai im I. D. Berkowitz, Hadoar*, vol. 49, 1969, no. 10, pp. 151–2; no. 17, p. 268; no. 19, p. 300; and no. 24, p. 389.

19. See *Moznayim*, vol. 24, April–May, 1967, p. 508.

Chapter 3

A COVENANT OF DEVOTION

As mentioned in the preceding chapter, Berkowitz and Sholom Aleichem enjoyed a very close relationship. Early in his career, Berkowitz had curtailed his own activity in order to apply his talents to the task of rendering Sholom Aleichem's Yiddish works into Hebrew. For Berkowitz, the significance of their relationship was immense. Moreover, the influence of this relationship upon the development and growth of modern Hebrew letters was considerable. It is through Berkowitz's translations that Sholom Aleichem's world has been incorporated into the mainstream of Hebrew *belles-lettres*. Much of the knowledge which present-day Hebrew readers have of *shtetl* life and of Jewish life in Eastern Europe in general is culled from Berkowitz's translations of Sholom Aleichem.

Berkowitz had been aware of the outstanding nature of Sholom Aleichem's work from the first. Each new contact intensified his admiration. Sholom Aleichem's consummate use of the Yiddish language offered Berkowitz a welcome escape from the patently amateurish works of other authors.[1] It is clear that he identified himself with Sholom Aleichem's fictional characters whose fates and moods he regarded as uncanny equivalents of his own. While his sensibilities were deepened by Sholom Aleichem's treatment of the tragedy of *shtetl* life, he was somewhat liberated from his own depression by the warmth and humour constantly to be found in the great Yiddish writer's work.

Much information on this subject may be derived from the frankly autobiographical *Ha-Rishonim Kivnei Adam*.[2] This gives

1. See above, p. 16. See also *Ha-Rishonim*, pp. 16–17.
2. This appeared as a popular series in the much-read Friday issues of *Ha-Aretz* (vols. 20–1, 23 April, 1937–June, 1938). It was published as a

a first-hand account of the international community of Hebrew and Yiddish writers, intellectuals, and Jewish leaders in whose orbit Berkowitz moved, and at whose centre Sholom Aleichem stood as one of the most inspiring forces until his death in 1916, the last recorded event in the volume.

The first contact Berkowitz had with Sholom Aleichem's work was the Hebrew story *Little Shimon*. This left him unmoved. His opinion changed on reading *Stempenu* which convinced him that the author of this story was 'full of compassion and pity for human tribulations as reflected in the animated dialogues. His language was lucid and precise; it overflowed with wisdom yet was unusually simple; it was resilient yet dynamic . . . his approach to his characters was personal and intimate, his view of human existence illuminating. He seemed to view everything, the vices and virtues alike, with an ease that could only emanate from real insight. . . . I had never come across such graphically portrayed figures and such exciting sketches. . . .'[3]

Even before he met Sholom Aleichem, Berkowitz had toyed with the idea of some day undertaking the monumental task of translating Sholom Aleichem's Yiddish works into Hebrew. A number of writers including Sholom Aleichem himself had attempted the task. None, Berkowitz realized, had succeeded in transmitting the force and simplicity of the original. Therefore, it is not surprising that when Sholom Aleichem suggested that he try his hand at one short story Berkowitz, though in a sense prepared for the task, was awed by the offer. He translated the story but refused to become his official translator. Only years later, when he was his son-in-law and had developed his own

separate volume in 1938 and republished recently as *Writings*, vol. 2. Sections were translated into Yiddish by Berkowitz and appeared in several volumes of *Die Goldene Keyt*. The first such translation appeared in vol. 3, 1951/2, no. 10. The footnote (p. 55) reads: 'A chapter from a yet unpublished volume *Unsere Rishonim*'—which still remains unpublished.

3. *Ha-Rishonim*, p. 15. *Stempenu* is available in an English translation by Hannah Berman (London, 1923). He had read *Shimale* (*Little Shimon*) in volume 5 of *Ha-Asif*, 1889.

career, did Berkowitz agree. Despite numerous misgivings about the effects of such an enterprise on his own artistic pursuits, Berkowitz seemed eager to return to this task under the imposing supervision and guidance of his meticulous master. He devoted himself to the work until his death.

He first selected *Tuvyah the Dairyman*, which, for a translator, presents particularly difficult problems. He resolved that, if successful, he would continue with the entire collection of works, but that if he failed, he would abandon the project. The obstacles that faced him are reflected in these remarks: 'The most difficult aspect of translating *Tuvyah the Dairyman*, it seemed to me, hinged upon the ability to transmit Tuvyah's special mode of speech. . . . If *Tuvyah* could not be translated adequately into a living European vernacular, rich in dialectical nuances and full of colloquialisms, how could it possibly be translated into a dead language such as ancient Hebrew? How could one create a low-brow, colloquial Hebrew for *Tuvyah*? It would need to be low-keyed; earthier and more robust than the majestic language of the prophets or the laconic, forbidding Hebrew of the Rabbis. How could Hebrew idiom depict Tuvyah as a noble yet unschooled Jew, who is both wise and jolly, when no such type exists in the Bible, and when for the Rabbis an untutored man was synonymous with vulgarity, stupidity and darkest ignorance?'[4]

It is evident, then, that Berkowitz, having made a careful study of Sholom Aleichem's works, was fully aware of the problems awaiting him. Sholom Aleichem was also attuned to the difficulties of the task. He insisted that Berkowitz was to feel in no way restricted by the Yiddish original. Berkowitz was not expected to produce a literal translation, but rather to create a Hebrew version that would convey the mood and evoke the sense of the original. In addition, Sholom Aleichem stressed that this Hebrew version should never violate any of the accepted canons of classical Hebrew prose.

Berkowitz was faced with the task of creating a Hebrew style

4. *Ha-Rishonim*, p. 242. On problems involved in translation see D. Patterson, *Hebrew Literature: The Art of the Translator* (London, 1958).

that was vibrant enough to portray convincingly the dynamic figures that filled Sholom Aleichem's pages. In quest of a suitable stratum of Hebrew, Berkowitz turned to the religious sources that were to be found in almost every Jewish home. These included the Pentateuch, the Book of Psalms, The Daily and Festival Prayer books, Rashi's commentary on the Pentateuch, and the pithy proverbs scattered throughout rabbinic and medieval literatures that had somehow found their way into the daily language of East European Jews. These familiar sources enabled Berkowitz to write in a Hebrew style that conveyed contemporary feelings in a non-stylized fashion. 'Most especially,' Berkowitz emphasized, 'I wanted this "Hebraized Tuvyah" to speak with Yiddish cadences, with the authentic rhythms vital to Yiddish dialogue that would inject simplicity, warm-heartedness and charm into the pathos of the prophets, into the constrained style of the *Mishnah* and the unadorned midrashic adages.'[5]

An astute student of Sholom Aleichem's techniques of understatement, description and dialogue, Berkowitz knew that, for Sholom Aleichem, puns and witticisms were more than parodies of ancient texts. They were often the keys to a real understanding of his characters. It was clear, for instance, that Tuvyah's malapropisms were not meant to conjure up a gruff illiterate who deliberately misquoted verses out of contempt for the learned. On the contrary, Tuvyah seemed to revel in *jeux de mots* with an almost scholarly delight. The reader was intended to gain the impression of yokels so conversant with the texts that they could reshape them at will, fully confident that their ironic intent would be grasped instantly by their equally proficient audiences. But whereas Sholom Aleichem could evoke a comic effect by having Tuvyah mistranslate a biblical verse, Berkowitz had to seek some other stratagem since the verses and adages were now to be presented in their original language.

At various intervals during the initial stages it appeared to Berkowitz that 'the ancient and immalleable Hebrew materials

5. *Ha-Rishonim*, p. 242.

could not be shaped to the demands of Sholom Aleichem's light-hearted style.'[6] At the outset frequent debates ensued between Sholom Aleichem and his young translator. They held opposing views about the nature and condition of the Hebrew language and, consequently, about the idiom to be employed in the translation. Sholom Aleichem held that, since Hebrew was not spoken by any group of individuals, the translator was to turn only to the available written sources and was not to project a Hebrew vernacular. He maintained, too, that the sacred texts were the exclusive sources from which the translator should draw. Hence he reacted violently against any attempt to reconstruct the idiom even when no fundamental rules were broken. Fascinated by the charms of ancient Hebrew's quaint, ornate figures of speech, he admitted only grandiloquent turns of phrase. He seemed beguiled by the artfulness involved in reshaping an archaic grammar to modern usage rather than by the artistic demands of aesthetic expression. Berkowitz, on the other hand, sensed that artfully used archaisms were hardly qualities calculated to transmit the full-bodied richness of Sholom Aleichem's Yiddish. Artificiality would inevitably detract from the spontaneity that was the hallmark of Sholom Aleichem's style. No doubt, the controversies between them about such fundamentals impeded progress and annoyed both parties, but at the same time, they compelled Berkowitz to defend his choice of nuance and expression.

According to Berkowitz's journal, Sholom Aleichem was eventually convinced of Berkowitz's methodology. After reading the finished draft of the *Tuvyah* translation, Sholom Aleichem exclaimed, 'It seems like a different Tuvyah, a very different Tuvyah but nonetheless my Tuvyah. Tuvyah's spirit still lives!'[7] Each revision prompted further compliments. Until finally, upon examining the Hebrew version of *Tuvyah's Daughter Held Captive Among the Nations*, Sholom Aleichem was so impressed that he exclaimed enthusiastically, 'The translation is far better than the original!'[8] Several years later, after Berkowitz had devoted himself almost exclusively to these

6. *Ibid.*   7. *Ibid.*, p. 243.   8. *Ibid.*

translations, he urged his father-in-law to engage someone else. Sholom Aleichem objected on the grounds that no one else possessed comparable talents, and he would not therefore permit anyone else to proceed with the work. He told his son-in-law, 'Without being told, you know what revisions I would have made, and you make them. . . . I will not allow anyone else to translate me!'⁹

In an interview conducted a few years after the publication of the Hebrew version of Sholom Aleichem's works, Berkowitz commented that, though many critics had applauded the *magnum opus*, no monograph had been devoted to a critical comparison of the original Yiddish version with the Hebrew translation. 'As a matter of fact,' maintained Berkowitz, 'I did not translate Sholom Aleichem's writings, I re-wrote them. During his lifetime I took greater liberties with the text than I permitted myself after his death. No humorist is translatable. Understanding this, Sholom Aleichem allowed me complete freedom to treat his works as if they were my own. Moreover, whenever I translated literally, he used to say, "I dislike translators who trail behind me like calves behind a cow."'¹⁰ A comprehensive study such as the one suggested by Berkowitz has not so far been undertaken. Such an analysis might also consider the direct and indirect impact of the then renascent Hebrew vernacular upon the Hebrew version. It might also prove interesting to note to what extent current Israeli usage and slang would be needed to update Berkowitz's versions, and to what extent the 'Yiddishisms' of Berkowitz's translation have influenced current Israeli style and usage.

9. *Ibid.*, p. 265.
10. See G. Yardeni, *Tet-Zayin Siḥot im Soferim* (Tel-Aviv, 1965), pp. 23–4. The interview with Berkowitz was held in 1954 and appears on pp. 19–26. In an unpublished letter from Berkowitz to P. Lachover, made available by the Tel-Aviv Genazim archives, Berkowitz deals with Lachover's queries about the proper translation of the word *nocknissel*. 'I do not recall how I rendered this word because I do not translate sentences literally. Rather, I find Hebrew equivalents.' The letter is dated Oct. 6, 1937.

The following brief outline of the central differences and similarities between the Hebrew and Yiddish versions of the opening section of *Tuvyah* purports neither to be exhaustive nor to present any final conclusions about Berkowitz's methods. However, even a brief introduction will suffice to illustrate the difficulties of the task Berkowitz had undertaken; although, for the English reader, even this elementary exposition is of necessity complicated by the fact that it is an explanation in English of a Hebrew translation from Yiddish.

As indicated above, Berkowitz strove to retain the wit and sense of the original and to present *Tuvyah* in a hebraized form without doing violence to the cardinal tenets of the Hebrew medium. The subsequent selection will, therefore, be translated as literally as possible so as to highlight the topics under discussion.

The Yiddish reads: 'A man toils, becomes so weary there's nothing left for him to do but to lie down,—a curse upon the enemies of Zion—and die; then suddenly, we know not why or how, things take a turn for the better. . . .'[11]

The Hebrew reads: 'Isn't this the way the world turns? You see a man whose entire life has been toil and trouble, who has been breaking his back and soul for a piece of bread, whose face has been charred like the rim of a pot, whose life has been hanging like a thread, whose sole solution seems to be the grave—then, suddenly, seven suns shine all at once. . . .'[12]

It is apparent that at such times Berkowitz felt that he could attain the best results only through lengthy embellishments.[13] Whereas the Yiddish opening description of the luckless man's weariness contains thirteen unadorned and commonly heard

11. My English translations from the Yiddish are based on Sholom Aleichem *Alle Verk Fun Sholom Aleichem: Ganz Tevyah Der Milkhiger* (New York, 1923), pp. 15–17.

12. My English translations from the Hebrew are based on *Kitvei Sholom Aleichem*, vol. 4, *Tuvyah Ha-Ḥolev*, trans. by I. D. Berkowitz (revised edition) (Tel-Aviv, 1956), pp. 9–10.

13. This method is briefly discussed in Y. Rabbi, *Min ha-Hekeifim el ha-Merkaz* in *Al ha-Mishmar*, Nov. 5, 1965, p. 5.

words, the Hebrew passage contains thirty-one words which are a kaleidoscope of biblical and rabbinic sources. Yet Berkowitz has captured Sholom Aleichem's intrinsic style to such an extent that these additions do not seem to impair the quality of the original. There is a natural quality about the Hebrew version which lends authenticity to the reconstituted *Tuvyah*. The additional length itself helps create the mood while simultaneously the asides and epigrammatic comments contribute no small measure of humour.

Berkowitz, struggling to recreate for the Hebrew reader the vigorous flavour of contemporary Yiddish, would occasionally employ end-rhymes which also imbued the dialogue with a certain air of lightheartedness. When describing his transformation on the Sabbath, Tuvyah remarks: (in the Yiddish) '... on Sabbath I become a king, I open a Jewish book, study a portion of the Pentateuch, Ethics of the Fathers, this, that, a noodle, an attic' (the last four words might be equivalent in English to 'a sliver of this and a snip of that'). The gusto of the Yiddish is transmitted in the Hebrew by end-rhymes. The Hebrew reads: 'When Sabbath eve is sanctified, who can compare with me and who is my equal then? I'm a king then, I rule the roost—look into a holy book, review the portion of the week according to the rules and regulations, that is I read the Pentateuchal text twice and Onkelos's translation once, besides the Song of Songs, Ethics of the Fathers, and hymns and prayers and other vegetables' (i.e. assorted goodies). The last four words of the Hebrew text are transliterated in the pronunciation of Eastern European Hebrew dialect '*òvis, zemìris, ushe' or yeròkis*' and were rhymed, it seems, in order to convey the flavour of the Yiddish original.

Berkowitz frequently omitted certain phrases altogether, while at other times he added such popular interjections as 'thank God', 'with the Lord's help', 'the Lord alone knows', and the like. These were evidently intended to simulate common speech and add a touch of colour.

When a humorous element in the original Yiddish depended upon a similarity of sounds between the quoted word and the

Yiddish comment, and this tonal equivalence could not be reproduced, it became necessary to invent alternative techniques. Towards this end, Berkowitz would build his pleasantries around new verses, deliberate blunders, or preposterous inaccuracies. Thus, to cite an example, when Tuvyah addresses Sholom Aleichem he says (in the Yiddish), 'If it's in the cards for someone to win, you hear Mr Sholom Aleichem, luck will come right into his house, what's the appropriate reference? *Lamenatzeiah al-ha-getes, as es geht—loift es*' (literally, if it goes—it runs). The witticism is based upon the similarity between the first line of Psalm 8 and the above 'reference'. An English analogue of this method, using the same verse would be: 'For the leader: Upon the *gittit*—you're the winner—if you *git it*!' Unable to reproduce the sound play in the Hebrew, Berkowitz substituted the following:

'Listen to me, Mr Sholom Aleichem, when fate begins to make its countenance shine upon someone, and the heavens take pity upon him, he is assured success in this world, as it is written in the High Holyday Prayer Book, "To everything there is a season," that is to say, everything depends on luck.' This verse, of course, is not found in the High Holyday Prayer Book but in Ecclesiastes 3:1, and its application here is patently and deliberately absurd.

The above examples demonstrate that Berkowitz assimilated the style and sense of the Yiddish while adapting them to accord with Hebrew expression.[14] In addition to serving as Sholom Aleichem's translator, confidant, secretary, and manager, Berkowitz was a foremost student and critic of his works. He had access to invaluable documents and manuscripts, and was also able to observe the master at first hand. Equally significant is the fact that Sholom Aleichem had found in his son-in-law a kindred spirit.[15]

14. See Y. Avinery, *I. D. Berkowitz, Oman ha-Signon, Gilyonot*, vol. 18, pp. 192-3 and B. Karu, *I. D. Berkowitz ha-Metargem, Moznayim*, June, 1967, pp. 12-15.
15. *Ha-Rishonim*, p. 129, where Berkowitz demonstrates that his knowledge of his master was sufficient to correct the date on one of Sholom

Berkowitz often had occasion to defend Sholom Aleichem from his more unreasoned critics whose limited literary sense had led them to see Sholom Aleichem not as a great and sensitive writer—but as a kind of buffoon. Particularly harsh were his criticisms against those members of the Jewish intelligentsia, dramatists and stage producers especially, who viewed Sholom Aleichem's work as nothing more than a mocking commentary on the plight of the Jews in Eastern Europe. 'Even today,' Berkowitz wrote in his memoirs, 'there are those interpreters [of Sholom Aleichem] who insist that Sholom Aleichem sketched what was grotesque in Jewish life, that he was the artist of distortion and excess. Our directors, either through misinterpretation or downright ignorance, stage Sholom Aleichem's characters as weird oafish bumpkins, dress them in an outlandish way and require the actors to perform with exaggerated gestures, the likes of which even extreme anti-semites could hardly imagine.'[16] Berkowitz often stressed that Sholom Aleichem, unlike Mark Twain, with whom he is often compared, never drew his material from the eccentric or abnormal in Jewish life. Day-to-day life provided him with sufficient inspiration and with an abundance of characters and situations, strange and amusing perhaps, but far from abnormal. His humour, Berkowitz maintained, has a sensitivity which transcends time and place because its inspiration was drawn from real and universal situations.

Unlike so many Jewish intellectuals, many Russian writers had a very deep appreciation of Sholom Aleichem's works. They recognized that his humour was not at all cynical, but rather that of a man of winsome disposition who viewed life with deep compassion.

Despite his admiration for Sholom Aleichem, Berkowitz was fully aware of the deficiencies in a number of his works, most

Aleichem's letters. Other errors of this nature are corrected by Berkowitz on pp. 83, 93, and 306. See also p. 83 where Berkowitz shows how Sholom Aleichem used historical and autobiographical material in his fiction.

16. *Ibid.*, p. 234.

especially in some of his plays. For example, he readily admitted that, though he had read and re-read *The Treasure* and
adapted it for the *Habimah* stage production, it was far from
satisfactory. The play *David ben David* disappointed Berkowitz
because of its weak dialogues and melodramatic subject. But,
while the early drafts of Sholom Aleichem's plays frequently
disturbed Berkowitz, who was often ready to suggest structural
changes, he was always fascinated by Sholom Aleichem's
imaginative experiments with film scripts, some of which,
Berkowitz felt, demonstrated a shrewd and sensitive understanding of the new medium.

In his work on Sholom Aleichem, Berkowitz had ready access
to the sort of information which is afforded very few literary
biographers and historians. From his own observation, and
from his close association with Sholom Aleichem, Berkowitz
concluded that, in addition to the considerable influence of
Mendele Mokher Seforim, there were indications that the then
popular Yiddish writer Yitzhak Yoel Linetzky had also made a
considerable impression upon him. Through critical analysis
and direct conversation, Berkowitz learned of the influence of
some of Sholom Aleichem's favourite authors, among whom
Knut Hamsun, Chekhov, Ibsen, Berenson, and Dickens were of
special importance.

Attempting to understand Sholom Aleichem's character and
explain his affinity to certain Hebrew writers, Berkowitz came
to learn of little known aspects of his career which seem, in an
oblique way, to explain something of Berkowitz's own affinity
to Sholom Aleichem. Berkowitz discovered that, although
Sholom Aleichem had abandoned traditional observance, he
remained a profoundly religious man. Only a close friend could
have known that a small Hebrew Bible always remained near
Sholom Aleichem's bed, and that the most worn pages were
those of the book of Job.[17] This illustrates strikingly the powerful perception of suffering that lies at the base of Sholom Aleichem's comedy—the permanent bond of suffering that linked
Sholom Aleichem to Berkowitz and to his people.

17. *Ibid.*, p. 47.

Chapter 4

STAGING THE PRESENT

COMPARED with other Hebrew literary forms, Hebrew drama
is in its infancy.[1] The first original Hebrew play, *Tzaḥut
Bediḥuta de-Kiddushin*, a comedy of love and marriage, was composed by Judah Sommo, an Italian Hebrew dramatist, in the
middle of the sixteenth century.[2] Hebrew drama was also to be
found in seventeenth- and eighteenth-century Italy and Holland.
For the most part it was patently imitative and limited in scope
to biblical themes. Hebrew drama of this period took the form
of morality plays and allegories that were clearly intended for
reading audiences and not for stage production. Linked with the
development of Hebrew dramatic art was an uninterrupted
tradition of Hebrew translations and paraphrased versions of
foreign plays. The nineteenth century saw a number of original

1. For a comprehensive survey of the history of Hebrew drama see D.
   Patterson, 'Hebrew Drama', *Bulletin of the John Rylands Library*, vol. 43,
   Sept. 1960, no. 1, pp. 88–108; C. Rabin, *Olelot le-Toledot ha-Dramah
   ba-Haskalah ha-Germanit, Melilah*, 1955, vol. 5, pp. 201–21. A complete
   list of early Hebrew plays is available in A. Yaari, *Ha- Maḥazeh ha-Ivri*
   (Jerusalem, 1956).
2. A critical edition of this play was published by Y. Schirmann, *Tzaḥut
   Bediḥutah de-Kiddushin*, 2nd ed. (Jerusalem, 1965). Although Patterson,
   op. cit., in footnote 1, cites two primitive dramas, one by a fifteenth-
   century Turkish Karaite and the other an early sixteenth-century Hebrew
   adaptation of Roja's *Celestina*, he also claims *Tzaḥut* to be the earliest
   full-length original Hebrew play. The *Jewish Encyclopaedia* lists M.
   Zacuto's play, *Yesod Olam* (1642?) as the first Hebrew drama simply
   because the text of *Tzaḥut* was unknown before Schirmann first published
   it from manuscripts in 1946. See, too, C. Roth, *The Jews in the Renaissance*
   (Philadelphia, 1959), chap. 11, 'The Jews in Renaissance Theatre,' pp.
   243–70.

Hebrew plays, none of which contributed significantly to the *genre*.

A unique dramatic form, the *Purimspiel*, deserves special mention if only for its prevalence throughout most mediaeval and even certain modern Jewish communities. At Purim time, Jewish leaders would sanction and often commission light-hearted satires, based upon the biblical book of Esther.[3] In this connection, it is noteworthy that of Berkowitz's minor one-act plays, the most successful was a *Purimspiel* subtitled 'A Farce in the Popular Style'. Berkowitz's introduction to the first edition stressed that this play was intended to be 'nothing more than a popular farce meant to amuse children of all ages during the Purim meal'.[4] In it, Ahasuerus appears as a drunkard, Vashti as a witch with a large, black wart on her forehead; Haman was endowed with one large and one very small eye and of the two courtiers, one was given a limp and the other a lisp. The playlet serves its purpose admirably and may well have sufficient charm to delight future generations of young readers.

His second one-act sketch, *Mi Navi ve-yeda* (Who Can Foretell) contains little of enduring value.[5] The two characters, both stock figures, Herzele Shpiel, a philandering cantor, and Sadie, an innocent young girl, engage in somewhat banal conversation based upon the popular belief that a girl should not marry a man who bears the same name as her father. Ignorant of the fact that both her boyfriend and father are called Herzele, although aware that they have the same name, he unwittingly undermines his own chances by convincing her of the absolute injunction against such matches. When the curtain drops Herzele is heard tediously trying to contradict his earlier claims. Both subject and exposition are contrived and trite.

Berkowitz's three full-length plays, however, command an eminent place in the history of Hebrew drama. Under the impetus of the national-cultural revival between the two World

3. See 'Purim Plays' in *Jewish Encyclopaedia*, vol. 10, pp. 279–80.
4. *Mikraot Ketanot*, p. 2. The text of the script without the author's prefatory remarks is provided in *Writings*, vol. 1, pp. 372–77.
5. The playscript is available in *Writings*, vol. 1, pp. 367–71.

Wars, several Hebrew theatre groups were formed in Russia and Poland. With the establishment of Palestine as the centre of Hebrew creative art, drama, too, seemed to develop more naturally. Reasons for this phenomenon are not difficult to find. Local audiences were anxious to further the cause of good theatre; a living vernacular was coming into being, and the *Yishuv* produced a number of playwrights who were anxious to present the vibrant issues of the day on the stage. Berkowitz's own plays, which were performed in Yiddish and Hebrew, and his translations of Sholom Aleichem, made a permanent contribution to Hebrew drama. It should be remembered that these efforts were made without the benefit of any substantial Hebrew tradition. The principles and techniques employed by Berkowitz, as by most of his contemporaries, were learned from the Russian realistic school and from Ibsen and Strindberg. The way was prepared for the realism of modern theatre.

Berkowitz was impressed by the new trends in the theatre and attempted to apply the new 'rules' for tragedy and comedy to plays with Jewish subjects. Though his work was not always free of melodrama, it succeeded nonetheless in raising the standards of Hebrew theatre. He is among the few Hebrew dramatists to describe the adventures and misfortunes of the Jews during the first decades of the twentieth century. Equally important is the fact that his scripts were meant to be performed. Full staging instructions pertaining to scenery, exits and entrances, and all the other details necessary for the production of a play were recorded in the most meticulous manner, and in other ways it is quite clear that Berkowitz was fully aware of the special demands made upon an author writing for the stage. In the two instances in which his plays are linked to previous short stories, he found it necessary to deviate completely from the original stories. He treated stage productions as distinct entities and not simply as variations of original prose narratives.

While still a relative newcomer to the field of dramatic criticism, Berkowitz wrote a scathing review of a performance of a widely acclaimed play by Jacob Gordon presented on Second Avenue in New York, the Broadway of the Yiddish theatre during the early decades of the present century. This review sheds light on the principles behind his own works.[6] After describing the production as tasteless, he attacked the audience for having applauded the work so immoderately, suggesting that anything more profound would have met with a less appreciative response. Berkowitz deplored the hackneyed moral and stilted style that seemed to constitute the backbone of plays such as this, and emphasized the importance of plays that tried to present on stage the obsessive drives and subconscious motives that actuate human conduct.

The three three-act plays are *Ba-Aratzot ha-Reḥokot* (In Distant Lands), *Oto ve-et Beno* (Him and His Son), and *Mirah*.[7] The first is a dramatized version of the author's short story *A Guest from Koslov* with certain prominent shifts in emphasis. The events of this fictional narrative are limited to a single evening in which Anton, a naïve young lad from Russia, arrives in Brownsville, New York, as a guest of the Cherniaks, who had come from the same town in Russia. Mr Naftali Cherniak, a recent immigrant to the United States, now a fruit vendor, is the father of four children: two sons, the elder Faivel (Philip) and an unnamed son, and two daughters, Bessie the elder and an unnamed sister. The main focus of the story is confined to Anton's initial introduction to what is described as a typical American Jewish immigrant household during the early years of the twentieth century. The background is provided as Anton is brought into the apartment, and as he and Mr Cherniak walk about the streets of the neighbourhood and the latter expounds upon the eminent role the Jews have played in the city's development. Naftali, apparently unaware of the calamitous nature of his circumstances, boasts endlessly about the 'American Dream'. His misuse of American phrases remains incomprehensible to his guest and impresses no one but the speaker.

6. A summary of this review appears in *Ha-Rishonim*, p. 152.
7. The scripts are to be found in *Writings*, vol. 1; *Ba-Aratzot ha-Reḥokot*, pp. 293–323, *Oto ve-et Beno*, pp. 323–45, *Mirah*, pp. 346–66. Yiddish versions of the first two plays were performed in Maurice Schwartz's Yiddish Art Theatre in New York and were highly successful.

Oblivious to the bleak realities of the 'sweat shops', Naftali glibly describes the wonderful conditions enjoyed by the factory workers. Anton's initiation concludes only after he has partaken of the 'American Dream'—in the form of such novelties as white bread and ice cream. Sated and bewildered, he falls asleep to Naftali's reminiscences with which the tale concludes.

The dramatized version, on the other hand, centres upon the children and specifically upon Bessie's romantic involvement with Anton. Consequently the play modifies the role of the father. At the prompting of her wanton friend, Rachel, who does not appear at all in the short story, Bessie is made aware of Anton's masculine charms. Slowly, she becomes infatuated with him, and begins to think of him as a potential husband, despite her family's vehement objections to her marrying a non-Jew. Her ardour is fanned by her girl friend's insistence that if Bessie does not run off with him, Rachel will abandon her Italian suitor and elope with Anton. At the end of the first act, after all these intrigues, the audience is made aware of the fact that Anton is married and the father of a young child.

Complications arise in the second act as Bessie's affection and endearments become obvious, and all members of the family, except the befuddled father, make every effort to put an end to her affair. Most adamant is her brother, Faivel, whom Bessie had financed through engineering school, and who now seems bent on ungratefully thwarting her only hope for a happy future. Events reach their climax when Sadie, the younger sister, announces that she has seen the pair kissing. When Faivel learns of this, he expels Rachel from the house, and prepares to avenge the insult. Meanwhile, Anton, overjoyed at hearing the news of the Russian Revolution, declares that he now intends to return to Russia, to his wife and child.

Beneath its humorous façade the play has tragic elements. The stage sets emphasize the humble surroundings of a poor Jewish immigrant who is unable to sustain his family. The weary young figures that he portrays seem frustrated and without hope. Faivel, a graduate engineer, feels restricted; his sister, no longer in her first youth, sees her long-held hopes of matri-

mony disappear before her eyes and begins to contemplate
suicide—a solution much favoured by Russian fiction and by
Berkowitz in a number of his short stories. Anton, bewildered
and alone, walks the streets of New York with no one to share
his excitement.

The humour both in the play and the story hinges, for the
most part, upon the repartee, the natural misunderstandings and
the foibles of Cherniak who tries to hide his identity but cannot
learn a proper pronunciation. He consistently mispronounces
certain words. He says 'Rockenfeller' for 'Rockefeller', 'in-
shineer' for 'engineer' and both he and his newly acquired companion, Anton, uniformly misuse such common phrases as
'Can't help it' or 'No ma'am'. Both are unable to cut themselves
loose from old habits, and their rough movements and gestures
are calculated to add to the overall effect. The final lines and
stage directions reiterate the tragi-comic tone of the entire
composition. Hearing the news of the revolution and Anton's
intended return they all join in singing, 'Praised be our God
who has created us for His Glory' as a toast to Anton and his
countrymen; all but Bessie, who is last seen with 'her shoulders
quivering with suppressed anguish!'

By far the best of Berkowitz's plays is *Him and His Son*
which was produced in Yiddish under the title *Untern Tzelem*
(Under the Cross) by the Yiddish Art Theatre in New York
and in Hebrew by the Habimah Theatre in Tel-Aviv. Through
its main character, Moshkele, it is directly linked with Berkowitz's prize-winning tale *Moshkele Pig*. There are however
great differences both of plot and structure in the play version.

The short story, written as a flash-back to explain the nick-
name *Moshkele Pig*, concentrates upon the unbearable plight
of the young Moshkele, whose half-demented father beats him
and locks him in the cellar as punishment for his pranks.
Physically intrepid, uninterested in his studies, tormented by
his father, Moshkele is driven to seek shelter in the house of his
Gentile friends who applaud his actions. In his new surroundings
he gradually sheds the yoke of Jewish ritual observance. He
meets Avdotia, a Gentile girl whose considerable charms do

not fail to have their effect. Anxious to hurt his father, he is converted and marries Avdotia. Moshkele, now ostracized by the Jewish community for his behaviour, regrets the sorrow he has caused his kind, ageing mother. Once a year, on the eve of *Yom Kippur*, the Day of Atonement, the most sacred day of the Jewish religious calendar, he forgoes dinner and wanders alone in the forest. One year on that day, he finds himself peering through the windows of the synagogue; he stands transfixed, until one of the worshippers recognizes him as the thirty-year-old, childless pig-merchant.

In contrast, the dramatic version presents Moshkele as a man whose intellectual capacity is evidenced by his large collection of books and journals and whose saintliness enrages his evil son Jacob and his graceless wife. By active participation in anti-Jewish pogroms, Jacob, the son of their ill-fated match, seeks to rid himself of all 'Jewish' vestiges that he may have inherited or acquired. Jacob feels persistently vexed by the delicate, book-loving wife, Tanya, whom his father had chosen for him. Instead he would have preferred an ignorant, but robust woman like his mother, Avdotia. His mother, for her part, feels she has been cursed and punished for her marriage to the incorrigible convert. She and her daughter-in-law bicker about their husbands; each begrudges the other her husband and is plagued by her choice.

All staged events occur during the twenty-four hours of *Yom Kippur*. This day of prayer and repentance emerges as a tangible presence that elevates the reported adventures beyond their specific context. The frenzied peasants, abetted by Jacob and incited by the call to revolution, initiate their forays against the Jews on *Yom Kippur*. This compels Meir Ber and Rehtze, his daughter, to beg asylum from the mob in Moshkele's home. The two are sheltered in his cellar, which soon resounds with the chanted prayers of *Kol Nidrei*. The next day, on *Yom Kippur*, their prayers apparently unheard, they are discovered, and despite pleas for mercy by Piatak the priest, and Tanya, they are dragged off and slaughtered. Provoked by this vicious act and incensed by the knowledge of Jacob's guilt, Moshkele vows revenge. He pulls his son into the cellar, where he sets himself, his son, and the house ablaze. Thereby, with atavistic submission and devotion, Moshkele, who mocked the Jews' suggestion of repentance through charity, prayer, and fasting, surrenders his life instead.

The biblical allusions in this play further accentuate its force. The title itself, *Oto ve-et Beno*, is a phrase which occurs but once in the Bible, in the immediate context of acceptable burnt offerings to be made to the Lord. 'And whether it be a cow or ewe, you shall not kill *it and its young* (*Oto ve-et beno*) both in one day.' (Lev. 22:28). In spite of the biblical injunction Moshkele, clutching the *Yom Kippur* prayer book, sets himself and his son afire on the day of *Yom Kippur*. Thereby, he purges himself and erases his son's name from among the children of God. Piatak's requiem that 'The sun sinks in flames . . . the Lord's wrath is ablaze. . . . They have led his children to slaughter, no one remains to chant a hymn of glory on this most sacred evening. . . .'[8] is heroically refuted by Moshkele bound now with the destiny of his tormented people.

The third drama, *Mirah*, is a totally independent work with no equivalent short story. Of all, this is the most typically Ibsenesque in that, by the final scene, each of the two central protagonists, the newly arrived Mirah and her fickle husband, David, has confessed a dark secret from the past.[9] The disclosure occurs in reaction to a third party, Florence, a dissolute divorcee whom David, assuming that his wife and son died in Europe, has been courting. Despite lapses into sentimentality both the characters and the dialogue are plausible and cogent.

In a style typical of Ibsen, the audience is put on its guard, from the first, in this case by Mrs Fradkin, the housekeeper hired by Nathan, David's elder bachelor brother and Mirah's ex-lover.[10] Everything is arranged in preparation for Mirah

8. *Writings*, vol. 1, p. 341.
9. On this feature as characteristic of Ibsen's plays see Francis Bull, *Ibsen the Man and the Dramatist* (Oxford, 1959), pp. 11–12.
10. This regular Ibsenesque technique is treated in U. E. Fermor, *The Frontiers of Drama* (London, 1945), p. 113.

and her son, who are due to arrive from Europe that evening. Mrs Fradkin intimates in her opening lines that in this new house she has forebodings of disaster. The feeling of impending doom is first suggested by a fur coat which Nathan had bought for Mirah and which Florence, who had bold-facedly thrust herself into the house while Nathan was away, now flippantly dons, to Mrs Fradkin's horror. Mrs Fradkin's inquisitiveness and innocence inject a humorous touch and advance the plot at the same time. One instance will suffice to illustrate this device. Mrs Fradkin inquires of Florence: 'Whom do you wish to see—the brother with the grey hair?'

> Florence: No, mine doesn't have grey hair.
> Mrs Fradkin: *Yours*—what do you mean *Yours*? Are you that close (relatives)?
> Florence: Very close, a cousin, perhaps closer than a cousin.
> Mrs Fradkin: What do you mean by perhaps? What is 'closer' supposed to mean? I don't understand you at all.[11]

The *double-entendre* of the word *karov* ('relative' and 'close', 'intimate') is the basis of the misunderstanding while at the same time it injects a touch of humour and arouses the audience's curiosity.

By the end of the first act, after Florence has told Nathan, 'There are no saintly women these days,—I can vouch for that. I know you were wild about your sister-in-law and still adore her',[12] she is introduced to Mirah as his fiancée, thereby avoiding the inevitable clash between the two women. The head-on encounter occurs in the second act when Florence, despite protestations from both the brothers, unabashedly reveals her true identity and the truth about her affair with David. She subsequently demands that Mirah divorce him and thus legitimize their relationship. She turns to Mirah and shouts, 'Why did you suddenly come? For years you have been hiding from your husband; you masqueraded as dead—what were you doing in the dark—with whom did you spend your time? It's not so straightforward as it seems!'[13] At this point Mirah, who does in fact have an intimate secret, feels threatened by this wanton

11. *Writings*, vol. 1, p. 348.   12. *Ibid.*, p. 351.   13. *Ibid.*, p. 360.

woman, and orders David to accompany Florence home. Upon
his return in the final act, he begs forgiveness for his conduct.
Mirah, in return, confesses that she had been raped by a Russian
revolutionary officer, after which she had hidden away and
had contemplated suicide. Upon hearing this story David,
delirious with rage, calls her a prostitute. Their son rebukes his
father for the insult and finally David falls helplessly at Mirah's
feet. They are reconciled—and in the final line of the play,
David addresses her as 'Miritchke, my good angel'.

All three plays are realistic dramas. None of the *dramatis
personae* is idealized or romanticized; the settings are authentic
and the general social and cultural milieu is convincing. The
backdrops and stage directions both combine to lend the
works an air of realism. Contrived 'conceits' are avoided.
The total effect, nonetheless, depends upon enigmatic lines,
sometimes even entire scenes, which are only understood as the
plot unfolds. Each work provides novel examples of the 'new
woman': in two of them, *In Distant Lands* and *Mirah*, the independent female is presented as licentious; in *Him and His Son*,
she is literate and sensitive, unlike the women of her immediate
environment.

Mirah and *Him and His Son* are constructed in accordance
with the so-called principles of the unities: in each, the action
spans no more than one day. In *Him and His Son*, the time portrayed is the day of *Yom Kippur*. The play opens on the eve of
the holiday, the second act depicts the next morning with its
impending climax evident, and concludes the same evening.
The time span in *Mirah* is confined to the evening of Mirah's
arrival. Act One occurs several hours prior to her homecoming,
Act Two takes place some time later after her arrival, and the
third act is at midnight. The opening act of *In Distant Lands*
relates scenes at the beginning of World War I, whereas the
events of the second and third acts occur consecutively, but
some three or four years later—towards the end of the war. Two
of the three acts fulfil the requirements of time-unity and thus
condense the time interval, thereby eliminating the need for
extra-dramatic, off-stage information.

All three plays were composed in accordance with the second principle of unity—the unity of place. That is, all staged events occur in one location. Consequently the need for change of scenery is avoided, while the audience's attention is focused squarely on the characters who appear, in this way, to be enclosed and circumscribed by an unchanging framework.

Berkowitz sub-titled the three works as follows: *In Distant Lands*: A Comedy in Three Acts, *Him and His Son*: A Drama in Three Acts, and *Mirah*: A Play in Three Acts. Despite their appellations, tragedy reverberates throughout them all. The curtain falls on *Him and His Son* as the desperate father has just taken his own life and that of his recalcitrant son. Despite the apparent reconciliation between Mirah and her husband—the direct outcome of the cathartic purge of mutual guilt—a sombre mood prevails as she dutifully aquiesces to living under one roof with her dispirited husband, their agonized son, and her elegant and magnanimous brother-in-law. *In Distant Lands* has the same superficial trappings of comedy, but nonetheless retains tragic undertones. After the final scene Bessie, a twenty-six-year-old spinster, remains in anguish after tasting the joys of love for the first time.

Yet, following an accepted pattern of tragedy, Berkowitz provided his audience with comic relief in the form of slapstick figures such as a gossipy housemaid or a half-witted watchman. Again, with almost classical precision, Berkowitz's plays are somewhat artificially divided into the 'required' three parts. Each play begins with an exposition in which the postures and attitudes of the protagonists and their various relationships are delineated along with some intimation of the particular conflicts about to transpire. The 'complication', or second phase, lays bare these conflicts and unfolds them in a confrontation of the adversaries, which leads directly to the final act, during which the tensions are relieved by some definite resolution.

It is noteworthy that in a period rife with social, political, and economic ferment, none of Berkowitz's plays is turned into a platform for doctrinaire comment. Berkowitz comes closest to this in his statements on immigration to Palestine. These may seem superfluous to some, but they are artistically plausible in their specific contexts. Each of the plays makes some reference to this topic. The most emphatic and potent declarations are those of Moshkele and Piatak in *Him and His Son*. Moshkele, being asked where he would like to go, replies, 'I'd like to go there [Palestine]; that's the place I yearn for. There I'll plough and sow and grind grain for bread; then I'll be like other men— not hunchbacked. There I'll purchase a plot of land and a house. I'll work and I'll be alone and not bother anyone else.'[14] This and similar statements, artistically integrated into the body of the works, neither detract from the plays nor from the charac- ters' credibility. In depicting the present, Berkowitz always sought effective means to portray the dilemmas and destinies of his modern Jews.

14. *Ibid.*, p. 337.

Chapter 5

SEVERED HEROES

THE purpose of this chapter is to analyze the characters, general themes, and plots found in Berkowitz's short stories and novellas. The next two chapters will concern themselves with language, style, and texture (chapter six) and fictional structures and patterns (chapter seven).

The tragic accents that dominate much of modern literature and prevail in modern Hebrew fiction, preponderate in Berkowitz's tales. His central characters are linked to one another by certain common characteristics that reflect the atmosphere of their age as much as the personality of the author. Several of these figures are linked to historical persons whom the author knew and who served as his models.[1] Whether due to identification with their lot, familiarity with their dilemmas, or awareness of their fictional potentialities, Berkowitz appears to have concentrated on isolated and hopeless Jews and Jewesses. These tragic figures, like their Russian counterparts, are defeated in their despairing struggles against hostile social and psychological forces. Chekhov's characters who suffer from *nadry* —overstrain, severance, and isolation[2]—are particularly interesting parallels to Berkowitz's figures.

1. These are specified in *Pirkei Yaldut*, p. 69; G. Yardeni, *Tet-Zayin Sihot*, p. 20; N. Chinitz *Misihotai im I. D. Berkowitz*, *Hadoar*, vol. 49, No. 1. Jan. 3, 1969, pp. 151–2. In an interview Berkowitz disclosed that he had several unpublished tales all of which are linked with people and places he knew as a child (Aviva Hazaz, interviewer for Oral History Division of the Institute of Contemporary Jewry, The Hebrew University in Jerusalem).

2. On the major moods in classical Russian realism see J. E. Simmons, *Introduction to Russian Realism* (Bloomington, 1965) and Sidney Monas's introductory comments to L. Shestov, *Chekhov and Other Essays* (Ann Arbor, 1966) and pp. 4–35. Simon Halkin in his Hebrew work, *Mavo*

While examining the dominant moods and postures of modern society, Kenneth Keniston has tried to create an 'index of alienation'. This seems so strikingly relevant that it may be worth quoting in full:

> Increasingly, the vocabulary of social commentary is dominated by terms that characterize the sense of growing distance between men and their former objects of affection. Alienation, estrangement, disaffection, anomie, and neutralism—all of these point to a sense of loss, a growing gap between men and their social world . . . The prevailing images of our culture are images of disintegration, decay, and despair . . . The index of alienation is measured by degree of distrust, pessimism, resentment, anxiety, egocentricity, sense of being an outsider, rejection of conventional values, rejection of happiness as goal, feeling of distance from others, subspection [the desire to look below appearances], self-contempt, and a view of the universe as unstructured and meaningless chaos.[3]

Thus, social estrangement and isolation stand out as hallmarks of modern man who, ill at ease with his immediate environment, knows no tranquility nor sees any sense in the pre-determined social surroundings into which he was born. Directly related to this general feeling of alienation and tension is a most sharply felt strain with the members of one's family. Disintegrating family unity and waning parental authority emerge as fixed motifs. The perennial 'generation gap', bringing with it widespread social disintegration and erosion, figures as both a cause and a by-product of communal and domestic breakdown. The awareness of rootlessness is sharpened by the increased ease of transportation and communication. Finding no peace at home, modern man is condemned to search for an eternally elusive utopia.

Dissatisfaction with economic conditions is another recurrent theme of modern literature. The economic factor looms as an almost insuperable obstacle in man's struggle for independence.

la-Sipporet ha-Ivrit (Jerusalem, 1958) discusses briefly Chekhov's impact on modern Hebrew fiction (pp. 431ff.).

3. K. Keniston, The Uncommitted (New York, 1960), pp. 3–25.

Disturbed by the external socio-economic constituents of human existence, modern man is further distressed by his inner dilemmas. Aware of the dimensions of his psychological condition, the modern hero is torn between two worlds—the conscious and the unconscious. The isolated hero is frustrated because he is unable to bridge the two planes of reality that constantly irritate him. The superficial he knows to be illusory while the permanent features of reality seem always elusive. Above all there is the abiding conflict between *eros* and *thanatos* between sensual love and death. Finally, he learns of the fated victory of death over love, of destiny over romance, of fact over fantasy.[4]

Berkowitz, as a young man, was very conscious of homelessness, rejection, and alienation. His crisis was symptomatic, not only of the general problems of twentieth-century man, but particularly of the plight of the Jews in Eastern Europe.

The theme of loneliness is boldly imprinted on Berkowitz's stories by the fact that the principal figures are often very young children, prematurely aged by oppressive circumstances, forlorn bachelors, unmarried young women in their prime, and widows. For example, in *In a Foreign Place* and *Confession*, baldly tendentious narratives, the main protagonists are forsaken bachelors who endure solitude because of their blind devotion to the revolutionary cause which has denied them friendship and affection. Disillusioned, they recognize that these movements were, in fact, no more than a series of insignificant intrigues and futile doctrinaire debating societies. Endeavouring to return to traditional ways and abandoned homes, they discover that all avenues of return are barred. One of these disenchanted rebels, Mark Syrkin (*Confession*), dies immediately after recounting the details of his vacuous life—and reciting to his girlfriend, Clara, a list of sins he has committed against his people and his family. He concludes his last testament with a touching per-

4. On these themes in modern fiction see, for example, L. Lowenthal, 'Literature and Sociology' and F. C. Crews, 'Literature and Psychology' in J. Thorpe (ed.), *Relations of Literary Study: Essays on Interdisciplinary Contributions* (New York, 1967), pp. 73–110.

sonal denial of the revolutionary objectives whose gentile adherents had betrayed their Jewish colleagues. The other revolutionary, Zibolin (*In a Foreign Place*), distraught that his fellow
travellers had acted insincerely and had rejected his efforts on
their behalf, withdraws from the arena and finds temporary
solace in a chant from the Jewish high holyday ritual. However this release is short-lived; his Jewish companions enter his
room and dash all hopes of personal retreat and restoration to
the Jewish people.

In a strangely contemporary way, all of Berkowitz's leading
characters are ill at ease with their environment, and fail to find
meaning and contentment in their routine lives. In one form
or another they all react against their immediate surroundings.
Nonetheless they all submit to their fate sooner or later, and
bemoan life's cruelty. Some wrest meaning from the bitter
contest and may even appear to have won the struggle, but they
all remain pathetic figures.

In contrast to the enigmatic backgrounds of many contemporary fictional heroes, however, none of Berkowitz's characters is presented as emerging from an anonymous social setting. In each case, the author describes the social, economic,
and intellectual milieu to which the character is bound, however tenuously. Nevertheless, the characters still retain a desperate feeling of non-commitment. They are related to their
background solely in a negative manner.

In one form or another *shtetl* life with its fixed institutions,
mores, and social structures serves as a constant antagonist with
which the characters must contend. In their determination to
assert their freedom from it, they never completely uproot
themselves, nor do they eradicate its reality from their consciousness. The *shtetl* serves as a foreboding background with
only its sombre aspects presented. When, however, by dint
of estrangement the hero has wandered far from his birthplace,
the *shtetl*, in retrospect, becomes the nostalgic nexus for which
he yearns; but having once spurned it, he is never able to return. Paradoxically, the closer, physically, the character is to
the concrete *shtetl*, the more dismal it appears—the further he

moves, the more idyllic it seems. Of these fugitives from Judaism who hardly ever arrive in the spiritual sense Professor S.
Halkin writes: 'They are the young Jews who come to the
metropolises of the world, seeking forgetfulness of the gravelike
home town. Yet they discover that they cannot forget it. . . .
These fugitives from the ghetto therefore forever remain in a
kind of no man's land.'[5]

In the decaying world of the *shtetl* old traditions are in rapid
decline, the families are disintegrating and migrating, the younger
generation need no longer fight for the right to partake of western
culture, for even the parents now proudly share their children's
new accomplishments. The problems these maturing individuals
face are those of the post-*Haskalah* era. The early *Maskilim*
endured the contempt and derision of the established Jewish
society but the youngsters in Berkowitz's tales no longer face
the same hardships. Their right is no longer contested.[6]

The contemporary struggle is subjective and psychological:
it is concerned with the impact of the tensions between the
dialectical forces of Jewish and western civilizations as they
converge upon and engage the individual. The focus has shifted
from the struggle between the generations for the privilege of
partaking in western enlightenment, to the inner struggles of
the adolescent Jew who for reasons now beyond his control is
severed from the old and yet remains somehow irrevocably
bound to it. He is alienated from one society yet cannot set
himself firmly in another. The centre of consciousness has
moved from the 'type' to the specific character who, though
sharing the same fundamental problems as other of Berkowitz's
characters, remains an individual as opposed to a stock
figure.

5. S. Halkin, *Modern Hebrew Literature*, pp. 87–8. Halkin in his Hebrew
   volume, *op. cit.*, analyzes the etymology of the Hebrew term *talush*
   (uprooted) and its inappropriate application to Berkowitz's heroes (pp.
   339–71). According to Berkowitz's daughter, Mrs Kahana, he preferred
   talush to be translated as 'severed'.
6. A sole exception is exemplified by the harsh comments expressed by the
   teacher in *A Proud Father*, p. 58.

Berkowitz's stories reflect the theme of the deteriorating family unit. Individual Jews, particularly members of the younger generation, are, for the most part, intolerant of and disgusted with their elders' inflexible views. The breakdown of the traditional Jewish family structure is heightened by the fact that in several stories the father has lost his role as the authoritative mainstay of the household and the bearer and transmitter of Jewish traditions. Divested of these functions and of his virility by reason of physical or mental disabilities, he is no longer capable of supporting the household, of educating his many offspring or of carrying on the ancient customs. The fathers, as in *Faivke's Judgement Day*, are often cast as weaklings, incapable of attaining their objectives and immobilized by their own personalities. The naïve Moshe Yosi, father of Leizer (*A Proud Father*), is frustrated in his efforts to gather an audience ready to listen to the joyful tale of his son's success.[7] Moshe Yosi is condemned to relate his joy to a puzzled youngster and ultimately to the wind, and Chekhov's Iona the coachman, finding no human ready to pay heed to the grievous story of his son's death finally repairs to the stable to tell the whole episode to an old horse. Unlike Iona, however, Moshe Yosi is portrayed as the weakling in his family. Though exuberant over his son's academic achievements, Moshe Yosi had little to do with them; he observes them all as an outsider. The mother, in this case as in several others, is the dominant figure both in business matters and in all household concerns.

Similarly, Yeruham the shoemaker (*The Letter*), deeply grieved by the news that his unmarried daughter is pregnant, pounces on a young lad of twelve whom he instructs to write a letter to his children in America. Thwarted by his inability to let the woeful news pass his lips, he releases his anger on the studious lad, whom he beats mercilessly. Shakhna Pandra (*The Minstrels*), left to raise his orphaned grand-daughter, and helpless in the face

7. Similar in theme to this tale is Chekhov's story, *Misery*, in which an old cab driver tries to tell his wealthy, preoccupied customers about his son's death. F. O'Connor, *The Lonely Voice: A Study of the Short Story* (New York, 1965), p. 83, comments on this tale.

of fresh problems, takes to drink. The father in *A Male Child* is bitterly reproached by his children for having sired another child. Pathetically hoping for vindication from his 'aristocratic' friends whom he has invited to attend a Friday evening party in honour of the new-born infant, he is broken by their deliberate absence. Without any support he remains listless under his own roof.

The conflict of generations also lies at the heart of *At the Table*, a rather trite but revealing sketch. Moshe Elyah, a boorish, surly father, insensitive to the disintegration of his family, controls his household by brutality. At the Sabbath table, noisily and greedily sucking at a meat bone to the utter disgust of those assembled, Moshe Elyah pauses in order to insult his son Raphael, whom he notices sitting at the table bareheaded. In like manner, Hayyim David, the hypocritical father (*Guests*), hastening eagerly to invite the patriarchs, who symbolically attend every *sukkah*, is appalled at the sudden arrival of his dumb brother Eliose. Only after his educated daughter's forceful insistence and persistent coaxing does he agree to have him join them at the festive dinner table. Likewise, Mariashka's father (*Mariashka*) is a pious but rather foolish man on the verge of blindness. Equally pitiful is Shifrah's father (*Cucumbers*), who has relinquished all familial responsibilities to his wife. Mad Michael (*Evil Spirits*) exemplifies degeneracy and impotence. As his name indicates, he is the victim of depressing and dementing melancholy. The father of a houseful of children, Mad Michael spends his entire winter oblivious of the world, rolled up in his blanket by the stove, in the grip of uncontrollable hallucinations. These are usually followed by terrifying nightmares which incapacitate him to such an extent that he is unaware of his infant son's death, his mature daughter's insanity and his whining children's needs.

Generally mated to the spineless and infirm father is a strong-willed but not very kindly mother.[8] In most of Berkowitz's

8. This is in sharp contrast to Berkowitz's portraits of his parents, who are described as understanding, affectionate, and gentle. *Pirkei Yaldut*, pp. 124ff.

narratives the mothers are harassed and fatigued by incessant economic hardships, extremely large families and disturbed husbands. Moshkele's mother cannot forestall his doom. Faivke's well-meaning mother seeks relief through prayer, but her prayers go unattended and, inadvertently, she becomes the cause of her son's premature death. In contrast, however, the memory of a compassionate mother ready at all times to console her prodigal son is all that remains for one dejected revolutionary. After her death, he realizes that he is ruined, for now he must live without any solace (*Confession*). Zevulun (*In a Foreign Place*) expresses this realization when, in the course of a soliloquy, he exclaims: 'While my mother was alive I still possessed a spot on earth to which I could return in my thoughts and dreams—now I am free, divested of responsibility, but barren and naked. . . .'[9]

The adolescents in Berkowitz's short stories seek to live their lives in accordance with their principles, which are inspired by contemporary ideologists and novelists. Popular Hebrew novels, essays and poems lead them to abhor the present, to revile the past, and to dream of a romantic world identical to the fictitious world of this literature which they read with such enthusiasm. Disregarding their past, these adolescents revolt against traditional Jewish habits as they anxiously seek entrance into modern anomian society.

The estrangement of the main characters is somehow related to socio-economic factors, which are frequently elaborated.[10] The *Power of Speech*, although one of the author's lesser works, relates the story of the rich upstart Mrs Mikhlin, who brings her smug, overfed son for a fitting to a newly-wed and rather simple tailor, called Bentzie. Upon completion of the garment, the robust mother puts relentless pressure upon the tailor in the hope of reducing the already minimal charge. Unable to express

9. *Writings*, vol. I, p. 76.
10. I. Rabinovich elaborates upon this topic in *Major Trends in Modern Hebrew Fiction*, trans. M. Roston (Chicago and London, 1968), pp. 150–2.

himself properly in the presence of the rich woman whose future patronage he needs, Bentzie accepts his fate and concludes that the way of the moneyed has always been to harass the poor. The socio-economic element also underlies the lamentable predicament of Moshe-Moti (*Maftir*), Avramtze's reticent father, who because of his poverty is thwarted in his efforts to outbid the rich grandees of the synagogue for a portion of the Torah reading. The class struggle and its consequences affect character development in several other stories. It is, for instance, a socio-economic conflict that lies at the root of Dr Winik's distress (*Severed*). As a poor egg-merchant's son who had persevered through medical school, he has been given a grudging welcome into Bourgeois society, which does not, however, forgive him his lowly origin. There are times when Dr Winik becomes disgusted with this circle and with Mr Berger, who represents it, and whose saccharine affection and unethical activities repel him. At such times he is once again attracted to his indigent brothers and their families who carry on their father's trade. But in their company, while yearning to be reconciled, he recognizes how far he has strayed. To the end he is irresolutely torn between the Bergers and his brothers: both attract and repel, both bewilder and provoke him.

Another manifestation of the class struggle presents itself in the intellectual's contempt and derision for the Jewish farmers. In *A Barbarian*, Hershl is from the outset dismayed by his potential employer's boorishness and ignorance. But since his poverty-stricken parents cannot afford to support him, nor satisfy his insatiable appetite for reading, he accepts the offered position. However, on the road to the farm, he jumps off the wagon and remains alone on the deserted highway. This is the only Berkowitz tale in which the hero acts in accordance with his principles and rescues himself—in this case from the monotonous existence of a tutor to the children of an uncouth farmer.

Another tutor, Levinson (*Mariashka*), dismisses his patron and family as 'inhuman and indecent'. Consequently they are unworthy of anything more than casual, subtly caustic remarks that are never fully understood by the illiterate rustics.

To add to the sense of aimlessness, most of Berkowitz's chief figures seem constantly on the move. Whether physically wandering from place to place, or mentally tortured, none finds respite or peace. Issachar Ber (*In Distant Lands*) is a tragic figure who has recently returned to the *shtetl* after a lengthy stay in America. The effect is devastating. He finds the *shtetl* unfamiliar and insufferably parochial. During his first winter he languishes in his hovel and agonizes on the irrevocable folly of his return home. Embittered, he finds no place for himself in the *shtetl* and knows no escape. He becomes bad-tempered and irascible and, to the disgust of his neighbours, never ceases making comparisons between the poverty of the *shtetl* and the delights of America. Similar pangs of isolation are felt by the aged Mrs Rabinowitz (*Twilight*) who, driven by her reduced circumstances to America to live with her insensitive and materialistic son, is condemned to listen to her son's constant boasting about his wealth. The more he flaunts his prosperity, the more she senses the distress of alienation. After sampling the vulgar social and religious life of America's Jewry she feels the emptiness of this new life and longs for the old.

Another example of a consuming sense of loneliness is to be found in the plight of the thrill-seeking, adventurous bachelor chauffeur (*The Chauffeur*), who, although living in Palestine, is the victim of desperate loneliness, while constantly driven in search of excitement and sensual stimulation.

It is necessary, therefore, to temper the conclusions of several literary critics who have pointed out the changes in Berkowitz's tone and themes after his settling in Palestine. Their generalizations about change in subject-matter hold good for his longer works, in which new attitudes are manifested. However, the anonymous chauffeur retains all the symptoms of the severed hero. The landscape and situations may have altered; yet, just as his European counterparts found the *shtetl* confining, he cannot tolerate the self-contained *kibbutz*, and is compelled to abandon it and roam the land in quest of the majestic open spaces which, he feels, will mitigate his loneliness.[11]

The distress of alienation is not restricted to those who have crossed the Atlantic or the Mediterranean. People who have left the confines of the Pale and tasted, for a while, the anonymity of big-city life express the same feelings. Thus Shifrah (*Cucumbers*), after spending some time as a seamstress in a great city, becomes homesick and returns to her family, whose entire existence rotates around the cucumber harvest. Initially she enjoys her stay. But she soon becomes aware of her miserable plight as an unmarried woman whose barren life now seems, in contrast to her experience in the city, doomed to eternal boredom. Aware of the hopelessness of her condition, she prays for death and even contemplates suicide.

The development of plot and character is predictable. The events portrayed do not purport to alter the static character's nature.[12] Rather, the behavioural patterns, through heightened dramatization, further delineate the basic features. Tormented and alone, the character degenerates in the face of misfortune until, with resistance gradually sapped, he ultimately relapses into a state of inertia and in the final scenes is heard bewailing his absurd condition.

One of Berkowitz's earliest stories (*Yom Kippur Eve*) portrays a disheartened child, Yosel David, who, upon hearing his parents bickering with their business partner on the day preceding *Yom Kippur*, feels himself, as it were, 'tossed in a sling by some cosmic force'. The boy is reconciled with his kindly father and shrewd business-minded mother in the course of the next morning.

Such reconciliation, however, is rare in Berkowitz's stories and is absent in his treatment of his more mature heroes and even in the case of another boy, Faivke (*Faivke's Judgement*

---

11. Berkowitz himself takes this literary metamorphosis for granted. This is expressed in his interview with Galia Yardeni, *Tet-Zayin Siḥot*, p. 20.

12. These terms, 'static' and 'developing' are discussed and illustrated in H. Fenson and H. Kritzer, *Reading, Understanding, and Writing about Short Stories* (New York, 1966), pp. 7ff.

Day). The latter is a mischievous, nature-loving boy of nine whose almost prophetic awe of the mighty hand of God arouses in him a feeling of isolation and fear in the synagogue, to which he is brought, against his will, on *Yom Kippur* eve. Together with his father, Matis the Blacksmith, he endures the insults of some local ruffians who, oblivious to the sanctity of the day, torment both father and son.

Berkowitz's unmarried women dream of romantic love affairs and are frequently driven insane. In *Mariashka* a major part of Levinson's adventures in the home of his charges concerns his involvement with Mariashka, a very attractive girl whose impoverished parents had sent her to work as a chambermaid in the same household. Struck by his good looks and his kindness, she finally goes to bed with him. Levinson, realizing that he has exploited her, seeks some means to console her. This he achieves by preaching to her about the nobility of menial labour and the equality of man. However, he can never bring himself to carry out the redemptive act that would have lent substance to his words. Instead, he fills her mind with empty thoughts and leaves her to her dreams. Shorn of hope, dignity and purpose, she too contemplates suicide.

The previously mentioned Shifrah (*Cucumbers*), experiences erotic fantasies because of the romantic novels she reads at every opportunity. Comparing her lot with that of her romantic heroes and heroines she curses her drab existence. Left to herself, she dreams of one moonlit evening when a handsome suitor will rush to her side and, taking her hand to his lips, passionately propose to her. She then goes on to dream of the sexual fulfilment that their marriage will bring. Her personal tragedy is intensified by these flights of imagination that never cease to torment her.

Dr Winik (*Severed*) notices the full extent of Miss Berger's beauty at his brother's funeral. However, in his relationship with her, as in his relationship with his new social milieu, he remains until the end ambivalent and indecisive. Whenever he considers the possibility of marriage, he is put off by the fear that women will court him because of his professional position and not because of his personal qualities. Winik flounders between reflections about his brother's death on the one hand, and romantic thoughts about young externs and their sweethearts on the other. The tension between thoughts of *thanatos* and *eros* is dramatized in the episode in which Miss Berger and Winik go for a stroll. He becomes intolerant of her prattle as he thinks about his brother's impending death. These reflections absorb and dominate him. He is convinced that he will never marry. In the final scene, walking behind his brother's bier, he notices Miss Berger looking at him from her balcony. She then appears to have 'kind, intimate eyes, full of grief and compassion'. In this dominantly pessimistic tale, kindness and compassion, two extremely rare words in Berkowitz's vocabulary, appear here for the first and only time. Winik is affected— but apparently it is too late. He continues following the coffin, aware that 'he would always be torn between these two forces, and would never know to which he belonged or in which of them his destiny lay'. This ambivalent anti-hero is not only alienated by the class struggle, but is also torn between the forces of love and death. His tragedy is without any ready solution.

In another instance, Zlotka, Michael the Mad's daughter (*Evil Spirits*), suddenly becomes deranged. After being subdued by her brothers, she peers through her window and imagines life's most unattainable delights. She is aroused to passion by erotic visions of beautiful, nude maidens enticing sexually deprived monks who had been stealthily observing them. Enraged by these projections of her own desires, she flees from her room only to be driven back by her brothers, who subsequently send her away for a cure. Exorcized of the 'evil spirits', her vitality is sapped and she sulks motionless, a pale apathetic figure quite unmoved by the world around her.

As has been indicated in several of these cases, suicide recurs as a constant motif. In despair, several of Berkowitz's characters contemplate suicide. Always the plot is similar; the hero stands on a bridge over a lake and considers throwing himself into the deep waters below. The act, although never carried out, exacts its toll from the sufferer. Faivke dies soon after entertaining this possibility, Mariashka and Zlotka never return to normalcy, and the grandmother in *Grandchild* becomes even more desperate as a result of the suicidal thoughts induced by her daughter's illegitimate pregnancy. Nowhere does Berkowitz try to soften the blows of all-powerful Fate—a force that wields absolute dominion.

Of all Berkowitz's leading characters only two can, in any sense, be termed leaders. His heroes are superior neither to other men nor to their own surroundings.[13] In fact even Mishael (*Mishael*) a possible leader type, is a teen-age lad who is annually rejuvenated when almost single-handedly he organizes and conducts the sale of *hoshanot*. He is a classic hero for one week in every year. He, too, in the end is circumscribed by the rest of the year, during which time he is a totally incapacitated cripple.[14] Of all Berkowitz's characters, Faivke alone approaches the stature of a traditional hero figure—perhaps, paradoxically, because of his total isolation. He is cast as superior to his father, mother, and the Jews of the synagogue into whose orbit he is tossed, and against which he instinctively rebels. His premature death also enhances his 'heroic' qualities. One might almost say that because his natural qualities were superior to those of his generation, the world drove him from its midst as an outcast.

Berkowitz seems intent on telling a story in as specific and stark a manner as possible. He presents a host of disinherited and irresolute figures, assaulted by external and internal forces which succeed in destroying them. Berkowitz's novellas are peopled by Jews whose vivacity has been sapped and whose efforts at self-renewal and re-dedication have at every turn been violently shattered. Defiant towards traditional religious and moral systems that have failed, and sceptical of all suggested

13. Northrop Frye suggests a classification of fictional genres according to the hero's 'power of action'. For details see his *Anatomy of Criticism* (New York, 1966), pp. 33ff.
14. Several details add to Mishael's mysterious nature: he is not considered human by the adult society, he is an outcast, and his energies are 'revived' annually in a way reminiscent of ancient nature-god myths.

panaceas, these tragic figures retreat into a shadowy world of fantasy.[15]

15. Frank O'Connor in his study of the modern short story pays particular attention to the 'submerged' and 'outlawed' figures who populate the narratives and have become, in his opinion, the focus of modern literary interest. F. O'Connor, *op. cit.*, 13–45. In this regard see, too, M. Krieger, *The Tragic Vision: Variations on a Theme in Literary Interpretation* (Chicago, 1966), pp. 14–20.

Chapter 6

THE LONELY IMAGINATION

THIS chapter seeks to provide an introductory analysis of Berkowitz's more dominant similes and metaphors, including his use, for aesthetic reasons, of various comparisons drawn from animal life. It also attempts to examine briefly the literary implications of the use of sacred Jewish terminology for describing 'secular' experiences and the stock phrases employed for depicting despair. Finally, reference will be made to Berkowitz's artistic application of dreams and his use of associations.[1]

All of Berkowitz's major stories, and a number of his minor ones contain as their essential vocabulary such words as *alone*, *foreign*, *strange*, and *despair*.[2] These determine the mood which is subsequently amplified and expanded by other artistic techniques. In *Severed*, for instance, the adjective 'strange' appears in at least ten different contexts. It is no less fundamental to the other tales.

In *Severed* the author, by means of a series of images, graphically conveys the anti-hero's persistent struggle to liberate himself from the grip of his family, his age and his erotic drives. At the outset of the tale Dr Winik is described as an apparently contented 'victor' who, by becoming a physician had gained

1. Critical examinations of these and other artistic considerations of the short story are provided in R. Wellek and A. Warren *Theory of Literature* (London, 1961), pp. 164ff; G. Trask and C. Burkhart, eds., *Storytellers and their Art* (New York, 1963) chapters 4 and 5; and S. O'Faolain, *The Short Story* (New York, 1964), pp. 227–34. The application of poetry analysis to prose narratives is treated, too, in D. Van Ghent, *The English Novel: Form and Function* (New York, 1953), pp. 110ff.
2. In an autobiographical aside the author mentions that even as a youngster he identified closely with Mendele Mokher Seforim's *Mendele* precisely because of his poverty, loneliness, and desperation (*Ha-Rishonim*, p. 15).

his victory.[3] At the same time, significantly, he is described as being 'not essentially a war-like man'. Towards the middle of the story, the military imagery shifts—he is now portrayed as 'one who has fled the battlefield, too fatigued to carry on the struggle'. In the final scenes he is compared to a 'crying infant'. These images, tracing Winik's decline from triumphant conqueror to exhausted renegade and finally to helpless child, underline most graphically the episodes which bring about his final disillusionment.

A closer look at these and other intervening images will disclose their relationship with the plot of the story. To the victor, the vanquished seem estranged. Yet in truth, the captor never fully succeeds in subjugating the vanquished people who carry on living on their land. Living on foreign territory among strangers, it is often the victor who remains alienated. In a sense, then, he paradoxically becomes their subject.

The ambiguity inherent in this primary simile is maintained in a description that follows immediately after Winik's appearance as victor. He is now compared to a 'sapling which, by some quirk of fate, has been uprooted from its rugged native abode and transplanted into fertile, but foreign soil'. Thus in a simple, but cogent image, the hero's victory is undermined and his eventual defeat foreseen. Winik is dominated by an unbearable sense of estrangement. His environment remains incomprehensible and unfriendly, and Winik the victor remains as rootless and disinherited as the transplanted sapling.

Soon after this analogy, the author temporarily abandons the military image and introduces another striking simile. Dr Winik's efforts to enter the élite circle and become established in society sap his energies. 'Superficially, he appeared as one of them, participating fully in their comfortable lives . . . But he was secretly plagued by an oppressive sense of loneliness mixed with envy and contempt for all that surrounded him, almost like the feeling of an incurably sick person who happens to come into the cheerful company of healthy people. . . .' The

3. An interesting comparative study could be made between this tale and J. L. Levin's poem *Kishron Ha-Maaseh* (published in Vienna, 1877).

full implications of his distress are concentrated into this last simile of an incurable doctor who cannot heal himself. The irony is clear—the doctor has become hopelessly sick. Moreover, in the presence of his female friends, Dr Winik is not compared to a victor. Among women he wins no laurels and knows no victories. Moreover, in this area his professional accomplishments, earlier considered an apparent victory, now prove the cause of his downfall. A whole-hearted relationship with any young woman remains impossible because he suspects that she will admire his professional status and not his personal qualities.[4] In the company of women the doctor 'would feel drunk with exuberance'. This is followed by the paradoxical statement that Winik seemed like 'the only sober man among a band of drunkards'.

Similarly his relationships with his working-class brothers and their families are no more successful. In their midst, Winik remains a stranger. A recapitulation of the similes to this point is provided in the description of Winik riding in his coach through the area of his former residence: Winik 'felt a painful tension spreading over his face—at one moment he smiled, at another his expression was clouded with sadness, and then again his face contorted as if in search of asylum.' The pleasant, smiling face recalls the images of the contented victor and the inebriated suitor; his dark, drawn expression is linked to the chronically ill person among healthy people. This description furthermore adds a new feature—the search for asylum.

A potent allusion to Winik's hopeless search for asylum follows as he contemplates the impending death of his brother Shlomo. 'At first he was horrified at the detestable idea which plunged him into a maze of countless evil thoughts that welled up from the depths of his mind and crawled over him like wingless flies.'[5] After his initial confusion he was again ensnared

4. One is reminded of Prof. Nikolai Stepanovich, who says, 'I want our wives, children and students, to love in us, not the fame, the label, the connection, but the ordinary man.' Anton Chekhov, *Ward Six and Other Stories*, trans. A. Dunnigan (New York, 1965).
5. Compare this with the following passage from Chekhov's *The Dull*

by the thought, like a fish 'caught in an evil net' struggling desperately but unable to get out.[6] All these creatures stand at the threshold of death; their hours are numbered, their struggle futile. Similarly Winik's efforts to liberate himself from his macabre thoughts are as ineffectual as those of the doomed creatures to which he is compared. The picture evoked is one of an heroic but unavailing contest with death.

This unavailing search for an 'exit' is further emphasized by the bedroom scene which follows close upon this last description. Winik, aware of his loneliness and unable to sleep, tosses and turns in bed. He walks aimlessly about his room, 'as if struggling to find an exit—any escape from these distressing suffocating thoughts.' However, realizing that there is no escape from the inevitable, and resigned to his destiny, he surrenders himself to his suffering.[7]

> *Story*: 'Sleeplessness, and the consequent strain of trying to combat my increasing weakness, have caused something strange to happen to me. In the middle of a lecture tears suddenly choke me, my eyes begin to smart, and I have a passionate, hysterical desire to stretch out my arms and break into a loud lament . . . New thoughts . . . are stinging my brains like mosquitoes.' (*Ibid.*, p. 174).

6. See Ecclesiastes 9:12. 'For man also knoweth not his time, as the fishes that are taken in an evil net, and as the birds that are caught in the snare, even so are the sons of men snared in an evil time when it falleth suddenly upon them.' (R.V.).

7. Winik's dilemmas are similar to those of Andrei Yefimyeh (*Ward Six*), who considers that life is a miserable trap. He knows that 'as soon as a thinking man reaches maturity . . . he cannot help feeling that there is no escape.' (*op. cit.*, p. 24). 'Burying one's head in a pillow,' a violent response to depression in several Chekhovian narratives, also occurs in many of Berkowitz's stories. The descriptions of Yefimyeh and Winik in their moments of contemplation are worth comparing. Yefimyeh 'felt layers of scum forming on the surface of his soul, and after each visit the scum seemed to rise higher as if it were going to choke him.' Winik wanted to bathe but 'knew that even then the viscid taint, the murky sediment that so oppressed him and made him pant for breath, would still remain.' The quest for an exit is a familiar theme in modern literature. See R. L. Shinn, *The Existentialist Posture* (New York, 1959).

Berkowitz frequently likened grown men and women to infants. In Western society young children have come to symbolize hope for the future, yet in Berkowitz's tales, children constantly appear in a state of frustration and hopelessness. This device adds a sense of impotence and futility and contributes to the macabre and nightmarish quality of much of Berkowitz's early work.

At various points in this story, Dr Winik contorts his face and scratches at his hair 'like a despondent child—and sighs "My God—My God".' The potency lies in the fusion of anti theses. Despair implies comprehension and awareness. Infants do not possess the necessary intelligence for despair. Their struggles, however, are viewed and interpreted by the adult world as desperate and depressing. Therefore, to describe an adult as a despondent child is to join the child and the adult in a double bond: the adult interprets the infant's reaction which, in turn, describes his own mood. Each element in this comparison, child, despair, and adult, contributes its specific effect to the total impact of this commanding yet contradictory image of Winik—the despondent child.

Between the stage of the 'despairing infant' and the weeping man-baby of a later passage several other forceful comparisons are made. He is first likened to a 'spoiled *mezuzah*,'[8] then to an orphan, and finally to a blind man groping in the dark. A *mezuzah* is rendered invalid not when its outer case is damaged —but when it is spoiled, in some way, inside. The outer case may sparkle—but a spoiled parchment inside renders it ritually invalid. Dr Winik is clearly in a similar state. As an 'orphan' Dr Winik is greatly in need of love and care, but there is no one to pity him. Finally, prior to his total breakdown among his kinsfolk, he gropes his way blindly into the barn. Lying in a wagon full of hay, reminiscent of a baby carriage, he bursts into tears. As he lies there sobbing he has a flash of insight. He

8. *Mezuzah*—(doorpost). Verses from Deuteronomy 6: 4-9 written on parchment encased in a small container and attached to the right doorpost of a Jewish home. It becomes spoiled when any of the letters are impaired.

sees himself as a 'deserted man who has torn himself away from his natural habitat . . . and has gone seeking foreign fields in which to sink roots—only to stray into a wasteland.' Realizing that he is still really a part of the society represented by his brothers, he admits 'that he had fled from the battle in weakness and now he, like the others, was too weak to fight.' The author thus concludes the story with the same kind of imagery that he used at the beginning, and so completes the cycle.

In other narratives the characters find themselves in entirely different situations. However, their reactions are strikingly similar to those of Winik, to such an extent that they become predictable and therefore less effective. On reaching the brink of despair, most of his heroes contort their faces, pull at their hair in great agony and are described as helpless infants. A few instances will illustrate the uniformity of reaction.

After his week of glory has passed, Mishael (*Mishael*), in the final scene, breaks down on the bench in the presence of his friends. 'He stretched out (on the bench), contorted his face, pulled desperately at his hair with both hands, pleaded with himself—and cried out in a strange wailing cry.' An almost exact replica of this scene occurs in the last chapter of *A Barbarian*. Hershl is alone in the forest into which he has escaped from the farmer who had engaged him to be a tutor for his children. 'Hershl felt alone and forlorn in a world full of wretched fear— abandoned by God and man. . . . Like a child, his face contorted, he began tearing at his hair with both hands . . . tormented by the fear of death, Hershl began running with difficulty into the darkness of the night sobbing rhythmically: "Mother . . . Mother!"' Thus it is apparent that facial contortions and so on, common reactions in many of Chekhov's tales, mark the psychological collapse of many of Berkowitz's heroes.[9]

We turn now to an aspect of Berkowitz's use of metaphor illustrated in *Faivke's Judgement Day*. Gershon Shaked has shown that the 'small animal' to which Faivke is compared

9. Shestov wrote of Chekhov ,'it is clear that he came to the conclusion that there was only one way to struggle—to beat one's head against the wall . . .' L. Shestov, *Chekhov and Other Essays*, pp. 52, 60.

constitutes the main image of the story.[10] A brief survey of the series of animal similes will show how deliberately and effectively the author employs the image that so graphically defines Faivke's affinity with nature. In the general introduction he is likened to 'a calf at liberty' roaming the fields at harvest time and leaping about carefree in the haystacks. His parents, we read, feel helpless since they are convinced that he is cursed and is growing up untutored and unmannered, 'as carefree as a wild young desert ass'. Close upon this description, but immediately before his fateful and final trip to the synagogue on *Yom Kippur*, he leaps at the opportunity of rescuing Mikita's runaway horse. The scene further impresses Faivke's feeling for animals and the agility with which he attempts to seize the unruly horse's harness and return it to its owner. Temporarily tamed by his parents he follows his father 'as quietly as a docile lamb'. But this 'lamb' is worried by the disturbing thought that he is being led to a fearful place, and as if by a sixth sense, he fears the place and the ominous hour. Instinctively he contemplates running off into the forest—the natural home for an untamed, carefree animal. However, forces beyond his control prevent him from carrying out his plans and he proceeds to accompany his father, again 'as quietly as a docile lamb'.

Faithful to the recurring motif, the author presents Faivke's young adversary in the synagogue as a 'young red-headed imp, who had freckles on his tiny bird-like face and small, pale, darting eyes.' Faivke, initially defeated by Leibke, stands like 'a small, angry animal that has fallen into a trap'.[11] The next morning, provoked by another of the youths, he turns 'like a little animal disturbed in its lair,' only to seek the proper moment for his revenge. Upon seeing his father tormented by the 'bird-faced lad', Faivke leaps up and curses him with a familiar formula that also includes a reference to an animal ('May wolves

10. G. Shaked, *Al Arbaah Sippurim: Perakim Bisodot ha-Sippur* (Jerusalem, 1963), pp. 11–33.
11. The names, to some degree, characterize their bearers. Faivke is a diminutive form of a Yiddish noun meaning 'spark', 'flame', or 'match'; Leibke—the diminutive of the Yiddish noun meaning 'lion'.

devour you'). In the most dramatic episode of this tale, the confrontation between Faivke and the red-head, the animal imagery dominates and amplifies the highly emotional conflict. Consequently we read, 'Faivke ... *pounced* on the red-head and *sank his nails into his* [*assailant's*] *bird-face*. At once he felt Lieb-nitz's heavy hands pounding on his head. Faivke was dazed and fell to the ground. Then, like a *tiny animal of prey*, he *jumped on* Liebnitz and *sunk his sharp teeth into his arm.*' This son of nature acts as impetuously as the carefree animals with which he spent his days in the forest and to whom he is likened. The common folk motif of an untutored boy who opposes civilized society takes on visual form by means of these artistically appropriate comparisons.

We find similar comparisons of human beings to animals throughout Berkowitz's narratives. Thus, for example, the crying of the unwed young woman about to give birth is compared to the lowing of a cow (*Grandchild*). Gedaliah the Mad's eyes are compared to the 'strange fire that burns in the eyes of a famished wolf, held in a trap, which is suddenly shown a piece of fresh meat.' (*Lashes*). In *Maftir* the unfortunate goat-bearded father and his naïve son are likened to lost sheep pursued by an enemy. Mishael's last outcry is like the whining squeal of calves led to slaughter.

In several narratives the identification of the character with an animal becomes a means of animating reactions or scenes. In them the hero feels complete empathy with a particular animal. *A Barbarian* provides a good example.[12] 'On the edge of a rickety fence ... was perched a lonely rooster blown by the wind and rain. Its reddish green plumage puffed up, it stood on one leg, trembling and dazed by its solitude, staring bleakly at its surroundings. Hershl sensed a comparable feeling of isolation engulfing him. ....' Such psychological projections into the animal world give insight into the hero's abstract speculations and fore-shadow his reaction.

Further on, as Hershl leaves his home town, 'from one of the

12. See Malkah Shaked, *Al Shenei Sippurim shel I. D. Berkowitz* (Jerusalem, 1969).

barns came the eager sound of geese screeching at the first sight
of nightfall. A lonely cow, abandoned outside the barn,
straightened its sombre face and lowed at the heavens—as
though protesting that the days were so short, the nights too
long, and the fields barren and desolate.' His own protest against
the heavens comes soon after he hears the cow's mournful lowing.[13] He flees the farmer's wagon and cries for his mother.

The feelings of Michael the Mad (*Evil Spirits*) are directly
related to the feeble cries of a lonely goat whose pathetic protest
is mingled with a wail of petition. The eyes of his starving,
half-naked children are like those of young cubs taught by their
mothers to hunt and prey. Animals, then, are not only useful
metaphors and similes but direct conveyors of human moods.
There exists a strong bond between the animal's condition and
that of its human observer who understands his own plight
better by reference to the animal.

Berkowitz adds another dimension to his tales by the frequent
comparison of modern secular phenomena with more ancient
religious equivalents. Thereby the profane is raised to the level
of the sacred while the sacred is profaned by the very process of
comparison. In *A Proud Father* the forces contending for Leizer's
allegiance—his devotion to secular studies, the day of the examination itself, the description of the oral test—are depicted
by means of a vocabulary rich in religious and traditional associations. 'At times Leizer would lower his voice as if pleading
for life'—is a description of Leizer studying his Russian vocabulary and grammar. The Hebrew words imply pleading before
the Lord for one's life and the implication is that Leizer studies
as diligently as the pious pray for life. Leizer's secular studies
that draw him further away from orthodox practice and the
synagogue are here made analogous to the prayers of traditional
worshippers. Although the secularization is complete, the
analogy also points to the possibility of transforming this secular study into an intense and sincere religious act.

In each of Berkowitz's longer narratives, dreams play an

13. In *Pirkei Yaldut* the author recalls his family's 'lonely, dejected, black
cow', pp. 151-2.

important role. They are presented in kaleidoscopic sequence and in general yield readily to decipherment. The dreams possess affinities with incidents already related or soon to be revealed to the reader. Faivke's trances are typical of the role that dreams play in these stories.

In his first dream Faivke sees himself as a human-faced tree growing out of the ground. Thereupon Aniske, the blind beggar, whom Faivke had previously tripped up, pursues him with a stick, carrying in his hand the same pebble that Faivke had previously thrown at the figure of Jesus, the 'son of God' on the white cross outside the cemetery. The fleeing child encounters a cloud behind which God hides in the vague shape of an icon-like Torah-scroll, wrapped in diapers. God is carrying his little 'son' in his arms. Faivke's feet feel as if they are chained to the ground, and he wakes up in a sweat. Each detail refers to an incident previously described and serves to review the previous narrative. Faivke, however, interprets the dream to mean that his sins against Aniske, his throwing the stone at the 'son of God', and his desire to stay in the forest, will soon be punished by God, who is also presented in a highly subjective manner.

More opaque is Faivke's second dream. In it he sees raging red rivers, but he is protected by a tall man wrapped in a *tallit*. This day-dream is a preview of a later incident in which Faivke is mortally wounded. The wounds are anticipated by the blood-red river. Later in the day, after the final encounter with the village lads, he dreams the same dream of red rivers and the protective giant. However, his last hours are approaching, and neither prayers nor worship can help him any longer. On the contrary, they join the foray against him: ' . . . prayers battered against his head.' The dream would soon be a reality.

Closely related to the dream is the contemporary technique of constructing details of a fictional hero's life through 'significant associations'. Events of the past converge upon the present; both are distended and integrated. Conventional boundaries between time past and time present are distorted and disrupted. The present leads to the past which again evokes the future. Two examples selected from *Severed* will demonstrate Berkowitz's use of this technique.

Dr Winik, while strolling along the city's main thoroughfare, frequently encounters a wealthy old gentleman. Upon returning home, Winik recalls that, as a youngster, he had been sent on an errand by this gentleman, for which he received an apple from the gentleman's wife. 'The apple was small, red and shiny. As if from some other world, the apple retained the remarkable scent of that lady's cupboard. . . . Musing over this apple, he became very upset: why had he accepted it from the woman? He now imagined that, if he had refused, his present relationship with this gentleman would be more candid.'[14] Thus a contemporary event leads to reflections about the past, which in turn substantially colour the present.

The second illustration is taken from the episode in which Winik, awake one restless night, observes two silhouettes and assumes them to be those of a suitor with his fiancée. 'Dr Winik suddenly realized that his youth had vanished never to return. . . . Now, he was merely a country doctor . . . a bachelor robbed of his virility...' Again, an incident recalls a former scene which in turn qualifies the present and gives it fresh meaning.

Not only does time disorientate modern man, but nature confounds and dismays him. It was almost axiomatic in classical literature that the macrocosm—the world of natural phenomena—was somehow synchronized and harmonized with the microcosm—the course of human events and behaviour. Berkowitz used climatic conditions and the seasons not only to create atmosphere and mood, but also to co-ordinate the various elements comprising the plot. Rain, fog, spring or hot summer days contribute tone-values to the narrative.[15] In *A Proud Father*,

14. Although Hebrew literary traditions do not associate the 'forbidden fruit' in Eden with an apple, one is tempted to elaborate upon the implications of this apple which retained its 'sweet, strange taste'. This brief description succinctly summarizes Winik's attitudes towards the second sex. Women remain, for him, sweet, attractive, but strange.

15. The two exceptions are *Minstrels*, in which Shakne's daughter died at the beginning of the summer, and *Severed*. Cf. *Writings*, pp. 29–30,

Moshe Yosi, frustrated in his efforts to relate the tale of his son's success, leaves the synagogue. The weather outside mirrors his mood: 'A stormy wind was blowing up outside, howling across the open fields. . . .' Furthermore, most of the events in the narrative occur during the dark rainy days of autumn. The external atmosphere reflects the dismal scenes within, and helps to create the aura of futility and pessimism. When, however, Moshe Yosi finally finds an attentive pair of ears, the weather reacts accordingly: 'For a moment the strong wind stopped howling over the fields. The whole world stood by in silence while Moshe Yosi the Simpleton poured out his heart to little Hershl.' Here, this device manages to accentuate, in a most sensitive way, the universal tragedy symbolized by Moshe Yosi's predicament. The day on which Hershl (*A Barbarian*) is visited by the farmer is a 'dreary, gloomy day. A raging autumn wind was howling as it drove low clouds above the shiny, wet, wooden roofs . . . stirring up the sewage in the open drains.' Subsequently Hershl takes on the mood reflected by the weather.

In view of these associations the sentence that joins the schematic introduction of *Faivke's Judgement Day* with the main body of the tale now takes on added meaning. 'The last days of summer had passed and autumn had now arrived.' This was indeed Faivke's last summer. The calamities traditionally associated with Autumn were soon to occur. The final chapter concludes: 'On a cold bright morning at the end of autumn when the road to town was being repaired and the sun was shining . . . the news spread among the Gentile urchins that Faivke had died in the city. . . .' Faivke does not live to witness the spring and the beginning of nature's new cycle.

However, the 'natural' parallelism no longer exists in the same way as before. On the day Faivke died the sun was shining. This detail suggests a curious disparity between nature and the course of human events. This ironic dichotomy in the antici-

52, 59, 69, 71, 73, 85, 105, 111, and 163. See, too, Chekhov's letter in Trask and Burkhart, *op. cit.*, p. 176 and S. O'Faolain, *The Short Story*, *op. cit.*, p. 93.

pated relationship between weather and human events is made more explicit in *Severed*. 'One pleasant morning, after a week of fluctuating between hope and despair, Shlomo died.' The intended irony is not left to the reader to infer but is explained several lines later in an unusual aside: 'It was astounding that on a fine summer's day, with the sun shining brilliantly from a cloudless sky, one small house was designated by the Creator of this splendid, wondrous world to be set in sorrow and mourning.'

The last quotation from *Severed* is one of the many sardonic comments about God found in these short stories. The modern God is no longer the All-Merciful Being who cares for his children or attends his flock. On the contrary, Berkowitz's narrative world, the contemporary scene, seems abandoned by God. Man is left to beseech an unresponsive God whose ways remain unfathomable and unpredictable. *Faivke's Judgement Day* may be interpreted as a direct refutation of the mercy of God. Faivke's pregnant mother sends her husband and intransigent son to synagogue on the Day of Atonement only because she relies on his mercy, and trusts that their prayers will bring relief and respite from the family's sorrow. Instead, not only do their prayers go unheard, but she becomes the immediate cause of her own son's death. Had she not insisted on Faivke's attendance his death might have been averted.

The manifest contradictions that arise from the conflict between a traditional, gracious Deity and the circumstances of contemporary human existence reverberate throughout several of his tales. Michael the Mad in *Evil Spirits* poses the problem in all its clarity. While idling on his bed, he hears the forlorn goat bleating hopelessly in the barn. He looks out of the frost-covered window and recalls that 'above this big, wide world, in the recesses of the heavens, dwells a mysterious, unknown God who is alleged to be compassionate and merciful.' Michael the Mad turns to God in the silence of the night, and hoping to evoke his justice and mercy addresses him simply as though in conversation: 'O Master of the Universe, look down from the heavens and see! It's such a pity for this unfortunate goat.' The point is clear. Though man would come to the aid of the bleating goat and ease her pain by helping her deliver her young, Michael's prayers to God go unheeded and his condition remains the same.

The lack of true religious feeling and sanctity even in the synagogue recurs as a *leitmotif* in several contexts. Callous in respect to human needs and feelings and to the essence of Judaism, the worshippers appear blatantly hypocritical in their observance. In order to stress these themes, the most awesome day of the Jewish calendar, *Yom Kippur*, was chosen as the setting for several tales.[16] In all of them the day is somehow profaned, its sanctity desecrated. The holiness of *Yom Kippur* is preserved only by a handful of sensitive people who are appalled by the general vulgarity expressed in the observance of the fast. Berkowitz suggests that the more a man has strayed from traditional observance, the more likely he is to be affected by the awesomeness of *Yom Kippur*. The strong element of criticism of religious life is perhaps best expressed in *Faivke's Judgement Day*. After the cruelty and hypocrisy of the *Yom Kippur* service, the atmosphere changes and a spirit of near-geniality pervades the evening celebration. 'The building was transformed. The putrid stench had subsided—holiness had given way to the profane.' The bitter irony of this remark is reflected in a number of Berkowitz's stories dealing with religious life.

These then are some of Berkowitz's devices. Cogent allusions, the juxtaposition of sacred and profane diction, classical gestures, overt questioning about a perplexing God and equivocal nature all contribute to the final effect. It must be stressed, however, that these disparate factors are essential constituents of larger structures, which when artistically arranged in definite sequence comprise the story. An inquiry into these larger fictional structures is the subject of our next chapter.

16. On the *Yom Kippur* motif in Berkowitz's writing see G. Shaked, *Motiv Yom ha-Kippurim be-Sippur, Maḥanayim*, 1961, pp. 130–5.

Chapter 7

MODES OF COMPOSITION

ONE of the main characteristics of the modern short story is the shortened introduction or, indeed, its total absence. Authors make every effort to open the story without any prefatory comments or introductory statements. Quite clearly the opening sentences are the most crucial in attracting the reader's interest and attention.

A survey of the opening sentences in Berkowitz's stories reveals that, in the majority of his narratives, the characters are introduced, the setting is established and the skeletal situation is defined in the opening paragraphs. Although he does not plunge the reader directly into the action or outline of the story, he uses the opening sentence to present the main character and his immediate dilemma. *Mishael*, for instance opens with the sentence: 'During the rest of the year he [Mishael] is not considered human.' As the tale unfolds, it becomes clear that this sentence, defining the hero's condition during the entire year, will serve as vital background to the hero's one week of glory, which is the tale's central theme.

The opening statements of most of Berkowitz's narratives include the central figure's name and some remark concerning his profession or trade, a brief and explicit statement describing his significant physical or emotional traits, and a hint at the central conflict which is to be elaborated as the story progresses. Accordingly, one of his minor stories, *The Letter*, begins: 'For a whole week after Yeruham the shoemaker's young daughter had borne an illegitimate child, Yeruham paced the house in a state of insanity . . .' Similarly, *Minstrels* opens, 'At the beginning of the summer, Shakhna Pandra's daughter became ill with typhus; a week later she died, leaving a five-year-old orphan daughter to her parents.' Both these instances illustrate

Berkowitz's use of condensation and expansion. Fifty-one weeks are summarized in a short sentence—and one week is condensed into a single phrase ('A week later she died') whereas the entire story revolves upon the events of a much narrower time span. These introductory statements serve as an essential setting for the fictionally more relevant time span which encompasses the main action of the story.[1]

Evil Spirits, however, may serve as an interesting exception to the general rule. This entirely bizarre tale begins with a full-length description of the house in which one cursed family lives. 'All that week,' the story begins, 'the tiny house which seemed on the point of collapse, stood isolated and separated from God's world.' Subsequently, each part of the house is described so that one is not made aware of Michael the Mad until the second paragraph. Yet, as the story develops, it becomes obvious that it is not a story which deals exclusively with the head of the family. The other members of the family are equally important. It is therefore appropriate that the attention of the reader should, from the outset, be centred upon the entire household symbolized by the ramshackle house, the sad state of which reflects the demented condition of its inhabitants.

An examination of the structure of *Severed* will reveal another aspect of Berkowitz's method in the longer narratives. The first chapter presents the hero's basic conflicts, the central issues at stake, and the fundamental antagonisms. From the second chapter on, the emphasis swings alternately from the brothers to the upper-class Bergers. Chapters Two and Four concentrate on Winik's relations with his brothers and other members of his family, whereas chapters Three and Five set Winik among the Bergers. The dramatic last chapter brings Winik face to face with both spheres. He stands in the presence of his brothers and the Bergers at the same time. The Bergers watch from the balcony as he, in company with his family, follows his brother's coffin in the street below. Winik catches a glimpse of Miss Berger, who now appears highly attractive to him. This mo-

1. Other instances of similar introductions are found in *Writings*, pp. 20, 25, 33.

mentary attraction, however, soon gives way to the indecision that has become so permanent a part of his relationship with both sides. This final confrontation of the two forces condenses the central dilemma into one scene. The curtain falls on the same sombre note with which the narrative began.

The characters in Berkowitz's stories are generally introduced in a direct way,[2] as the following section from *Yom Kippur Eve* may serve to illustrate.

The child's father is presented as 'a tall, stately man with a long, curly, black beard: his Sabbath caftan always looked new and his boots were always shining.' This is followed by a list of ethical virtues and psychological traits. The mother, on the other hand, is an unemotional peasant woman, 'whose every thought and deed was purposeful and practical.' Grunam, his father's partner, introduced in the fifth chapter of the story, is described as 'a short man, with a long beard resembling an old brush, the bristles of which have become worn and shrivelled with age. He had cold, expressionless eyes that denoted neither friendliness nor harshness: his voice was quite devoid of passion, monotonous and with a grating edge, and yet it was as firm and decisive as the most irrevocable contract.' Grunam's wife on the other hand is described as 'tall and robust with a red face and blond hair, fleshy arms, thick, hairy, masculine legs and a gruff male voice.'

These descriptive passages are typical of Berkowitz's prefatory remarks. As a rule, however, the one-chapter short stories do not contain any introductory descriptions. The sole example in the short stories is in *Guests*. Eliose, the dumb brother, is considered the black sheep of the family, and is described as a freak with 'ravening red eyes, which gleamed foolishly, and a pinched red nose, a gaping mouth and a hairless

2. S. Niger, a Yiddish literary critic, correctly claims that, at times, the minor characters are presented more fully than the central figures. However, he also makes the unfounded claim that the technical aspects of the smaller works are more effective than those of the major compositions. S. Niger, *Vegen Yiddishe Schreiber: Kritishe Artiklen* (Warsaw, 1913), p. 136.

upper lip that quivered as if suspended in air.' In order to classify the brother's reactions, and to offer some explanation why he was so repelled, Eliose's grotesque features are recorded in detail. In so far as his physical appearance is necessary for a proper understanding of the relationship between the brothers and their families, the description given is an integral part of the story's development.

In addition to the elements enumerated so far, each of Berkowitz's stories includes a key moment which brings all the events into focus and reinterprets them. To cite one example, in *Severed* Winik's unexpected visit to his sick brother Shlomo compels him to reconsider his attitude towards his family, to reflect upon the deteriorating *shtetl* and thence upon his individual plight. This crucial encounter also prevents his whole-hearted association with the upper-class society of the town, and has a serious effect upon his personal attitude towards the poor as well as the rich. Winik's return to his original social environment is, as a result, more personally traumatic, perhaps, than his brother's death.

Most of Berkowitz's stories include a moment of illumination when the underlying unity of the tale becomes clear. In the third chapter of *Faivke's Judgement Day*, for instance, Faivke's transition from the world of nature to urbanized life is represented by his walk through the forest to the synagogue. An additional moment of illumination is presented with Faivke's first horrifying experience in the synagogue, as he dumbfoundedly observes his father being whipped in preparation for the observance of *Yom Kippur*. These two crucial 'moments' are central to the development of the story.

Short stories require a certain degree of repetition, which may or may not be mechanical. Repetitions that modify the plot and introduce new psychological dimensions are essential: they are evident in every one of Berkowitz's short stories. The author also makes use of mechanical repetition in order to heighten tension, arouse curiosity and intimate the future. The opening chapter of *Faivke's Judgement Day* contains the ominous sentence: 'Faivke's father and mother, Matis the smith and his wife, paid no heed, and made no attempt to rebuke him. They felt that God's curse hung over this lad, who was growing up untutored and unmannered, as carefree as a wild desert ass.' The sense of foreboding, here felt only by the parents, is repeated in the next chapter, but now as a matter of 'objective' truth. Faivke is described as 'an untamed, untutored lad over whom a divine curse hovered.' This repetition colours each episode and becomes a link in the final fulfilment of a preordained curse, which predictably takes the form of the boy's death. His doom, first anticipated by his parents and then gradually by the reader, finally seems inevitable even to Faivke.

With rhythmic insistence, two other elements are reiterated in this story: the bridge scene and the portrait of Faivke's mother standing on the threshold of her home. The bridge, an obvious link between the two worlds of nature and urban civilization, appears twice in this tale. On the way to the synagogue, Faivke crosses over it and contemplates suicide in an effort to avoid the awesome confrontation with the Divine. On the way home from the synagogue after *Yom Kippur*, he faints on the bridge and is unable to return to his natural surroundings, having seen the Mighty Lord and having personally experienced man's brutality to man. The bridge becomes a symbol of the incompatibility of the two ways of life.

A scene in which Faivke's mother stands at the door by the *mezuzah* occurs once at the beginning of the tale, as she sends her husband and son off to the synagogue, and is repeated almost verbatim in the brief final chapter as she stands alone while they carry her dying son to the city hospital, from which he never returns. Grasping the inevitability of this last journey she stands by, calm and reserved, whereas in the earlier episode she cries out in the hope that God would answer her prayers. The resultant comparison is striking and serves as a *leitmotif* linking the first and final scenes.

Dialogue is another important element of most short stories. Berkowitz succeeds in creating dialogue which is both natural and artistically satisfying. Often accompanied by vivid gestures that add dramatic dimensions to the conversations, they cast much light upon the participants. In an age in which Hebrew was not yet spoken as a native language, and when colloquialisms and slang were not available, it was a rare feat to have created authentic-sounding dialogues. In the main, the author achieved this effect simply by translating the slang of current Yiddish vernacular. These translations bear the ring of authenticity. At times, moreover, long monologues are used for comic relief. At other times, the author makes use of characteristic mannerisms or malapropisms to distinguish individual figures. So, for example, the yokel in *A Barbarian* repeats his ludicrous rhymed refrain, *Ma-sheyesh ba-kalaḥat, sim al ha-tzallaḥat* (whatever's in the can, put in the pan) which is clearly the equivalent of the English idiom 'to put one's cards on the table'. This is his substitute for conversation which is another source of annoyance for the intellectual Hershl.

One of Berkowitz's favourite methods of controlling effect is the use of irony. This device is employed to some extent in each of his compositions. The title, for instance, is often calculated to provoke a reaction contrary to that created by the tale itself. As Shaked has indicated, the title *A Proud Father* prepares the reader for a happy tale about a joyous father. As the story develops we find that the 'proud father' is disappointed and frustrated by his inability to find an attentive ear to his tale of pride. On the individual level the father remains proud and happy, but his joy is diminished by his disillusionment with a callous society. The title serves as an ironic counterpoint to the entire story. Moreover, the reader senses both the father's happiness and his frustration as the unexpected harshness of an unreceptive audience becomes apparent.[3]

A Barbarian exemplifies another use of the author's ironic choice of title. This instance differs from *A Proud Father* in that the title is, itself, applied by two of the characters, Hershl's father and the yokel farmer to Hershl, the young tutor. The yokel uses the term 'Barbarian' in the final scene when Hershl runs off in order to escape serving as instructor to his unruly children. From the very first encounter and initial conflict between

---

3. See G. Shaked, *Al Arbaah Sippurim*, p. 12.

the intellectual Hershl and the boorish farmer, this derogatory name appears to be intended for the farmer and seems grossly misapplied by Hershl's father. Thus the title serves an ironic-comic function.[4]

A third illustration of irony of title with comic effect, but this time with tragic overtones as well, may be found in *Grandchild*. The immediate impact of this title is to conjure up thoughts of affection, love and the warm feelings of grand-parents for their grandchildren. This mood is shattered by the opening scene as the reader becomes aware of the child's illegitimate birth. In this way the author has made ironic use of the reader's initial response and has turned it into a literary device to enhance the total effect of the tale by contrasting the expected outcome with the actual development.

Further, Berkowitz makes frequent use of irony of situation. In *Severed*, the Burial Association's members who come to prepare the body of Dr Winik's brother are the same types of Jews that Berkowitz frequently criticized for a spiritless and mechanical observance of Jewish rituals. The description reads: 'They were all craning their necks and holding their breath without taking their eyes off the people performing their sacred duties in so coarse a fashion. They treated the corpse with disgusting contempt, turning it from side to side on the cleans-ing slab, almost like butchers tossing flanks of meat onto the butcher's block.'

A fine blend of ironic situation and statement is provided in the scene where Matis, Faivke's simple-minded father, during the *Yom Kippur* service, looks admiringly out of the window at the tree tops glowing in the setting sun. Oblivious of the tradi-tional service, which was being performed by an exhausted cantor, Matis weeps aloud. Noticing his outburst some lads turn to him and inform him that one is not supposed 'to cry at this place'. The *double-entendre* is very poignant: no one cries at this point of the service, and no one ever genuinely cries in this place—the synagogue. The worshippers are incriminated.

4. For a somewhat different interpretation of this facet, see M. Shaked, *Al Shenei Sippurim shel I. D. Berkowitz*, pp. 19–20.

They remain to the end untouched by nature, prayer, or *Yom Kippur*. The scene also affords another example of how, in a large number of Berkowitz's works, the synagogue plays an ironic role. Instead of representing a sanctuary from daily cares, it serves in a number of his tales as a cause of friction and antagonism.[5]

Any study of Berkowitz's artistic methods must contain some consideration of the focus of his narrative. But for three exceptions (*Yom Kippur Eve*, *In A Foreign Place* and *My Birthplace*), all the stories are presented through the eyes of an omniscient author.[6] These three stories, however, are told through a narrator-protagonist who relates his 'personal experiences'. Perhaps the most consummate of the three first-person narratives is *Yom Kippur Eve*, which is related as witnessed by a young boy, now a more mature student, who recalls a past *Yom Kippur* eve during which his father and partner had disagreed on some financial matter. His affections shift from mother to father, both of whom appear to have erred against his grandfather's maxim of 'guarding one's tongue from slander'. The tone, atmosphere and diction are all highly suggestive of the thoughts of a timid and confused child.

As indicated, most of Berkowitz's stories are written in the third person. No effort is made to give the reader the impression that the narrated experience is occurring in the present or that the reader is to re-enact it. Neither is the reader required to experience the situation in the manner sought by the 'stream of consciousness' school.[7] Berkowitz records the intimate

---

5. The synagogue is drawn in a negative fashion in *Maftir*, *A Male Child*, *Moshkele Pig*, and *Twilight*.

6. The first-person Palestine-based narratives are treated in the next chapter.

7. The original, first printed editions of Berkowitz's early tales show signs of primitive attempts at this type of writing. However, under the influence of Mendele Mokher Seforim, Bialik and others, these tendencies were subdued and a more classical style and diction were adopted. A thorough analysis that traces the variants and emendations from edition to edition is still a desideratum.

secrets of his characters. In most tales he concentrates upon the psychological and emotional elements.

Often, summary 'telling' is preferred to dramatic 'showing'.[8] For instance, in *A Proud Father*, instead of dramatizing Moshe Yosi's strained relations with his children, the author chooses to describe them. Accordingly, the account reads as follows: 'The other members of his family [in addition to his wife] also treated him scornfully and addressed him in an insolent manner which is unusual, since children generally obey their fathers and respect them. In his heart of hearts, Moshe Yosi was sometimes hurt by this, but would bear it in silence, for he was a quiet man who seldom expressed his thoughts aloud. In short, he was a meek and humble person ignored by everyone.' This description, taken from an introductory passage, displays the author's method. Another aspect of this same summary practice is illustrated further on in the story. After Moshe Yosi has been fondly nurturing the fantasies and visions of the welcome he will receive from the frequenters of the *Beit-Midrash*, he enters the synagogue only to hear Avram Itze's tales of adventure. The author adds, 'No-one knew that Moshe Yosi was not interested in a tale about a snowstorm or about Avram Itze's barking dog. Moshe Yosi's heart was aflame. He was desperate to tell his story.' Again, his speculations are presented in the form of summary statements.

Such summary statements of essential thoughts and characteristics comprise only a part of the author's literary means. Revelatory monologues can also be found in almost every one of Berkowitz's short stories. Ordinarily, these take the form of questions to elicit the trends and processes of the character's thoughts. The following instance may illustrate the point. In this passage the author presents Faivke's musings during the most momentous day of his life. Faivke reflects: 'Why had his father put on his ragged, Sabbath coat on a day that was not Sabbath? Why was he carrying his *tallit* and that wide, white

8. For a discussion of the limits and artistic deficiencies of this contrast, see W. C. Booth, *The Rhetoric of Fiction* (Chicago-London, 1961), pp. 16, 19.

smock? The awesome fateful, ominous hour from which no one escapes had apparently arrived.' The questions delineate the process of thought, and explain the conclusion which stems directly from it. Furthermore, these questions give rise to a sense of immediacy and participation despite the objective presentation.

Yet Berkowitz's objectivity does not prevent him from occasionally interjecting an implicit condemnation of such evils as religious hypocrisy and social injustice. These ills become the target of his satire, although he manages to retain a mask of objectivity by never appearing as an exclusive spokesman for any specific sect or movement. Berkowitz was of the opinion that no story should provide a platform for propaganda. The closest Berkowitz, the short-story teller, comes to infringing the delicate area between *belles-lettres* and propaganda is in his two anti-Russian Revolutionary tales (*In a Foreign Place* and *Confession*) in which the heroes and heroines bare their souls and confess their sin of participating in the revolutionary movement. Even in these stories, the historical background is accurate and the hero's regrets are described with sincerity. The human predicament of disillusionment and frustration remains Berkowitz's centre of interest—and in the works that deal with these themes there is little commentary.[9]

For the most part intellectual heroes, Berkowitz's characters engage in reading or discussing popular novels or dramas. These are sometimes in a foreign language but, more generally, they are drawn from modern Hebrew *belles-lettres*. These works always serve as powerful motivating forces in the characters' development and in the rejection of the *status quo*. Authors

9. On realism, objectivity, impassibility, see R. Wellek, *Concepts of Criticism* (New Haven, 1963), pp. 240–54; also D. Daiches, *A Study of Literature for Readers and Critics* (New York, 1964), pp. 99ff. so, too, E. Auerbach, *Mimesis: The Representation of Reality in Western Literature*, trans. by W. Trask (Princeton, 1953), pp. 457–84. On the nature of Chekhov's objectivity, read J. Hagan, 'Chekhov's Fiction and the Ideal of Objectivity', *Publication of the Modern Language Association*, vol. 81, no. 5, Oct. 1966, pp. 409–17.

cited include Maimonides, Smolenskin, Sheikowitz, Berdi-
chevski, Aḥad Ha-Am, Marx, Engels, Chernyshevsky and
Pisarev. Among the volumes mentioned are: *Kevurat Ḥamor*
(A Donkey's Burial), *Fathers and Sons, What is To Be Done?*
The History of English Civilization, The Collected Works of
Pushkin, Thus Spoke Zarathustra, A History of Philosophy,
Graetz's *History of the Jews* and Krylov's *Fables*.

An interesting example of a quoted work is the mention in
Severed of Lermontov's *The Demon*.[10] This dramatic poem
presents the loneliness of life through the experience of the
fallen angel. Aimlessly wandering about the universe, unable
to find solace, the fallen angel is rejected by God and man, and
indulges in every sin only to find them all unsatisfying. Life
has lost its meaning—he has no one for whom to live and no
purpose for which to endure. He finally contemplates love and
thereupon, seeing the voluptuously beautiful Tamar, falls in
love with her. Their love is short-lived, for she dies as they
embrace for the first time. The despair and loneliness inherent in
Lermontov's poem help to reinforce the underlying theme of
the short story and augment the plot.

The social background to the stories is realistically and objec-
tively depicted, while the social *mores* of the *shtetl* are meticu-
lously described. Of the various Jewish institutions, the *Beit-*
Midrash is the one most often portrayed. It reflects the decline
of the entire *shtetl* society whose religious, social and cultural
centre it had once been. The elderly Jews who still frequent the
Beit-Midrash are portrayed as decadent and insensitive sufferers
in a decaying order. The walls of the *Beit-Midrash* crumble with
decay—and the foul stench of decay is to be found inside.
Similarly the houses in every tale are on the point of collapse,
the interiors are decrepit, the doors swing loosely in the wind,
the windows are broken, the roofs have gaping holes. The entire landscape is one of desolation and ruin.

Berkowitz's short stories and novellas rarely end on a happy

10. There are two English translations of *The Demon*, one by R. Burness
    (Edinburgh, 1918) and a more recent one by G. Shelley (London,
    1930).

note. The only tale to conclude in an optimistic way is *Yom Kippur Eve*, at the end of which the youthful narrator regrets having cast aspersions upon his mother's integrity. His faith is restored in her and in his father, both of whom had seemed, until the final chapter, guilty of hypocrisy and immodesty. All the remaining tales, however, leave the hero more despondent at the end of the story than at the beginning. The events and situations all converge to increase the hero's frustration. By the final scene the unheroic hero is usually alone, in a state of oppressive remorse brought on by the sufferings he has endured. Mishael, inebriated from drinking too much at the celebration marking the conclusion of his week of triumph, rambles on incoherently about his unenviable future now that his days of glory are terminated and the annual cycle is about to recommence. 'I could have had a beautiful bride', he ponders in the final scene, 'and prayed with a *tallit;* but now who will have a rump, who wants a ne'er do well . . . with torn trousers. To my dying day I'll wander about like this . . . abandoned and alone . . .' Thus the full impact of the hero's predicament is conveyed by this self-awareness, which concludes the story but does not resolve the central character's permanent dilemma. Mishael's final complaint pinpoints the fact that his condition will be perpetuated, as another year of misery and idleness begins for this young man who only knows joy one week each year.

Similarly Moshe Yosi's rueful isolation is emphasized in the concluding scene which finds him pouring out his heart to the little Hershl, a youngster who can neither comprehend the proud father's conversation nor participate in his joy. *Twilight* concludes with an equally despondent scene in which the aged Mrs Rabinowitz is left shaking her head and moaning to herself. 'She was helpless and hopeless as a wretched young orphan, deserted by man and God.' An air of futility is retained in the final words that impress the pain endured throughout the narrative.

With this inquiry into a number of the basic textual components, we conclude our introductory survey of Berkowitz's themes, style and dramatic techniques. These chapters have attempted to present some of the elements that constitute the author's contribution to the development of the modern Hebrew short story.

Chapter 8

NEW HORIZONS

WHEN asked whether the gloom that pervades his European-centred tales reflected a fixed attitude on his part, Berkowitz replied that these stories mirrored conditions as he had experienced them. However, he stressed the fact that 'when I came to *Eretz Yisrael* the pervading mood in my tales was altered, better still I was transformed. Here, in *Eretz Yisrael*, I experienced a new spark of enthusiasm, the effect of which is evidenced in everything that I have written since. Even when I criticize certain negative aspects of our life here, this life remains purposeful and vital, filled with hope and promise, a cause to which one readily adheres and for which one is willing to endure pain.'[1] By reviewing the works composed under the impact of Palestine and Israel, the last two chapters of the present volume examine the degree and nature of the effect of contact with the land on the author's literary achievement.

Three short stories, *The Chauffeur*, *An Innkeeper in Tel-Aviv* and *The First Swallows*, two travelogues in quasi-diary form, *America Comes to Eretz Yisrael* and *Yesterday*, and a major humorous work written in epistolary form, *Menahem Mendel in Eretz Yisrael*, together portray a voyage to Palestine in the 1920's and life in various settlements and cities there during the first three decades of the present century. All the works, written in or about Palestine, are first-person narratives, in which the narrator relates personal and immediate experiences. Of the short stories, the most satisfying artistically is *The Chauffeur*.[2] In this story, the anonymous narrator, on his first

1. Quoted from G. Yardeni, *Tet-Zayin Siḥot im Soferim*, 1965, p. 20. See above chapter 5, note 11.
2. The citations quoted here, but for slight variations, are from the translation of this story by I. D. Berkowitz's daughter Tamara Kahana,

visit to Jerusalem, engages a chauffeur to tour the Jericho-Dead Sea area. Incorrectly assuming the narrator-passenger to be a rich, untutored American tourist who knows no Hebrew, the driver-guide speaks throughout in flowery Hebrew style which the narrator obligingly pretends not to understand.

The melancholy humour of *The Chauffeur* relies for its effect upon the dichotomy between its lofty language and crude content. For instance, fully convinced that neither his attractive companion, Edna, nor the narrator comprehends what he is saying, the driver turns to her with swashbuckling histrionics declaring: 'Edna, how thankless thou art! I remember the kindness of thy youth, when thou wentest after me in the Emek, in the land of Jezreel, when I came to the house of thy aunt to take thee with me to the Dead Sea on our final, farewell journey. Suddenly, thou hast despised me and preferred to warm thyself next to America's capital, next to a bagful of dollars.' The parody based on Jeremiah 2:2 is poignant.[3] It evokes a sense of melancholy humour by raising a smile even while giving vent to the chauffeur's double-edged loneliness. His solitude and seclusion are heightened first by Edna's preference for the American passenger and secondly, by his certainty that his passenger neither understands the content of his lament nor appreciates his flowery style.[4]

From the very outset the driver's physical appearance, like his ostentatious diction, lends him a mysterious air. The blood-red scar that runs diagonally across his right cheek 'marred the contours of his face but lent him a virile charm; a hidden light seemed to radiate from his face.' This scar is intended as a gateway to his personality, for his reactions can be gauged by the

published under the title *The Heart of a Chauffeur*, in *Commentary*, vol. 15, 1953, pp. 159–65.

3. The full text is: 'Go and cry in the ears of Jerusalem, saying: "Thus saith the Lord: I remember for thee the affection of thy youth/ The love of thine espousals/ How thou wentest after me in the wilderness/ In a land that was not sown".'

4. For other expressions of this loneliness see *The Heart of a Chauffeur*, loc. cit., pp. 161, 163–4.

transformations brought about in the scar. The driver himself underscores this enigmatic quality when he refers to his scar in a monologue addressed to Edna. 'What is the meaning of the bloody mark on my face?' he inquires rhetorically, 'Is it a mark of Cain or of heroism . . .? What weighs upon my heart will never ever be revealed to you.' So, the mark that attracted Edna to him remains unexplained. As he claims, it can be the mark of Cain, the need to wander about, or the mark of valour.[5]

The striking rift between language and content, physical appearance and inner struggle, that points to the chauffeur's estrangement and inability to unify his world, is strikingly emphasized by the technique of verbally colliding the spheres of the old and the new. The guide refers to his escapades in the wild desert as 'midnight lamentations', to his automobile as a 'light flying chariot' or 'blue eagle'. In the total context these puns, parodies and associations are more than simple word-plays. They indicate a clash—between the two worlds: Europe and Palestine; between the urge to wander, generally associated with Jewish existence in the Diaspora, and the quest and inability to attain security and tranquillity in Palestine; between his superficial callousness on the one hand and his tense and tender soul on the other.

Although the depressing sadness of the old world is not entirely alleviated, the positive influence of Palestine, his new world, appears to outweigh the negative features allied with the old. Thus, like his fictional predecessors, the guide—a swaggering, lusty fellow who fled his parents' home disgusted with their values and habits—has come to Palestine; but, nevertheless, by his own admission, he remains a lonely and uprooted man constantly in search of thrills and diversions. In this respect he closely resembles the whole array of Berkowitz's

5. *Ibid.*, pp. 159, 162. The biblical verses concerning the mark of Cain are: '. . . a fugitive and a wanderer shalt thou be in the earth . . . And the Lord said unto him: "Therefore whosoever slayeth Cain, vengeance shall be taken on him sevenfold." And the Lord set a sign for Cain, lest any finding him should smite him.' Genesis 4:12–15.

European-based characters. Unlike them, however, he finds solace not in books, but in his automobile, the vehicle which enables him to race recklessly about the country as a guide, in fulfilment of the Cain-like urge to pursue an insatiable pleasure. This automobile, a solace unavailable to his European fictional counterparts, is his only source of comfort and joy, the only 'heart' that understands his plight.

Further, this young man also bears some resemblance to Berkowitz's earlier figures in his inability to tolerate the pressures of his immediate surroundings—neither those of his home nor of his kibbutz. As he confesses to his passengers: 'I could not bear the eternal stillness of the rocky mountains around me. I could not bear the dark serious faces of my comrades who had vowed never to smile like human beings until their ancient fatherland was liberated from its withered stones. Even the stormy Hora dance could not still the storm in my breast.'[6] In the same way that Berkowitz's intellectual heroes are incapable of uprooting themselves entirely from their past, this driver, too, is torn and tossed 'from the dark fields of Ukraine,' his birthplace, to the 'white deserts of our stupendous fatherland Eretz Yisrael.'[7] Akin to the heartrending cry that is almost a conditioned reflex for Berkowitz's European characters are this driver's tears and laughter. In his confession to Edna, he declares, 'I love the lofty resounding word, the expansive echoing cry of the soul, the clear shrill laughter which rolls over the distant desert with an echo that replies from all the ends of the skies ha-aha-ha-ha! But I know weeping, too. Not the soft weeping that is choked into a pillow between the narrow oppressive walls of a room—but the high wailing that rends loneliness into shreds, shakes the soul to its foundations, makes the heart tremble to its depths. Sometimes, there comes a night, one of those marvellous moonlit nights of Jerusalem, our beautiful

6. *The Heart of a Chauffeur*, loc. cit., p. 162.
7. Themes related to the difficulties of acclimatization recur throughout the Hebrew works composed by the poets of the *halutz* period—particularly during the twenties and thirties. On this central topic see S. Halkin, *Modern Hebrew Literature*, chap. 6, especially pp. 119–30.

city, when I cannot find peace. Then I rise . . . to make my midnight lamentations, I let my blue eagle loose . . . and wail aloud
the deep sorrow of my heart which is deeper than the seas, and
my weeping accompanies the heart-rending wails of hungry
jackals howling for their prey.'[8] 'The soft weeping that is
choked into a pillow' and 'the narrow oppressive walls of a
room' are direct references to the instance where such is the response of so many of the central figures in Berkowitz's other
short stories.[9] Nonetheless, this character is different. He prefers
'the high wailing that rends the loneliness' that occasioned it. In
contrast to the 'European' characters who are not relieved by
their weeping, but whose agony is aggravated by a reaction
that intensifies their perception of loneliness, this hero in
Palestine is capable of rending his solitude by uniting his wailing
with that of the jackal, the desert animal that symbolizes the
country's barren and desolate areas. This alliance with nature
may be contrasted with the various animal metaphors and similes that mark the author's earlier writings in which nature has
no redemptive power. In the diaspora narratives the animals
are mere symbols; in the Palestine stories they somehow alle-
viate and liberate the hero's sufferings.

   Throughout this tale there are direct erotic elements. A comparison of such references with those in *Mariashka*, *Cucumbers*
and *Evil Spirits* shows that the erotic elements in *The Chauffeur*
are normal whereas in the other stories they are always clandes-
tine and even degenerate. Furthermore, like several of Berkowitz's 'new women', Edna possesses 'a peculiar suppressed,
mischievous charm'. This helps explain the driver's comment
after swimming together in the Dead Sea. Having delighted his
eye with her slender figure he exclaims, 'Edna, thy bathing
suit has drawn us closer physically and spiritually—This is the
first time, my pure one, that thou hast cast off thy garments
before me in all the purity of thy young body . . .'[10] Again,
the chauffeur expresses his painful solitude in tragi-comic tones.

8. *The Heart of a Chauffeur*, *loc. cit.*, p. 162.
9. See chapter 5, pp. 60ff, chapter 6, pp. 69–70.
10. *The Heart of a Chauffeur*, *loc. cit.*, p. 164.

The overall humorous tone, the atmosphere of expansiveness and freedom, the delight in the landscape and the pleasure derived by the chauffeur when he speaks poetic Hebrew, combine to make this story unique. It may, indeed, have served as a transition to a new style. But whether because of an inability to fathom the psychological complexities of the *Yishuv* or for some still unknown reason, the fact remains that Berkowitz wrote no tales in which the *ḥalutz* serves as subject for a full-length story.

The dominant theme of *The Chauffeur*, the search for roots and solace, is also the main theme in *The First Swallows*. The early swallows referred to in the title are American *ḥalutzim*, who come to Palestine either to witness for themselves the miracle of the century, or to find peace of mind. All in all they are more successful than the chauffeur, for they derive stimulus and significance from their new lives.

The light-hearted tone that softened the melancholy element in *The Chauffeur* prevails in *An Innkeeper in Tel-Aviv*. This narrative, hardly a short story, is rather a series of humorous anecdotes related by a stalwart *Maskil*-Zionist innkeeper for his guests' entertainment. These light-hearted accounts afford amusement and engender an atmosphere of hospitality.

America Comes to Eretz Yisrael is a travelogue which realistically presents a cross-section of Jewish passengers travelling to Palestine. The problems that divide them are described in a light and humorous fashion. The impassioned discussions about ideologies and politics are presented in a witty and pleasant vein. Little effort, however, is made to delineate character, probe psychological motivation or provide a forum for subjects other than those related to Palestine and Zionism. The author, instead, seems intent only upon exhibiting a fair sampling of types, for which purpose he chooses a popular journalistic style.

The collection of serio-comic essays, *Yom Etmol Ki Avar* (Yesterday)—originally a continuation, in serial form, of the author's first-hand reports *America Comes to Eretz Yisrael*—were written soon after his arrival in Palestine from

America.[11] The volume is divided into four large sections, each of which is subdivided into chapters that deal exclusively with a single subject. The sections are entitled 'Tel-Aviv' (ten chapters), 'Jerusalem' (seven chapters), 'Touring the Land' (sixteen chapters) and 'Odd Types' (four chapters). Each chapter contains the author's personal impressions of his first confrontation with the land and its people. His personal feelings are blended with finely written descriptive passages. With great sympathy for and deep pride in every manifestation of reclamation and restoration, the entire work reads as a song of praise to the *halutzim* and the resurgent genius of the Jewish people.

It seems that the positive forces which emerged in *The Chauffeur* and gained strength in *An Innkeeper in Tel-Aviv* came to full flower in *Yesterday*. In the meeting of the old and new there is no longer a clash but rather a positive blending. The old forms take on a renewed vitality in the author's reminiscences. This can readily be seen in his comparison of the Sabbath in the past and present. After dwelling on the delights of the Sabbath in modern Tel-Aviv he remarks, 'I still cannot fathom how this miracle occurred—how the ancient, austere Sabbath has been transplanted with such extraordinary ease upon Tel-Aviv's carefree new life . . . Gone is the observant Jew's unendurable bitterness toward non-conforming youth. It seems that there is no longer the compulsive fear lest the essence of Sabbath should fade away.' (p. 362) Even more striking is the contrast of the *sabras*, the native-born Palestinian Jews, with the Jews of the Diaspora. The author notes happily, 'the malignant

11. First published as a separate volume under the full title, *Yom Etmol Ki Avar* (Tel-Aviv, 1962). Then published in *Writings*, vol. 2 *Sippurei Zikhronot* (Tel-Aviv, 1963), pp. 353–439, with the abbreviated title *Yom Etmol*. The page numbers will follow directly the citations from *Yom Etmol*. Since, as Berkowitz explains in an apologetic preface, these essays mirrored contemporary realities too closely, he preferred to delay publication until 1962. That is, until after he had recast them in the light of a more objective historical perspective (p. 351). Consequently, this text is a re-edited volume that contains the author's revisions and supplementary comments.

features of Diaspora Jewry: melancholy eyes that reflect the fear of foreign rule, too keen a shrewdness that serves as a shield against fear, crass intolerance, the competitive urge and the incessant drive towards excellence—all have disappeared.' (p. 414) Even the railway trains seemed to reflect the changed Jewish ethos. Externally, of course, they exhibit no difference, but the Jews aboard them appear so much at home that a discerning observer would find it difficult to believe that these 'non-Jewish'-looking faces are in fact Jewish. (pp. 369ff.)

The initial flush of excitement and admiration seems not to have waned with the passage of time. Having for years been sceptical about the glowing reports of progress in Palestine and having dismissed them as excessively enthusiastic, Berkowitz was now delighted to learn that these accounts were not exaggerated. As he admits, 'Although I have been living in Tel-Aviv for a year and I have experienced all sorts of moods, one aspect of my life here I still cannot comprehend rationally. I, too, go about my daily affairs as I did in Odessa or in New York—nevertheless, I feel now as I did the day I arrived—that is, the feeling that somehow after years of meaningless existence I have come upon a perpetually festive environment . . . ' (p. 355) His home in Palestine also combined the amenities of modern urban life with the *shtetl's* traditions. 'The *mezuzot* that stare at you intimately from the doorposts remind you of your childhood when you kissed each *mezuzah* as you crossed the threshold and serve, too, as trusting guardians of bygone days as they soothe your "immigrant spirit".' (p. 359) Fond memories were awakened, too, when walking along streets named after various Hebrew writers and famous persons whom Berkowitz had known personally.

An organic element of this nostalgia becomes clear from the similes employed. By recalling traditional-religious elements, the author bridges the chasm between the still unfamiliar present and the well-known past. In addition, these comparisons evoke a genuine, good-natured humour which, in turn, creates an air of joviality that pervades almost the entire work. When portraying the hand signals of the Jewish traffic policeman in

Tel-Aviv, for example, Berkowitz compares them to the gestures
of the *kohanim* (priests) as they bless the congregation.[12] The
same is true of the passage about the vegetable vendor who 'raises
his strong, youthful voice in a pleasant chant like a trained and
accomplished cantor . . . as if he were reciting psalms . . . or
intoning the chapters describing the fragrance of the sacred
incense for the Temple . . .'

However, to some extent Berkowitz felt that *Eretz Yisrael*,
the seat and symbol of redemption, had itself been defiled. The
shock of the collision between dream and reality occurred
most sharply when he visited the famous cities about which he
had heard in his childhood. Under Arab control, these holy
sites make every Jew, according to the author, feel a bitter sense
of despair. After a visit to the Cave of Makhpelah, the grave of
the patriarchs, he pondered, 'Is this the Cave of Makhpelah? Is
it here that our forefathers rest under the oppressive guard of
foreign mercenaries?' He writes further, 'The Cave of Paradise,
the final resting place of those unblemished souls of old, was
pointed out in a most vulgar, crass and profane manner—by
bakshish seekers . . .'[13] He was similarly repelled and sorely
disappointed by his first visit to Jerusalem. The thought of this
journey had set him astir because, 'there was an awareness that
you are about to traverse the abyss that lies between legend and
reality.' He gleefully records how he had imbibed the sacred
air of Jerusalem and been amazed that he had not grown faint.
Instead he had fallen into a trance in which past, present and
future, the finite and infinite, had converged as his sense of
reality melted. Nevertheless, he had walked the streets and
alley-ways with a broken heart, for after the exhilarating experiences in the all-Jewish city of Tel-Aviv, he had felt tossed
again into foreign territory. 'When one realizes,' he sadly declares, 'that on the mountains of the prophets stand foreign
holy sites . . . a deep depression descends upon the observer . . .

12. *Yom Etmol*, pp. 359–60.
13. *ibid.*, p. 340. See, too, description of a visit to Safed, pp. 404, 416. On
    the problems that arise as a result of the doubtful historicity of these
    sites, see *ibid.*, pp. 382ff.

Only here does one realize with final clarity that Jerusalem . . .
the last refuge for homeless spirits . . . has been seized . . . only
now does one fully comprehend the sad and bitter humour of
the Diaspora: all the sated, glutted and gorged nations . . .
pounced upon our inheritance with their bared fangs, ripped
it to shreds and divided it among themselves, while they granted
the Jews permission to walk about its ruins, to rest content with
one desolate corner [the Western Wall], the sole remnant of
the destruction, and to wail there like forsaken dogs before their
ruined house . . . ' (p. 372) Yet, he is consoled by the very realization that, miraculously, Jews are still deeply attached to the
Wall. Personally, he confesses, he was unable to weep at the
Western Wall, although he lamented the fate of the Jewish people.

Nevertheless, although the land itself may temporarily be
defiled, it may still be fully redeemed. Thus, for example,
Berkowitz holds that the renascence of the Hebrew language
despite all odds, attests to the spirit of the people who are a
living testimony to the overall revival now in process.

The resilient and reanimated Hebrew language had, as the
author puts it, 'rekindled belief in the resurrection of the dead'.
Tel-Aviv, too, by its very existence was a constant source of
comfort, for it attested to the Jewish people's latent but as yet
not fully realized powers, and lent a certain credence to the
hope for a more splendid future.[14]

At the root of the last of these works, *Menahem Mendel in
Eretz Yisrael*, there is a serious dilemma. Having returned to
their homeland, the Jews—except for the idealistic *ḥalutzim* on
kibbutzim—have apparently largely retained the *mores* and
traits they had acquired in the Diaspora. This is illustrated
humorously by Menahem Mendel who, unlike the Jewish
inhabitants of the land, has been himself transformed.[15] Berkowitz's contemporary, Menahem Mendel is an adaptation of

14. For Berkowitz's critique of modern Hebrew theatre, see *ibid.*, pp. 372ff;
    of present condition of modern Hebrew *belles-lettres*, pp. 384–5; and
    comments on education in *Eretz Yisrael*, pp. 369–70.
15. Menahem Mendel's humour is essentially that of the original Menahem
    Mendel and consists largely of incorrigible naïveté, innocent misadven-

the quixotic character created by Sholom Aleichem to repre-
sent the comic and the grotesque in *shtetl* life. Sholom Aleichem's Menahem Mendel seems endlessly engaged in business
ventures in which imagination and fantasy play a larger part
than financial acumen. He becomes, in turn, an unsuccessful
broker, a business agent and a real-estate solicitor. Each involvement evokes humour because of the farcical discrepancy between Menahem Mendel's flights of fantasy into the world of
affairs and the harsh reality to which they seem totally unrelated.

Berkowitz employs a modernized Menahem Mendel to lay
bare the less desirable features of the *Yishuv* in Palestine during the
twenties and thirties of the present century. The butt of the
author's most scathing comments are the land-speculators and
unscrupulous business adventurers who rushed to the country in
the hope of retrieving the fortunes they had lost during the
economic depression following the First World War.

Although on the surface Menahem Mendel symbolizes the
old, degenerate, society, and the population apparently represents a new utopia, the truth is just the opposite. Except for the

tures that lead from one ephemeral business deal to another, and his
pipe dreams that are smashed by the realities of the business world which,
however, never seem to discourage him. The entire volume consists of
twenty-four letters sent from *Eretz Yisrael* by Menahem Mendel, now
forty years older than his original namesake, to his wife Shayne-Sheindl
in the Brownsville section of New York City. The greeting formulas in
these letters are exact replicas of the Berkowitz rendition of Sholom
Aleichem. A postscript follows every letter as in the original. However,
Sholom Aleichem provided the wife's replies whereas Berkowitz does
not, but simply hints at them. Also, the original Menahem Mendel's
garrulous mother-in-law is still alive and her pithy folk maxims and
proverbs are cited by her daughter. The new Menahem Mendel keeps
her memory alive by quoting at least one of her *bons mots* in each letter.
A critical comparative study of the original Yiddish Menahem Mendel,
his hebraized transformation in Berkowitz's rendition and the modern
application in *Menahem Mendel in Eretz Yisrael*, remains a desideratum.
For an English rendition of Sholom Aleichem's Menahem Mendel see
The Adventures of Menahem Mendel, translated from the Yiddish by
Tamara Kahana (New York, 1969).

farmers, the inhabitants are portrayed as decadent and dis-
honourable, while he is described as being completely innocent.
'Menahem Mendelism' now ironically suggests someone involved in speculative and chimerical business ventures, while
the new Menahem Mendel personifies the naïve tourist, always
on the verge of becoming involved in fanciful projects, but
saved in time from committing such disservices to the rehabilitated land. In fact, Menahem Mendel is appalled at the degree of
'Menahem Mendelism' that has permeated the country and is
undermining its well-being. At times he is caught in its web,
but he tries to take every opportunity to expose and ridicule it.
At one point Menahem Mendel reflects upon the typical
'Menahem Mendel' mentality that has been spreading through
the *Yishuv* and how detrimental it will be if it continues. 'What
good,' he wonders, 'will the national homeland be if each one
of us here relates to his fellowmen without love and mutual
respect, devoid of Jewish and human feelings—if each one is
concerned only with personal gain, with animal desires, and is
prepared to snatch whatever he can from his brother? How
detestable that would be to the God of Israel, the Torah and the
Land. . . .' (*Writings*, vol. 1, p. 255.)

In his foreword to this volume the author outlines what
comprises 'Menahem Mendelism' as it is found throughout
Sholom Aleichem's works. This original portrait made Menahem Mendel more than a fictional character; he came to symbolize the helplessness and lack of substance in East European
Jewry's economic and social structure. The 'new' Menahem
Mendel is intent upon exposing similar injurious developments
in Palestine. The author remarks that 'despite the fact that he
[Menahem Mendel] is guilty of the same evils, he stands above
them by dint of his naïveté, imagination and innocence.'
Above all, unlike the 'real' counterparts, he is free of petty
selfishness. The fictional Menahem Mendel is capable of laughing at himself and observing his actions with a smile. As the
author indicates, his Menahem Mendel differs from the original
'in his thoughts, manner of expression and outlook.' 'I have
adopted the basic externals, family ties, customary salutations

and so on . . . More precisely I have adopted Menahem Mendel, the literary symbol, as a literary technique and device, but I have injected fresh content in accord with the needs of a different time and place.' (*ibid.*, p. 215).

Throughout *Menahem Mendel in Eretz Yisrael* the settlers express revulsion at the mere mention of the familiar 'symbolic' Menahem Mendel. Wherever the new Menahem Mendel appears, people recognize him and are anxious to chase him from the country. Consequently, he feels condemned by his past. Some, however, pay him a back-handed compliment by telling him that were it not for him they would never have left Europe. His spirits are restored at a reception at Bialik's home. Bialik, Menahem Mendel writes to his wife, publicly declared that the Jewish people has far too long considered Menahem Mendel a symbol of decadence. 'But we have forgotten that Menahem Mendel belongs to the family of restless individuals who continually search for the unknown, who strive to reach the unreachable . . . Who knows if we could have endured the long, bitter exile were it not for the many Menahem Mendels who strengthened us with their soaring dreams . . .?' (*ibid.* p. 267.)

However, more than in the other narratives, the sadness is alleviated by the humour with which even the most heart-rending scenes are presented. At the most basic level, the sentences are so constructed that they evoke a smile and thereby soften the sadness of the content. Thus, for example, after a long and arduous journey Menahem Mendel finally meets up with his son. He reports to his wife that his son 'Moshe Hershl, known here as Moshe Tzevi, the *halutz*, gave me such a warm welcome that I could have buried myself alive—he practically threw me out. To tell you the truth, he did throw me out, may it not be counted against him, and I was just about to turn around and return to Tel-Aviv when an angel of God in the shape of a *halutzah*, appeared to console me. Not only did she reconcile father and son, but she gave me the opportunity of meeting a good and pleasant young lady (our daughter-in-law).' (*ibid.* p. 238.) An examination of this selection demonstrates the regular use of apostrophic phrases (to tell you the truth, may it not be counted against him) which were part of the Jew's conversational jargon. This passage also emphasizes another stylistic feature: the juxtaposition of two or three contradictory elements that provoke comedy by the surprise outcome (he gave me such a warm welcome that I could have buried myself alive, an angel of God in the shape of a *halutzah*). In addition, the author parodies words and phrases whose original religious contexts were very familiar to the readers.

As the contemporary Menahem Mendel travels about Palestine, first in search of his son and then, having found him, in search of building sites for a number of outlandish projects, he is overwhelmed by the country's natural beauty. He consistently relates his personal experiences to some biblical or rabbinic passage, and thereby achieves an added comic effect. As usual in Berkowitz's compositions, the humour relies upon the language, which is generally a mixture of misquoted biblical verses, rabbinic sayings and popular proverbs—all part of the common vocabulary of the semi-learned Jew. The delightful experiences and inspiring accomplishments far outweigh all other considerations, and exhibit Berkowitz's exuberance and the country's electrifying effect upon resident and visitor alike. Because of the light humour and delicate wit, the fine descriptions of the country's landscapes and a consuming interest in the positive facets of the renascent life—this volume expresses hope for a brighter future for the dedicated pioneers, and sincere pride in their achievements.

Chapter 9

MESSIANIC DAYS

Messianic Days, Berkowitz's only full-length novel, was first published in serial form as a weekly feature in the Sunday Literary Supplement to the Yiddish *Daily Forward* printed in the United States. The series ran from August 5, 1934, to August 25, 1935.[1] Tragically and ironically, the Thursday issue of this newspaper immediately prior to the first instalment, carried the headline, 'Hitler becomes President'. During the months that the story ran, news reports of the rise and spread of Nazism served as a terrifying counterpart to this novel of romance and reclamation. The serial proceeded regardless of events that were to lead to the destruction of the entire European Jewish community and to bring its destitute remnants to the shores of Palestine.

No comparative analysis of the original Yiddish version and the Hebrew edition published in 1938 has yet been made. However, without citing illustrative examples, one may conclude that aside from any differences determined by the peculiarities of the respective languages, the overall tone, style, mood and plot remain the same. The basis for all the remarks in this chapter is the more readily accessible Hebrew version.[2]

Structurally, *Messianic Days* may be divided into two large sections: scenes before the arrival in Palestine and events subsequent to it. Approximately one-third of the volume, the first seventeen chapters, describes the three-week voyage of Ameri-

1. Because many critics and readers of the original tried to guess the 'living people' who had served as models for the novel's characters, Berkowitz stressed that any such similarity was absolutely coincidental. See *Writings*, p. 381.
2. Published in *Writings*, pp. 381–518. The Yiddish original has been published under the title *Baginen* (Tel-Aviv, 1968).

can Jewish passengers travelling on an ocean liner to Palestine. The remaining thirty-six chapters concentrate on events in the week following disembarkation.[3] The overall emphasis is on the return to the land which is the focus of the entire narrative. The early chapters serve to introduce the cast, and to describe their physical features and basic attitudes. In its broad outline, the first section resembles Berkowitz's novella *America comes to Eretz Yisrael*. In fact, the opening lines parallel each other. However, in place of the novella's quasi-allegorical stock figures, the novel is peopled with more realistic characters.

The novel's central themes are clear: the joys and tribulations attendant upon the individual's anticipated metamorphosis from an uprooted, Diaspora Jew to an integrated citizen of *Eretz Yisrael*, living permanently upon his own land. The process of transformation is the novel's main theme. The career and biography of Dr Menuhin, the novel's central hero, is paradigmatic and symbolic. His initial solitude and rootlessness are accentuated by his bachelor state. He is cast as a modern, Jewish intellectual who, after many years of doubt and frustration, is led to the threshold of a new life. In Palestine he hopes to find roots, a reason for his existence, and personal joy in a double union: in marriage and in agricultural life.[4]

Other motifs are complementary. The novel's general structure indicates a movement away from a temporary, perilous and exposed life aboard a ship towards *terra firma et sancta*. The former typifies the precariousness of Diaspora Jewry, while the latter is synonymous with security. Consequently more than

3. The time covered by the action of the novel spans a narrow range: chapters 1–17 span the three-week voyage aboard ship, 18–46 cover the first week: 18–31 the first day [Sunday] after arrival in Haifa; 31–5, Monday; 36, Tuesday; 37–42, Wednesday, during which period the heroine's past is divulged; 43–5, Thursday and Friday; 46, Sabbath in Jerusalem; 46–52, a brief visit to the Emek; 53, the wedding day—a few weeks after the first week.

4. A new form of uprootedness and estrangement felt by Berkowitz's heroes even in Palestine, their homeland, is discussed in G. Shaked, *Ha-Telishut ha-Ḥadashah, Moznayim*, vol. 11, Nov. 1960, pp. 431–8.

half the volume is devoted to the life on land—to the middle-aged hero's quest and need for sources of regeneration for his personal and national existence.

Throughout the volume *Eretz Yisrael* represents the anticipated fulfilment to which all the characters strive. Each person represents a different kind of Jew with individual ideologies and attitudes, for whom the country will serve eventually, if not immediately, as a transforming power. Thus, notwithstanding the many *dramatis personae*, Palestine remains the centripetal force that constantly attracts the people involved and gathers them together. Each character reacts to and draws sustenance from it. The land, thereby, becomes the dominant axis around which all actions revolve, and towards which, whether obliquely or directly, the entire complex of interactions is directed. The whole story is, however, only a first stage, as is indicated by the fact that the Yiddish version is captioned 'Part One'. It was the author's apparent intention to carry the story beyond the initial phases, during which the characters still maintain a somewhat superficial and unnatural relationship to the land and its people. It can only be assumed, based on the initial reactions of these characters, that Palestine would continue to play an ever more prominent role in their search for self-fulfilment, thereby actuating the 'messianic days'.[5]

Throughout the composition Berkowitz devotes a wealth of detail to the description of the *dramatis personae*. In part this may be due to the origin of the work. It is clearly Berkowitz's intention to identify the various characters in the novel with social, economic, political or intellectual positions. From an aesthetic or literary point of view many of these details are superfluous and might merely have been hinted at. But for the fact that Berkowitz wished to present life under a microscopic lens that is shifted slowly from segment to segment, the back-

5. This caption reads 'Part One *Oyf Der Zunniger Zeit*', 'On the Sunny Side'. Clearly it is difficult, if not unwise, to attempt to guess whether volume two was to be even 'sunnier' than the first, or to be an exposition of the negative aspects that followed close upon the initial contact with the dire realities of Palestine.

grounds of many characters need not have been so thoroughly exposed. Moreover, at several points, the novel's mainstream is abandoned for the sake of ornamental digressions, which undoubtedly detract from the general impact of the work.

A summary of the novel's contents may serve to support the view that Berkowitz wished to record a spectrum of prevailing Jewish types, ideologies and attitudes rather than adhere to literary-aesthetic norms. The first two chapters set the scene on board ship, and concentrate on one adult, Mr Cederbaum and two American Jewish teen-agers, Amos and Shulamit. The third chapter is entirely given over to Cederbaum's biography and the fourth and fifth focus upon Amos and his relationship with Shulamit. Only at the conclusion of the fifth chapter is the chief character, Dr Menuhin, introduced. From this point on all crucial plot developments revolve about him, and chronicle the agonies and delights of his highly romantic courtship with Miss Gordon.

The novel presents a number of characters most of whom are representatives of types and partisan positions.[6] The first, chronologically, is Mr Cederbaum, a forty-year-old Hebrew schoolteacher from New York who is returning to cultivate the groves he has purchased. Encouraged by the number and calibre of the Jews aboard he declares, 'the messianic days are upon us'. As the only passenger who converses in Sephardi Hebrew, with his wife and daughter Shulamit, he immediately becomes the centre of attraction and information about Palestine. Discounting the rumours about the latest Arab pogroms, he encourages his attentive listeners and comforts himself by citing biblical verses which he considers relevant to the present situation. Thereby, too, he substantiates his claim that since God gave the land to the children of Israel no harm can befall them there.

Shulamit, raised in a Hebrew-speaking home and nurtured

6. They include: Shulamit, Amos, Pini Dubrow, Menuhin, Cederbaum, Judith, Mr Gordon, Mr Hanina, Daniel Gordon, Miss Zackheim, Dr Scheinin, Mr and Mrs Shimshelevitz, Berl Shimshelevitz (Shimshi), Prof. Rabinchik, Dr Birenbaum, Mr Pedahzur, Shimon Heller (Bar Giora), Yohanan Meisel (Yohanan Ish Gush Halav), and Ishtov Goodman.

on traditional texts and the classics of modern Hebrew literature, is a refined, sophisticated, intellectual American-Jewish
teen-ager. She, like her father, dreams of a reconstituted life
in Palestine where she will be able to mix with children of
similar interests and backgrounds. She does indeed find contentment and significance in her new life, although she continues
to long for her friend Amos Dubrow, whom she met aboard
the ship.

Amos, a seventeen-year-old dreamer, identifies mystically
with the prophet Amos. He comes from the American West
where he had been a lonely and delicate lad who, until he met
Shulamit, had spent most of his time studying and dreaming.
Shocked into a realization of the Jewish plight by reports of the
Arab riots against the Jews in Palestine, he had begun to delve
into Jewish history. Ultimately he announces his intention to
join his mother's brother in Palestine. After reading many
volumes about the Messiah, he fashions himself in the role of
saviour, and dreams of building an atom bomb that will bring
eternal peace to the world. As the boat approaches Palestine, he
fears that his dreams will be shattered against the routine demands of daily life. That is precisely what occurs. Only because
of Dr Menuhin's assistance does he find a home on a *kibbutz*
whose members, he finds, live their lives according to biblical
principles of social justice and equality.

Amos's father, Pini Dubrow, typifies the Jewish pseudo-
intellectual, racing rapidly from one ideology to the next, from
one extreme to another; from the *yeshiva* to the *Bund*, to the
radical labour party, to bolshevism, and then to pacifism. Of all
the characters depicted, he alone is disappointed and disenchanted. He feels impotent because he has arrived too late
to make a real contribution. Constantly overshadowed by his
famous brother-in-law, Berl Shimshi, he longs to return to the
States. At the end of the volume, his fate is left unclear and his
dilemma is unresolved.

The central figure is Dr Israel Menuhin.[7] The name itself

7. Menuhin is a minor figure in a short-story version of this novel. See

bears connotations symbolic of the quest that binds the novel together. *Menuhin* derives from *menuḥah*—rest, tranquillity, and peace. The surname is patently emblematic and requires no amplification. Throughout the composition Menuhin's individuality is blended with the search of the people of Israel for roots. His career in the medical profession, as well as several other aspects of his life, associate him with Dr Winik in *Severed*. Like Dr Winik he finds no satisfaction in his life of solitude and craves for a life of normalcy—of marriage and family. Menuhin composed a book on Jewish history, *Eternity of Israel*, in which he attempted to unravel the mystery of Jewish existence. In it he defended the Diaspora and praised Jewish achievements there. He later discarded this view and in its place adopted Zionist ideology, concluding that only in *Eretz Yisrael* can he rebuild and revitalize his life.

On board ship he falls deeply in love with Miss Judith Gordon. With her he plans a totally new adventure—a life of married bliss as a farmer. Hearing that she has been married before, he leaves her only to discover that the further he goes from her the more attracted he becomes. The more he considers her previous marriage, the more he recognizes the defects evidenced by his own acts of infidelity. The novel concludes with the marriage ceremony in which Menuhin pays special attention to the traditional blessings recited on this occasion which he sees as reflecting his affection for his bride and for *Eretz Yisrael*.

Judith (Yehudit) is also symbolic of the Jewish national fate. Yehudit is the feminine form of 'Jew' (Yehudi). By her former marriage to a non-Jew she personally embodied the Jewish assimilationist ideal. Her marriage failed as many attempts at total integration seem to fail. Judith finds her happiness with Israel Menuhin, the scholarly scion of Rabbis. Together they find their way back to the land and its people.

Ha-Toren, vol. 4, no. 20, *Al Kiddush ha-Ḥayyim*, pp. 8–9. His book plays a more dominant role here—see *ibid.*, vol. 4, no. 26, pp. 10–12. It would be interesting to trace the development of this work from its early phases as a series of short stories to their integration and reconstitution as a novel. On this book and its place in the novel, see *Writings*, pp. 399–400, 466.

Many relatively minor characters are involved in the plot. Each again represents a specific aspect of Jewish life in Palestine or in the Diaspora. Mr Hanina, a former American and now the mayor of Shaananah, the village in which Judith and Menuhin will reside, typifies the established farmer who rests content with the fact that he is able to till the land and seeks no greater benefits. Judith's father, Mr Gordon, typifies the upper-class Russian-Jewish immigrant to the United States whose 'astute business sense blends easily with proper social behaviour'. Daniel Gordon, Judith's brother, and his colleagues 'Bar Giora' and 'Yohanan Ish Gush Ḥalav', are spokesmen of the new party that is dedicated to reconstituting the ancient kingdom of Israel on both sides of the Jordan. Their many discussions provide Berkowitz ample opportunities to air his views and counteract such positions. The unattractive Miss Zackheim serves as comic relief, and as the third corner in the triangle of romance between Judith and Menuhin. Conceding victory to Judith she disappears to a *kibbutz* and does not reappear until the end of the novel when Menuhin chances upon the same *kibbutz*. It is here that Judith and he are reconciled and decide to marry. Dr Menuhin's brother-in-law Ishtov Goodman is cast as a typical, insensitive land speculator whose presence is a decided detriment to the *Yishuv*. Unmoved by moral or national considerations he is ready to defile his fallen son's memory in order to advance his financial interests. Except for Dr Menuhin, the other characters tend to be possessed by a single idea and do not veer far from it. Dr Menuhin is a more 'complicated character' to the extent that he bears within himself the dilemmas and perplexities consistent with and characteristic of the type he represents. Although he changes, from the outset the seeds of this transformation were implanted and merely come to fruition in the course of time. Menuhin moves from dejection to elation. This process and its concomitant problems make for 'roundness' and more human qualities.

Not only are people rehabilitated and the land reclaimed, time is also regained. Although the entire action is limited to several weeks, by means of flashbacks a much greater time span is covered. Several historical events serve as immediate, relevant and realistic backdrops. These include the economic depression in the United States during the late 1920's, and the Arab riots in Palestine and their aftermath.[8] The flashbacks recall, in general, the post-World War One era and, more particularly, the community of Jewish émigrés who had fled from Berlin to Copenhagen and then to America—the precise route taken by Berkowitz and Sholom Aleichem. Also mentioned is the second-generation American-Jewish community which, the author underlines, no longer feels a sense of estrangement and is, therefore, caught up in the quicksands of acculturation that are about to engulf and destroy it.

Due to the abundance of characters and its implicit purpose the novel is loosely constructed and episodic, and it creaks with ideological contrivance. In this respect there is a real difference between Berkowitz, the honest chronicler of the Diaspora in his earlier stories, and Berkowitz the unsuccessful novelist, once artistry gives place to ideology. The central conflicts comprise an interplay of external and internal forces, the external ones being the vicissitudes of Menuhin's affair with Miss Gordon and the demands of *Eretz Yisrael* while the internal conflicts centre upon Menuhin's interminable tensions and demands for a changed life. The steady progress of his romance—from its mercurial beginnings to the dramatic complications caused by the news of Judith's former marriage to a non-Jew, to the readjustment and finally to resolution in marriage—forms the novel's basic framework. From Menuhin, Judith and their respective families and friends, threads radiate along which the action turns towards the periphery and eventually return to the centre—to the hero or heroine.

Since Palestine is the focus of the novel, the major actions take place either there or on the way from America to Palestine. In order to achieve the necessary compression, the author employs the techniques of retrospect and anticipation. One of

8. Mentioned specifically are such historical events as the British ban on visas to Palestine and the Madison Square Garden protest rally in New York.

the more common aspects of retrospect employed extensively throughout this work is recall, whereby a specific experience stimulates the recall of a similar situation in the individual's past. The response is spontaneous and simultaneous with the current event. This is a primitive application of 'subjective' time, through psychological flashbacks initiated in the hero's mind. The technique differs slightly from Berkowitz's usage in his short stories in which the recall is mechanically and, at times, artificially introduced by the author. To cite two illustrations, Menuhin, upon hearing Russian spoken on the ship, recalls the 'forgotten sounds of his birthplace', which sounds in turn initiate a host of reflections upon his youth and his escapades with young Jewish girls. Here the sense of sound sets off a continuum of responses. A second instance involves the sense of touch. Upon accidentally touching Judith's body, he feels a tremor pass through his entire body which reminds him of similar sensations experienced during his youth. These natural, biological responses help transcend the present and link it to the past. In charting the romance of Judith and Menuhin, the author also uses anticipation. For example, even before Dr Menuhin decides to marry, the author hints at the future relationship, and thereby, early in the work, indicates that in the end, regardless of the concatenation of events, all will be resolved. To a degree, the element of mystery is mitigated. On the other hand, the scattered references to Judith's affairs with other men, which are mentioned long before her father exposes them to Menuhin, arouse the reader's interest because of their intrinsic ambiguity. Only after the 'news' is reported do these previous clues take on a new meaning as indications of some future event that will affect the relationship.

The forces that motivate the characters are not limited to human ones, but also include drives that lie 'beyond human control'.[9] The irresistible determinants include external as well

9. As Forster writes, 'There are in the novel two forces: human beings and a bundle of various things not human beings and it is the novelist's business to adjust these two forces and conciliate their claims.' E. M. Forster, *Aspects of the Novel* (London, 1927, 1954), pp. 45ff.

as internal forces. To cite a few examples of external forces: Judith's physical attractiveness that stirs Menuhin emotionally, and arouses hitherto suppressed sexual urges and propels him to seek traditional fulfilment in marriage; the murder of Menuhin's nephew by the Arabs which prompts him to abandon everything for *Eretz Yisrael*; and finally the revolutions and wars that compelled the complacent to seek new asylums and forced them to reconsider the meaning of exile and the Zionist ideal. Note that all these elements are related to the characters' convergence upon Palestine, the central force, and their eventual regenesis there. The internal drives are subconscious. Hence, for example, the author describes Mr Dubrow's resolve to settle in Palestine: '"Pini" Dubrow's decision to leave for Palestine with his family at first seemed a hasty, spontaneous act ... even though, in fact, it was the result of very deep sentiments, of subtle psychological pressures which he himself might not have wished to admit.'[10]

If the unconscious can be inferred only from the symbols, memories, and associations that emerge in man's conscious expression, Berkowitz provides a number of leads into the subconscious areas of at least the two chief figures, Judith and Menuhin. Menuhin's subconscious comes to the surface when the circumstances are propitious—in his dreams, at moments of deep anguish or in times of frustration. The most obvious illustration is Menuhin's long dream to which an entire chapter (fifteen) is devoted. The dream *per se* requires little commentary—it is self-evident in the light of the preceding chapters. A brief outline of this dream sequence will highlight its erotic nature, which forms an integral part of all Menuhin's reflections.

'As the boat approaches Palestine, Menuhin sees himself seated in his cabin with Miss Zackheim who flirts with him but does not excite him. Soon he becomes totally absorbed in a Hebrew primer which is suddenly changed into a large

---

10. *Writings*, p. 355. By revealing the hidden life at its source, Berkowitz fulfilled one function as novelist. See Forster, *op. cit.*, pp. 45ff. Forster defines a character as real 'when the novelist knows everything about it.' *Ibid.*, p. 63.

Talmud, the tractate *Ketubot* (Marriage Contracts) opened at the first page, with the word 'virgin' printed in bold type. This word turns into a beautiful princess, Menuhin's ideal female, the bearer of *The Eternity of Israel* in her womb . . . He lands on the Tel-Aviv beach where he is astonished to see Judith's nude body. To his chagrin, this figure is actually his sister who pleads with him to recite *Kaddish* for her deceased son. . . . Returning to his cabin for his hat in order to be able to pray, his father appears and tells him: 'Your *Yahadut* (Judaism) doesn't suit me!'—but by a slip of the tongue he said 'Your *Yehudit* (Judith) doesn't appeal to me!' The virgin disappears and is transmuted into a newspaper obituary in which he reads 'Professor *Eternity of Israel* is dead—thereupon he recites the *Kaddish*.'

Upon awakening, Menuhin realizes how the web of this dream has been woven from the threads of reality, although some of the strands remain undeciphered for several weeks. The merging of blurred contours and the disregard for causal links which are replaced by psychologically plausible connections of past, present and future, the interaction of *eros* and *thanatos*, all combine to give the dream a surrealistic and authentic quality.

It is clear even from the above passage that this dream contains eroticism which mirrors Menuhin's mystical relationship with Judith and *Eretz Yisrael*. Throughout the work his attitude is expressed in highly sensuous terms and tactile sexual images. Menuhin is from the outset attracted by Judith's physical beauty. He is aroused at the mere sight of her shapely and sensual body. Each intimate encounter brings him unanticipated pleasure. Judith too, is thrilled by the touch of his strong, masculine hands. Menuhin who had always considered womanhood in a purely mystical way, feels guilty and embarrassed by his carnal thoughts. Although he seeks opportunities to beg her pardon, he is never able to express his feelings.

The eroticism intended for Judith is often transferred to the land. In several passages this nexus is made explicit.[11] Two

11. Such passages can be found in *Writings*, pp. 385, 393–4, 401–2, 416, 461, 492, 500, 503. Add to this Amos's first involvement with sex, pp. 393ff.

examples may serve as illustration. Once, while standing with Judith and staring into her eyes, Menuhin's heart fills with love 'at the sight of the round ripe fruits . . . he visualizes the heads of lovely, innocent children, which he will soon sire from this stately and exquisite tree . . .' Immediately afterwards, Menuhin is embarrassed by this train of 'animal thought'. In a second dream he again sees Judith lying naked on the sands. She is rapidly transfigured into a beautiful ripe tree. Bound to a metal bed, he is unable to reach her. Again too, he sees his name within the black borders of an obituary notice.[12] The frequent association of death and sex in this novel is indicative of Menuhin's efforts to circumvent death, and even overcome it by marriage. All efforts to avoid reflecting upon death lead him into Judith's arms. Furthermore, as he prepares for his wedding day, he attempts to rid himself of all sensual considerations by total purification—hoping to enter marriage in a sanctified state.

When Menuhin had mused in private over Judith's previous marriage, he had of course visualized it in highly erotic terms. Horrified at the thought that 'she had offered her body and soul to a gentile and thereby desecrated the unstained bed of her modest matriarchs' he wonders how he can 'aspire to chaste progeny when the tree trunk has been defiled—the sap drained forever?'[13] He then recollects his own past affairs with gentile girls, the memory of which still affords him erotic pleasure.

The novel's style, humour and techniques are similar to those used in his other stories. Modern ways are compared to traditional Jewish rites and habits.[14] The humour is based primarily on the incongruity of language. The characters' reactions are not very different from those expressed by the characters in his

12. *Ibid.*, p. 486.　　　　13. *Ibid.*, p. 492.
14. To illustrate, the terms used to describe the entrance to the gambling casino at Monte Carlo (one of the stops *en route* to Palestine) derives from biblical passages describing the sanctuary and the Temple. After the visitors 'prepared themselves in the corridor they finally entered the inner sanctum and then to the sanctum sanctorum.' 'To prepare oneself in the corridor' comes from *Ethics of the Fathers*, 4:10.

short stories, they tear their hair, cry aloud, recite the high holy-day prayers and identify themselves with places and with animals.

In short, the novel's overall trend is towards resolution, reconciliation and purposefulness, as befits the emergence of messianic days. It proceeds from transience to permanence, from bachelorhood to marriage, from gloom to joy. By the final chapter each character has resolved his problems. Dr Menuhin marries Judith; Miss Zackheim finds happiness with a member of her *kibbutz*; the young dreamer, Amos Dubrow, discovers in the *kibbutz* a utopian society to which he hopes to bring Shulamit Cederbaum. The die-hard, revolutionary, Mr Dubrow, discovers new and more significant movements in which to become involved. Beneath the surface of the volatile bickering that permeates the work, there is a growing tolerance, so that the characters, despite all partisan sympathies, learn to endure and even admire each other.[15]

Although Berkowitz's influence upon the writers of his own and subsequent generations has been limited, several of his works are of permanent value. It is generally agreed that his best short stories and novellas are those that were composed in accordance with the traditions of the Hebrew, Yiddish, and Russian realists. While remaining faithful to their aesthetic modes and objectives, Berkowitz introduced new themes and structural patterns, and expanded the use of symbolic landscapes, metaphors and literary allusions. The central focus of his narratives, however, remained fixed on the psychological upheavals which his alienated heroes suffered in the face of the powerful forces which shook the *shtetl* to its foundations and victimized its residents. From an artistic standpoint, both his novels—even the suitability of the term 'novel' is questionable—are only of middling quality. His plays, all faithful in some measure to the principles of realistic drama, range from superior to banal. The memoirs of his childhood, of his association with Sholom Aleichem and of life in *Eretz Yisrael* bear

15. On this work's thematic and literary contribution to modern Hebrew writing see S. Halkin, *Arai va-Keva*, New York, 1942, pp. 104-9.

interesting witness to their author's experiences and tastes. Regardless of any estimate of the virtues or limitations of Berkowitz's operative principles and original writings, his rendition into Hebrew of Sholom Aleichem's collected works deserves special attention. It is a *tour de force* in metaphrase, an inventive contribution to the development of modern Hebraic wit, and a major source for the infusion of Yiddish rhythms, diction and idiom into the mainstream of modern Hebrew usage. A master of the many strata of Hebrew literature, Berkowitz utilized them as effective media for depicting contemporary dilemmas. Thus, by rendering the Hebrew language more flexible and resilient, he prepared it for further literary experimentation and achievement.

PART TWO

TRANSLATIONS

Severed

AFTER the many trials and failures, the misgivings and anxieties that marked the start of young Dr Winik's new life in his home town, he gradually acquired a secure and comfortable position as a conscientious physician and a keen intellect. He was cordially received in the homes of the wealthy whom he joined on winter evenings for tea, small talk on literature, or card games, and with whom he sometimes dabbled in community affairs. But basically he was lonely and aloof in a world of his own. Gone were the early years following his triumphant return from the university when he was still enthusiastic about his new role in his forlorn birthplace. The years also witnessed the cooling of his youthful passion to realize his full potentiality, to succeed, excel, to make all the townsfolk gaze at him with admiration, awed by his talents and proud of his achievements. All the teeming plans that had demanded fulfilment from the moment he had first conceived them seemed, at the critical moment, to retreat before the cold, disapproving stares of the fashionable people, before the condescending glances of the 'respectable' members of society at this *parvenu* who had climbed from the bottom of the ladder and was now frequenting their salons in the hope of bringing about reforms and innovations. Since he was not essentially a war-like man, he eventually came to loathe such a wearisome occupation and, out of weakness and dejection, began to be drawn into the stagnant stream of small-town life—to become one with the many. The few young idealists who had at first surrounded and pinned their hopes on him, presently became disenchanted and one by one lost interest in him.

'He's nothing more than a careerist!' they declared in tones of condemnation, making derogatory signs behind his back.

The young doctor swallowed the insult and retreated further into his shell. Stripped of all grandiose dreams, he sought comfort in trivial matters. At times he would stroll along the city's main street

and meet a rich, old gentleman, strolling unhurriedly, not as someone on business, but as one walking for pleasure in the afternoon
breeze. Dr Winik would greet him with some hesitation. The old
gentleman would acknowledge him with a friendly smile. Afterwards, upon returning home, the doctor would ponder over the
encounter for a long time, without ever reaching any satisfactory
conclusions. Once, while Dr Winik was still a poor young *yeshivah*
boy, this gentleman had sent him to his home to check if the
samovar had been heated and had told him to ask his wife for an
apple as a reward. The apple was small, red, and shiny. As if from
some other world, the apple retained the scent of that lady's cupboard. To this day he experienced a thrill whenever he recalled the
sweet, strange taste. Musing over this apple, he became very upset:
why had he accepted it from the woman? He now imagined that, if
he had refused, his present relationship with this gentleman would
be more candid and straightforward.

He still did not feel quite at ease with upper-class folk like them.
Born of poor, humble parents, he was raised in dismal surroundings
under a low, charred roof and had lived a life of dire poverty.
Whenever he came into the company of these self-satisfied local
worthies and their pampered children, he felt like a sapling which,
by some quirk of fate, has been uprooted from its rugged native
abode and transplanted into fertile, but foreign, soil. Superficially, he
appeared as one of them, participating fully in their comfortable
lives, in their casual strolls, in their conversations and jokes and in
the many mannerisms which they had grown up with. But he was
secretly plagued by an oppressive sense of loneliness mixed with envy
and contempt for all that surrounded him, almost like the feeling of
an incurably sick person who happens to come into the cheerful
company of healthy people, and when they are at their merriest,
secludes himself with his secret and attends to the illness which is
secretly devouring him.

This may perhaps explain why he was still a bachelor. Often as he
looked at one of the women desirous of his friendship, he uncon-
sciously thought of his younger sister who had tried to worm her
way into his social life until, through his assistance, she had left for
America. She was unable to find a husband equal to her social status

—the status of a doctor's sister. She used to be seen with a veil over her face even on winter days; she would confuse *toilette* with *toilet*, and would walk alone every evening on the main street so that she might meet *him*—'the doctor'—walking with the city's aristocracy.

When surrounded by lovely upper-class ladies competing with each other for his affection, he would feel drunk with exuberance: yet even then he was not at ease, for at the crucial moment he appeared to be attacked by some bug that whispered, so it seemed, to the only sober man among a band of drunkards, that this success was not the result of any intrinsic merit, but rather of the professional reputation which he had attained after much toil and tribulation. He would marry none of these, but would buy a wife as one would buy something in the market—at the proper price.

As from a nightmare he fled and hid from the indigence in which he was raised and in which he got to know the world. When among the poor he felt as if he had severed almost all the links that bound him to them and their kind. Yet, whenever he visited one of their sick, he was not at all estranged from them, nor did he act haughtily. On the contrary, he treated them affably, sprinkling his conversation with jokes and pleasantries, chatting with the womenfolk and showing marked affection for their children. All of this he affected not as one of their kin, who had come to survey cheerfully the scene of his own past, but rather as a distant philanthropist or benefactor who had brought the bounty of a world other than their own. Even the Yiddish he spoke sounded somewhat foreign because of its unique inflections, as if it had been forgotten in that other world on account of its insignificance and was recalled not for any personal need or pleasure, but solely because of those who spoke nothing else. Nevertheless, he still felt certain bonds of affinity not totally effaced. Even the youngsters knew by hearsay that this doctor, who now rode his coach on the Sabbath in public,[1] was really one of them, that is, in his childhood he ran barefoot to the *Talmud Torah*[2] and

1. Riding a coach in public or in private on the Sabbath was in flagrant violation of the Sabbath.
2. *Talmud Torah*, originally the obligation to study Torah (the entire corpus of Jewish sacred literature). The term subsequently came to indicate the

was always called 'that clever little devil, Leibl',[3] because of the enthusiasm he applied to his studies and to his youthful pranks. The elders still recalled him jumping down from the synagogue attic where he had been pulling down birds' nests. To this time they resisted his prescriptions and stammered, as if bewitched, when they had to address him with the respectful 'You',[4] or call him 'Herr Doktor Winik'.

His brothers, who still carried on their father's business, lived on a street at the foot of the hill. They sold their wares in the village and eked out a meagre livelihood. Whenever he passed through this street, perched aloft in his open carriage, he was embarrassed by the stares of former friends and acquaintances who now gazed at him from every courtyard and window. He felt a painful tension spreading over his face—at one moment he smiled, at another his expression was clouded with sadness, and then again his face contorted as if in search of asylum. Sometimes, he would have liked to jump from the carriage and hide in a corner in the shadow of the old familiar broken-down fence as he used to do in those far-off childhood days when he took refuge from his pursuers.

Here was that most cherished corner on the whole street—the little, old house with its sagging roof darkened by moss stains—his father's poor home. The coach drew near. Dr Winik looked around and wondered—would any member of his family be there to greet him? Yes, both his older and his younger brother were busily engaged in their work—that all-too-familiar task—packing eggs in long wooden crates. Both had removed their long, black coats and were standing in the middle of the narrow court that was full of crushed straw and sawdust. They were sorting eggs with special care and

community-sponsored educational institution for orphans and poor children. See M. Zborowski and E. Herzog, *Life Is With People* (New York, 1952), pp. 102, 103 and S. Baron, *The Jewish Community* (Philadelphia, 1942), vol. II, chap. 9.

3. The suffixes 'l', 'le', 'ke', 'chik' as in 'Hershl', 'Shlomole', or 'Shlomke', or 'Gideonchik' are diminutive endings of endearment.

4. 'You' of respect: in Yiddish 'ihr' or 'etz', in German 'Sie'; in Hebrew either the second person plural form is used or the person is addressed in the third person singular.

shooing away the children who were constantly getting under their feet. With one glance Dr Winik observed the red, hairy neck of his older brother, Moshe-Aharon, who had bent down to thrust his head and beard into one of the crates; the round, black patch on the pants of his younger brother Shlomo crouching on the balls of his feet as he counted the eggs in the straw, and the grimy infant clinging to his father's side and pulling at one end of his leather belt. At the sound of the coach-bells the brothers raised their heads. Dr Winik looked down at them from his perch as he forced a wry smile, like that of a stranger who has chanced unwittingly upon a long-forgotten spot. The work in the courtyard ceased at once and the two brothers stood flustered in front of their crates. At his master's command the coachman, in blue uniform and shiny, black hat, halted the coach which was drawn by a handsome, glossy horse, holding the reins in his hands and looking down with all the hauteur of servants in livery. Smiling, the doctor turned to his brothers and addressed them in the very words he used with his patients:

'Well, how are we doing? We're working, eh?'

Moshe Aharon, the older brother, moved slightly as though about to advance towards the coach, but suddenly changed his mind and answered from where he was:

'Working.'

Moshe Aharon looked angry. Keeping his distance opposite the coach, he had the air of a man who has been unnecessarily disturbed. With his shirt sleeve he wiped the sweat from his face and waited silently as if curious to know what this was all about.

'Well, very well!' exclaimed the doctor, searching unsuccessfully for words as he twisted his thick, black moustache. Shlomo, the other brother, who had served in the army for four years, stood looking as embarrassed as a soldier who has disgraced himself before his commanding officer. His large red hands clung to his waist as if they too had been reprimanded. He felt the doctor's eyes on him, and in confusion blushed all over, and bent down to catch hold of his little son, who was standing in front of him, as a drowning man clutches at a straw.

'Shlomo, is this the son born of your old age?' asked the doctor, finally finding words to address his brother.

'Um, hum,' Shlomo grunted in response as he bent his blushing face to the child and pulled him on to his knee.

'A fine young child,' the doctor praised his disgustingly filthy little nephew, still twisting his moustache and standing with a bland smile that had frozen and soured on his face.

After Dr Winik had gone some distance from his father's house, he contorted his face in a grimace of self-disgust and felt somehow tainted. He reflected upon his childhood, when as a dirty child he had run barefoot about that yard. He continued to puzzle over the black patch hanging from his younger brother's pants as if to mock the poor wretch, and over his older brother's stubborn silence that contained no small measure of hidden animosity and obvious alienation from him, their brother, the physician. Then, too, he recalled the elder Mr Berger, a rich money-lender to whom all the gentry's estates were mortgaged, and the father of the young Dr Berger who had recently returned from the University at St Petersburg and had opened a magnificent practice here. When his young colleague had introduced him to his father, the latter inquired of his family background and was shocked:

'Your father's name, you say, was Avraham Winik? Wait, wait just a minute: which Winiks are those?... You say he was an egg dealer? With which of the lords did he deal? I know almost all the Jewish merchants who gather around the gentry's courts. Ah, he traded in the village with the farmers? Then he wasn't really a merchant, he was a hawker... And he sent you to study in a *gymnasium*?[5] Ah, you studied on your own and passed the matriculation exams? Well, that is commendable and speaks well of you. It proves that you're very clever.'

2

One summer day Dr Winik was informed that his brother Shlomo was sick. Upon returning home from his visits in the city, he found a girl waiting for him. Slightly bewildered at his sudden entrance, the girl got up from the chair, curtseyed and said,

5. *Gymnasium*—a government secondary school.

'Mama sent me to tell you that Shlomo took sick. Mama asks that you come right away.'

'Who's this Shlomo?' the doctor inquired.

'Shlomo . . . your brother . . .'

'Ah, Shlomo! Very well . . . immediately.'

For a moment he admired her pleasant flushed face, her neat clothes and the small parasol in her hand and then asked:

'And whose daughter are you?'

'Menaker's daughter. My mother is Malkah Menaker.'

'You're Aunt Malkah's daughter?' he asked with amazement. After a brief pause Dr Winik decided to walk to his brother's house and thus not accentuate his comfortable life in view of his family's desperate condition. On the way the young girl informed him that Shlomo had been in bed for four days. At sunset on Friday evening he had returned home from one of the villages 'as black as the earth' and began to complain of severe pains in his chest and back. Her mother, thinking his condition dangerous, had urged the family to call Dr Winik. However, the patient insisted that he did not want him to come—and he was not really sick. But now . . .

'How is Moshe Aharon?' the doctor inquired.

'Moshe Aharon is in Shlomo's house. Day and night he tends to the patient. Since he has a grown daughter and doesn't have any dowry for her he planned to leave for America this week. Sheindl, that is Zena, your sister Zena, sent him the passage money. But Shlomo's illness has delayed the trip.' The girl rambled on about her brother Benjamin Menaker—Dr Winik certainly must have heard about him; he passed the fourth-year *gymnasium* examination and did very well—anyway he lives in London. He works for a printing firm and earns three English pounds a week, that is thirty Russian roubles, and sends home enough for her and her mother. He writes letters practically every month and suggests that she, his sister, engage a private tutor to teach her English, since he plans to bring them, her and her mother, to London. Consequently, she's asking Dr Winik's advice: Who is the best English teacher in town, someone really fluent in English?

The doctor walked alongside her, distressed by the thought that there were, in fact, better brothers than he in this world—even in his own family. He cast frequent glances at his young companion walking with her quick stride under her white parasol. Her dark, yearning eyes which she opened wider as she spoke reminded him of his talkative, robust Aunt Malkah. He feared an encounter with his aunt, for he knew he would not emerge unscathed.

When they entered the house, they found Moshe Aharon sitting near his brother's bed, conversing with him softly. The shutter on the window facing the street was closed in order to shelter the patient from the heat of the sun, while from the darkened corner where the bed stood there rose a cellar-like stench of decay. At first the interior of the house appeared to Dr Winik as through a mist; only very gradually did the extreme disorder become more apparent. Crates big and small, heaps of dry skins, bundles of onions lay strewn in every corner. The low ceiling and blackened walls were covered with strings of mushrooms hung up to dry for eventual sale, which filled the air with a hot, choking smell. The patient, covered with quilts and blankets to induce sweating, lay on dirty linen. A large bowl of unfinished soup stood on the chair at his head.

Dr Winik looked around confused, without knowing how to conduct himself or what to say in this house which he was visiting for the first time. Only as he approached the patient's bed did he speak to his squat Aunt Malkah who was standing near the chest-of-drawers with her arms folded—her ageing, wrinkled face as enraged as that of a child who has been admonished without reason. The doctor nodded in her direction.

'Good morning, Aunt Malkah!'

'Good morning, a good year! Hmm . . .,' Aunt Malkah sang out her blessing and then groaned hoarsely.

She said no more. From some hidden corner a pregnant woman with a green, swollen face appeared carrying a filthy two-year-old infant in her arms. The child was sucking a dirty thumb, breathing with difficulty through a stuffed and runny nose. It seemed almost as if it was not being held in its mother's arms, but was somehow crouching quietly and securely on her protruding belly like some inseparable organ. The patient, raising his head from his pillow, exclaimed 'Rachel-Leah, you should've brought a chair . . . take away the bowl . . .' He looked ashamedly at his brother the doctor. His

gaunt cheeks were inflamed, the hair of his short beard seemed to
have thinned out and withered, his parched lips trembled and revealed
large, dry, crooked teeth; his whole face twisted with strange con-
vulsions, half-smiling with pain, half-asking forgiveness for the
audacious act that his family has committed on his behalf—for having
troubled his distant, elegant and fortunate brother at this hour of
distress. The pregnant woman with the small child approached with
a sullen face which was flushed despite its green pallor. With her free
hand she removed the bowl. The doctor sat down on the chair.

'How come you're sick?' the doctor asked jovially, trying to ease
the burden of silence that hung all about. 'Do you think this is the
proper behaviour for an old soldier like you who served in the im-
perial infantry for four years? It's time you stopped such nonsense!'

The doctor realized that his banter was out of place and cast a wan
smile at his older brother Moshe Aharon who had left his chair near
the patient and had sat down near the table. Moshe Aharon continued to sit quietly, a sombre expression on his face. Meanwhile
from over by the chest-of-drawers Aunt Malkah was saying:

'Nonsense, you say Leibl? To you this is nonsense, to me this is
God knows what—murder, real murder! For four days non-stop,
day and night I stand and argue with them, arguing and pleading,
cajoling and begging mercy: Villains! Are you blind? The man is
lying in front of you at death's door! Hurry up and call Leibl, that
doctor of yours! . . . They pretend not to hear. I say to them, it's
nothing—your doctor can afford to spare two minutes of his precious time for his sick brother. It's no skin off his back, if he comes
once, and especially since, thank God, he owns his own coach with
bells, and he needn't burden his legs . . . On the contrary, let him
come and look, and give himself a treat! . . . With my simple mind I
don't understand: does he cure only his "aristocrats"? are the "aristocrats" closer to him than his brother, his own flesh and blood? Or is
there any reason to be ashamed of him? He is a brother—he can't
deny that, even if he wants to. Whether he likes it or not he's a
brother! . . . That's what I keep telling them, but they don't budge!
. . . Did you ever see such fools? . . . Just imagine: The Lord blessed
you with a brother who's a doctor; what more do you want? What
tremendous luck! But what do you say? True, everybody knows

that our brother is a doctor, but what shall we do if, for our sins, the doctor is not a brother? Not only that, but the doctor won't even acknowledge his own aunt, his father's sister, as if, God forbid, his father, may his soul rest in peace, were a wild plant in the desert or a stray stone in some forgotten field! Perhaps he has completely forgotten the time when he was a *Talmud Torah* student, and his aunt, instead of giving him *Ḥanukkah* money,[6] bought him a pair of new boots that winter for his bare feet... Anyway, that should be my greatest worry! My life doesn't depend on him! Thank God who has not forsaken me in my old age. My Benjamin, my comfort and my solace, may he live a long life, is enough for me. He, too, is a learned man and an "aristocrat", but he, God forbid, isn't ashamed of his old mother; he sends her English money and writes to her regularly every month. That's what I pleaded with them for four whole days, but they wouldn't move—as if they couldn't see that a man was lying deathly sick and "black as the earth" upon the bed . . .'

All the while her daughter, standing near the table, angrily implored her mother: 'Mama, enough . . .' nervously glancing at Dr Winik. He smiled pathetically and was unable to record the patient's pulse.

'Enough, Aunt Malkah . . .' Moshe Aharon shouted aloud, and then immediately quietened down and returned to his seat. Aunt Malkah stopped talking, folded her arms over her bosom, and with a satisfied expression glanced at Dr Winik from the other side of the room like an insulted child once it has vented its anger against an antagonist and is now satisfied. The sick man's wife sat heavily on the bench in the corner and put the baby down on the floor. She seemed to be uninvolved in all that went on in the house. Her sole duty was apparently to be pregnant and to care for this dirty child. Upon seeing her, Dr Winik suddenly felt violently disgusted with this life of poverty, and shuddered at the thought that this woman with the green resentful face was his sister-in-law.

He helped his brother open his shirt buttons and began examining him and listening to his chest and back. The patient lowered his

6. *Ḥanukkah* money—*Ḥanukkah*, a holiday celebrating the victory of the Maccabees. It is customary to give young children *Ḥanukkah gelt* (money).

head in shame, staring at his fingers as he placed his body in his brother's hands. His feverish face continued grimacing pitifully; he was very careful not to make the slightest movement. The patient's confusion seemed to extend to Dr Winik whose gestures during the examination were hesitant and uncertain. Presently, he recalled a long-forgotten scene of his distant childhood. Once, when his father had fallen sick, his Aunt Malkah urged them to fetch the best physician of that period, the old Pole, Dr Franciskiewich. The whole family, himself included, stood in the room at a distance, listening in fear and trembling to the insults of the old Pole who spiced his speech with Jewish rhyme-words: 'fire-mire, curse-worse'. Moshe Aharon, hat in hand, stood in front of him, bareheaded. Who, then, could have imagined that the day would come when he, the barefoot youth, dressed in rags, a pupil of the wretched *Talmud Torah*' would replace the esteemed Dr Franciskiewich? Indeed, his had been a strange fate, so different from that of his relatives who now surrounded him; it was almost like a dream. But when he put his ear to his sick brother's back and his smooth-shaven face touched the feverish, unbathed, worn-out skin of the wretched man, he was repelled. The amusing problems of his complacent existence were replaced by a disturbing and oppressive mood. How strange and painful the situation was! How odd that this thin, emaciated body with its protruding bones, which could be felt immediately upon contact, was the transfiguration of his younger brother. This was the same body as that of the once healthy, gay, mischievous, daring lad who was known to everybody on that street for his audacity. This sickly Jew, this poor, humiliated man with the black neck, sunken hairy chest and feeble hairy arms was none other than the little, red-cheeked Shlomik together with whom he would greedily swallow the groats which his mother used to serve them in a big bowl, and with whom he slept in one bed, each of them pulling the blanket over to his own side and kicking the other.

'Pneumonia,' Dr Winik whispered to his older brother and aunt who followed him to the door after he had written the prescription. Aunt Malkah wrung her hands and exclaimed, 'My God, My God!' For several minutes the three of them whispered together by the door. From her seat, the pregnant woman looked at them with glowering eyes. The sick man lifted his head from the pillow and restraining his anger shouted at her with a hoarse voice. The young child sitting at his mother's feet suddenly began crying. From every corner sorrow enfolded the all-pervading poverty. The doctor took his wallet out of his pocket and told his brother. 'Here, Moshe Aharon, . . . this will pay for the medicines and the other expenses . . . I'll send a woman from the hospital to look after him. . . . If you notice any change, call me immediately. I'll be here again tomorrow morning.'

He pushed a gold coin into his brother's hand, looked somewhat confusedly at his cousin who had not taken her eyes off him, and quickly left the house.

3

Towards evening Winik took a stroll outside of the city with the Bergers—the old father, his son and his young daughter who had recently returned from the city. Dr Winik walked alongside the tall, attractive young woman, listening to her in silence. She told him of her many experiences in the metropolis from which she had re-turned with many bright ideas. But from all that she had seen and experienced there, she concluded that nothing was being done in this God-forsaken provincial town. Passionately the girl discussed the poverty and illiteracy impeding the proletariat's progress, the intelli-gentsia's responsibility for the indigent, and the celebration that would take place in the city on the occasion of the dedication of a public library for the 'enlightenment' of the masses. Her Russian was fluent and quick; however, she gave particular stress to foreign words. She never tired of a certain marvellous, new word which she had apparently imported from the city: 'intensive'. If only the farm-ers would be more 'intensive'! From time to time Dr Winik raised his head and looked into her pretty eyes with their dark brows and lashes that accentuated her beautiful, white forehead, her soft red cheeks, and the beauty of her delicate round chin. At that moment he thought that this young woman, despite her naïve and somewhat boring talk, was the most splendid of all the women he knew in the city. He had, moreover, reason to believe that her father and brother deemed him a fitting suitor. Perhaps, too, some day he would decide to change the pattern of his life and marry her. She would become his wife and the sister-in-law of that pregnant woman with the green face and those sullen eyes whose dreadful image pursued him wherever he turned.

The elder Berger, walking behind them with his son and listening to their conversation, commented:

'Listen to what I'm telling you, my girl. Let this nonsense alone! "Library", "intelligentsia", "proletariat", "celebration" . . . the whole lot of them are not worth a penny piece. Do you really think that the poor will thank you for all the good you're doing them? I know them better, and I understand their mentality. I still remember how they treated my father, of blessed memory, who was a *gabbai*.[7] Now, it's euphemistically called "chairman", "treasurer" or "secretary". In our days they'd simply say *gabbai*—"the *gabbai* of the *Talmud Torah*", "the *gabbai* of the Free Loan Society", "the *gabbai* of the Visiting the Sick Society", etc.[8] But what was I talking about? Those beggars used to come with sticks and thunder at the door, as if we had stolen their inheritance! In brief, it was then that I made a vow which I have kept ever since: they're none of my business! I don't want to be a *gabbai*. . . . And you, too, my dear daughter, if you want to live in peace, avoid them like the plague! Just think how much money and energy I have spent on your education! Don't tell me you are going to waste your training and knowledge on garbage like them in the hope that they may eventually like you. I ask you, is it fair? What do you think, Herr Doctor Leib, Leib . . . Abramovich?'

'What?' Dr Winik asked, feeling the blood come rushing to his face. All of them stood bewildered and then walked on slowly. Miss Berger cast an anxious glance at Dr Winik's harrowed, still blushing face. While walking, she tapped her small parasol against the trees and bushes at the side of the road. Finally she broke the heavy silence and began to describe a performance of the opera *Demon* which she

7. *Gabbai* (collector)—a synagogue officer or public official.
8. There were many and various societies in the Jewish towns of Eastern Europe. On these societies see, for example, Zborowski and Herzog, *op cit.*, pp. 202–13.

had recently attended in the magnificent theatre in the city.[9] The young Berger pulled at his father's sleeve and both of them sat down to rest on a convenient bench between the trees. Dr Winik passed them by as he walked absentmindedly alongside his companion only half listening to her chatter. All about there brooded the silence of dusk, blending with the ceaseless croaking of frogs in the meadow and the hum of beetles in the hot overcast air. Far away in the distance, darkening the edges of the horizon in the thick woods, night was falling.

'Perhaps Shlomo will die of this illness?' The thought suddenly struck Dr Winik. At first he was horrified at the detestable idea which plunged him into a maze of countless evil thoughts that welled up from the depths of his mind and crawled over him like wingless flies. After his initial revulsion he was again ensnared by the thought, like a fish 'caught in an evil net', struggling desperately but unable to get out.

'If only you could have heard that singer who sang the part of Tamara,' continued Miss Berger with feeling, 'that was sublime art! How aesthetic, how graceful each movement was! Especially her pathos, the pure ring in her voice, her intense ardour!'

Dr Winik walked at her side with downcast eyes, deep in speculation: he had rid himself of his bothersome sister, Moshe Aharon was about to leave for America, Aunt Malkah would soon join her son in London, and Shlomo would die. The last cords that bound him to the past would thus be severed of their own accord, one by one. After this precise summary his thoughts became hazy; everything seemed distorted and baffling. Suddenly he wanted to leave this chatterbox of a young lady who so smugly took for granted the pleasures of life which had come to her so very easily. If only he could shut himself up in his room and be alone with his dilemma.

9. *Demon*—A Russian work by the poet Lermontov (1814–41). In this opera, Demon, king of the fallen angels wanders aimlessly and despondently about the earth attempting to sate himself with sin. He finds no purpose to life until he meets innocent, passionate Tamara who dies immediately after he has kissed her. The dominant moods are despair and loneliness. For English translations see those by R. Burness (Edinburgh, 1918) or Gerard Shelley (London, 1930).

Winik looked ahead; night had already fallen and had darkened the surrounding fields.

For hours on end Winik tossed on his bed, unable to sleep. His mind wandered aimlessly in the impenetrable darkness of his bedroom as if struggling to find an exit—any escape from these suffocating thoughts. From time to time he would throw the blanket off and rest his feet on the bedstead—but he found no relief. Finally, he jumped out of bed, pushed the shutters open and went back to rest. A pale light, the glow of the moon after midnight, flooded into the room, playing on the shadows in the corners and showing up the whiteness of the washbasin near the wall. For several minutes his moist eyes squinted at the white marble basin and the bright towels that hung above it. How wonderful it would be to overcome his tiredness and rip off his nightshirt and bathe his tortured sleepless body in cold water! But he knew that even then the viscid taint, the murky sediment that so oppressed him and made him pant for breath would still remain. He shut his eyes again, determined to forget it all, determined to divert his attention from everything that had transpired during the day, to eradicate the wretched thoughts that plagued him incessantly. But what could he think of now? What had he left to cling to, to console himself with, to ease his distress, to distract him from that lonely corner at the bottom of the hill, his childhood nest, his family home? . . . Now he saw his sick brother's face, flickering like a wretched tallow candle with eyes blazing in a final splutter, with a humiliated smile on his face which seemed to ask mercy for his miserable life. Next he saw Moshe Aharon's face set in the stubborn mould of suppressed hostility. Then he saw his Aunt Malkah taking up her aggressive stance, and heard her trenchant protests, with her bitter, but justified criticisms that affected him so deeply . . . Winik contorted his face, scratched at his hair like a despondent child, and sighed:

'My God, my God!'

Had he not been ashamed, he would have cried aloud to find relief from his repressed self-pity. How strange his fate, and how odd this life that God had made so tortuous! What was there between him and Shlomo—that shy, naïve pauper who lived secluded in a remote hovel and who had done him no harm, that he wanted him to die?

Had he ever thought about his life as he was now brooding over his death? Even after his brother's death, would he ever be at rest and content, knowing that he had been contaminated and defiled by such vile reflections? What was the solace which he was seeking so eagerly, and for which he misused those who had been ordained to be closer to him than anyone else? To desire this Miss Berger, the daughter of a coarse, despicable money-lender, who finds this wretched world so pleasant! . . . Winik spat in anger at the thought of Berger's name. He leaped from his bed, put on his bathrobe, and went out on the balcony. Having given vent to his anger by spitting, he calmed down slightly as if his pain had been relieved.

Outside, the heavy silence of night hung over everything. The houses on the street, some one storey and some two storeys, separated by gardens, dreamed away in the shadows cast by the street-lamps. Suddenly between the clefts of the white, soft, snow-like clouds there appeared for a moment a full moon moving in its mysterious orbit through the heavens. Sitting on a chair, Winik leaned his aching head on the balcony rail. In the hazy mist a light, cool, refreshing breeze rustled through the lonely trees in the yards. The trees' shimmering shadows blended with the moonlight that hovered over the green grass between the houses, and climbed over the walls and the closed shutters. At a distance could be heard the faint, pensive crowing of an inexperienced young cockerel which, aroused from its dreams, had miscalculated the time of day. Footsteps could be heard. Two silhouettes approached the corner of the street, a tall, grey figure and a short one, white from the middle up. The couple were holding hands as they conversed. Then they separated, each one headed in a different direction. The tall grey figure was a young man who passed quickly by Winik's house, holding his hat in his hand. His rapid steps re-echoed for several minutes—they were the steps of a person confidently striding towards the future. 'Most probably an *extern*[10] leaving his girlfriend,' the doctor guessed and imagined the young man walking in the centre of the city until late at night with some innocent middle-class girl who would listen eagerly to his high-flown talk about improving the world. His young, sensitive

10. *Extern*—A student who prepared himself on his own for the matriculation examinations outside the *gymnasium*.

girlfriend would now be running up the stairs of her father's home, groping in the dark, furtively knocking at the door, as she whispered in a soft, guilty tone—'Open up'. Dr Winik suddenly realized that his youth had vanished never to return. Not so long ago he himself had been an *extern* courting innocent middle-class girls and talking excitedly about his plans to reform society's ills. Now, he was merely a country doctor or, as the young folks called him, a careerist, a kind of spoiled *mezuzah*,[11] a bachelor robbed of his virility. His cheeks had grown flabby, his moustache had thickened, and his face had a constant blue shadow from over-shaving. Here he was, on a sleepless night, snugly wrapped in his bathrobe, sitting on his balcony, musing about *externs* and their girlfriends, and never associating them with any of his former desires that were slowly fading away.

4

One pleasant morning, after a week of fluctuating between hope and despair, Shlomo died. When Dr Winik arrived at his brother's house he found sorrowing neighbours crowding about the small yard. Some sat on the dirt-ledge along the wall and mumbled to each other; others milled about, coming up to the fence round the vegetable garden near the house to examine the well-tended rows of cucumbers, beets, and beans, nodding as they expressed their grief for the deceased who had been such a good householder. Alone, during his spare time, he had tended his garden, built his own fence around it, seeded it and weeded it. The merchants among them, however, were not distracted from more mundane matters: they walked out into the street looking for marketable produce, and peered into some farmers' wagons that were passing slowly by. Occasionally, from within the house, the wailing of mourning women would pierce the windows. It was astounding that on a fine summer's day, with the sun shining brilliantly from a cloudless sky, one small house was designated by the creator of this splendid, wondrous world to be set in sorrow and mourning.

When Dr Winik came to the door, the people assembled near it silently moved back to make room for him. He stood near the door

11. See above p. 69, n.8.

for a short while, with the indecision of a man whose task is done. In the centre of the room, on the dirty wet floor, the dead man, covered over with a black ragged overcoat, lay on a thin pallet of straw. At his head flickered two candles in rusty, brass candlesticks. On the empty bed two old women sat sewing the shrouds, while their coarse, hard faces expressed a cold anger with all that was going on. Several women crowded around the table, some standing and others sitting as they whispered together and piously shook their heads and justified God's ways. The older women blew their red noses into their aprons; the younger ones used handkerchiefs. The deceased's pregnant wife stood in the arched corner between the burner and the stove and sobbed loudly; her big belly danced and shook in a bizarre motion that seemed more like that of a laughing woman. At her feet the dirty child sat banging his stick on the ground. To her right and left the two older children stood like two dazed lambs. The face of the elder son (a lad about nine) was dirty with tears. With open mouth he cried aloud; he neither looked about nor wiped his running nose. His younger brother stared with wide, frightened eyes at his dead father's feet that protruded from under the black covering. The profile of his innocent, baby face was so similar to his father's that Winik flinched in pain and remorse. Moshe Aharon stood by the wall, and leaned on the chest of drawers, burying his face in his hands. Aunt Malkah was regarded by the other women as the chief mourner; her whole body denoted profound and total grief as she held her wrinkled, tear-drenched face in her hands and swayed back and forth. Even after the doctor entered, she did not stop shaking her head as she stared straight at him. It seemed to Winik as if his aunt were chiding him without a word, as if to say 'Look at what you did to us!'

All eyes were now fixed with curiosity upon the doctor-brother. The room was so crowded that he was pushed from side to side, and, having attended his dead brother through many sleepless nights, Winik now began to feel dizzy. His Aunt Malkah's daughter stood out from the other young women who now gazed at him with the shy longing of simple folk. She looked at him with eyes full of tears. Her eyes were tender and intimate, and her lips were compressed in a smile full of sorrow that they both shared. Feeling a little relieved,

Winik, unwittingly, smiled back. Immediately, however, he turned his face away and his smiling eyes converged upon his pregnant sister-in-law's tearful, furious eyes. In confusion the doctor withdrew into the hallway and the whispering neighbours fell silent and made room for him. Only one of them, a bearded dwarf-like old man, plucked up courage to approach him. Winik recognized him at once. He was the sexton of the synagogue on this street. He had aged, the matted beard had become sparse and white.

'So that's it!' the old man began, shaking his head. 'Well, what can you do? It's a pity on the deceased. . . . A young man, dead in the prime of life. . . . A fine Jew who always worked hard for his livelihood. . . . A great pity, indeed! . . . young children, a pregnant wife . . . .What can we do?. . . . Perhaps the doctor has a cigarette? I think the doctor smokes. I still recall the old days. . . .'

Winik quietly opened his cigarette case, and, not wishing to offend the old man, asked him a simple question:

'What do you have to say, Reb Zechariah?'[12]

'Eh! It's not worth mentioning,' the sexton replied, and encouraged at hearing his name mentioned he put out two fingers, took a splendid cigarette with an unusually long tip from the case and continued, 'I recall a silly incident . . . When Leibl was a young boy . . . I was always around the synagogue and I witnessed all kinds of strange things. The gentlemen used to smoke and throw away their butts . . . Boys will be boys—he looked them straight in the eye and snatched them right up from the floor . . . Yes, the world has changed.'

The old man sighed happily as he twisted the doctor's long cigarette around in front of his eyes as an example of the changing world, 'I suppose Leibl has a match too?. . . Yes . . . a pity for the deceased. A great pity . . . !'

The doctor gave him a light finally and, wanting to evade the curious bystanders who were eavesdropping on his conversation with the sexton, left the room.

'Here comes Reb Yosef Shmuel!' one of the men sitting on the

12. Reb—A title given to a respected man. Also used as equivalent of Mister.

dirt-ledge announced. A fat, stooping, bow-legged man came slowly up the street, his old bearded head nodding from side to side. He looked like an ox staggering under the weight of its yoke. It was Reb Yosef Shmuel, the *gabbai* of the synagogue who owned empty lots, ran a brickyard on the outskirts of town and supplied the city with cement and bricks for building stoves—the same *gabbai* who served as cantor for the Additional Service on Sabbaths and Festivals and who, on weekdays, between the afternoon and evening services, instructed the congregation in the *Ein Yaakov*.[13]

'What are they waiting for? Why don't they cleanse the deceased?'[14] Reb Yosef Shmuel bellowed from afar even before he entered the yard. 'Why do they permit the women to howl away unchecked? Isn't it forbidden to delay burial in the heat of summer? Where's Moshe Aharon?'

Of all the people assembled on the grass, only Reb Yosef Shmuel dared raise his voice. Obviously, he was a recognized expert in these matters and his decisions were final. At the entrance he stopped, looked at the crowd with sad, resigned eyes and shook his beard in mute rebuke. Then he noticed Dr Winik, 'Ah, here's Leibl! Well, very good then . . . I say, why don't they prepare the dead? Why all this excessive weeping? Does it improve one's health . . .?'

He looked at the doctor with a troubled, concerned face as if he felt for him, all the while examining him from head to foot. He gave the men standing around him a look of silent reproach, and then said:

'Well, well! Why are you standing and staring? Did you come here to look? Well?'

Dr Winik glanced with bewilderment at Reb Yosef Shmuel. The old sexton pushed his way forward and came closer.

'What's all the noise about, Reb Yosef Shmuel?'

'You're here, too? "What's all the noise about," he asks! Did you come here to stand around with your arms folded and smoke long

13. *Ein Yaakov*—A compendium of religious tales culled from the Babylonian Talmud composed by Jacob b. Ḥabib of Zamora (15th–16th centuries).
14. Washing the body according to a fixed ritual pattern is part of the duties of those who prepare the body for burial.

cigarettes? Can't you see that he hasn't rent his clothes yet? He's a brother, isn't he, and he's required to observe the rites of mourning! "What's all the noise about?" . . . Bring the knife!'

Reb Yosef Shmuel with the stern glance of a man who knows his duty and performs it to the letter, quietly surveyed the people standing idly by. He looked about and shook his beard. Even after he had taken hold of the knife and begun cutting the lapel of the doctor's jacket he did not stop grumbling to himself.

'They just stand around and stare. . . . He himself, thank God, doesn't know . . . he isn't used to this . . . a medical doctor . . . for him it's enough that he treats human beings before they die . . .'

He then handed the torn lapel to Dr Winik and motioned that he rend it further. 'Like this, this way . . . a little more . . . as big as a span . . . it's a rule in the *Shulḥan Arukh*[15] . . . after thirty days you can sew it up . . .'

One detected a cautious, soft, paternal tone in Reb Yosef Shmuel's voice. In his supervision of the doctor's rending his garment, he treated him in the same way as kind people treat a young, abandoned, helpless orphan. Indeed, at that moment Winik's trustful, willing face looked like that of a pathetic young orphan. After Reb Yosef Shmuel had gone away, Dr Winik remained standing among the men who had gathered around him; he touched the lapel where the rent had been made and looked at them with a sheepish smile. It seemed as though for the moment the chasm that separated him from them had been bridged and their faces, lined by poverty and toil and hidden behind thick, tousled beards, had suddenly become as kind and familiar as in the past.

Dr Winik found a seat among the men squatting on the ledge. He sat down among them self-consciously, as if he meant by this act to express some special relationship. He then sank into a reverie. Noon—the street was hushed in the heat of the day. Occasionally one could see a lone wagon that had been delayed on its way to market and was moving along ponderously in the dry sand, trailing behind it a thin cloud of dust. In the courtyard across the road on the well-worn crooked stone floor which surrounded the well, pools

15. *Shulḥan Arukh* (Prepared Table). The most popular compendium of Jewish religious practices compiled by Joseph Caro (1488–1575).

of spilled water sparkled and shimmered with rainbow colours in the bright burning sun. A tall, barefoot lad, wearing short, torn pants which reached to his knees, stood near the well with a yoke for two pails on his shoulder. With one hand he pulled on the rope, and with the other he held a large cucumber which he kept biting, all the while looking in bewilderment and listening very attentively to the unending cries of the wailing women. The barefoot boy standing near the well, the bitter, exhausted wailing of the women in the house, the silence in the street and the noon heat—all seemed to Winik like some marvellous dream that he had once seen in his childhood which was now repeating itself before his eyes. Maybe it was not a dream, but the only reality of his confused existence which had continued from then to now, and the pleasant dream was merely the hiatus of his student days, of his stay at the university, when he served as doctor far from his birthplace, far from his indigent brothers from whom he had become estranged without cause or reason and against whom, he had, thereby, committed an unforgivable sin.

'Oh, oh, oh! Daddy, oh, oh, oh!'

The doctor was roused. The black-draped coffin now stood at the entrance to the house, and Shlomo's eldest son stared at it from the threshold and burst out crying. Opposite him stood several young boys who looked at him with the peculiar expression which fresh orphans evoke in their friends.

'Come here,' the doctor called to the lad as he motioned to him with his finger.

'Come here, son . . . What's his name?' he asked his friends.

'Avram'l'

'Ah, Avram'l? Of course . . .' Winik was flustered when he heard the boy's name, since he realized that the boy was named after his father. He arose and overcome with compassion said, 'Come here, Avram'l! Don't cry, don't be afraid of me . . . I'm your uncle!'

The boy resisted his uncle's overtures. When the doctor wanted to pat his cheeks, Avram'l looked at him with the same sullen eyes as his pregnant mother. Without saying anything he stubbornly evaded him and ran off to the yard. Confused, the doctor followed him, but, in the meanwhile, he took out a white scented handkerchief from his pocket and with it wiped the boy's snot from his hand. The lad went some distance away and hid behind the stable and the doctor went back into the house.

As he entered, he found himself pushed into the midst of a group of excited, sweaty men, all crammed together to see the naked corpse that was now entrusted to the hands of the *Ḥevrah Kadisha*[16] who were preparing it for burial. They were all craning their necks and holding their breath, without taking their eyes off the people performing their sacred duties in so coarse a fashion. They treated the corpse with disgusting contempt, turning it from side to side on the cleansing slab almost like butchers tossing flanks of meat on to the butcher's block. 'Why don't they bring more water?' one of them screamed angrily. 'Where are the relatives? Is there no more water in town?'

Dr Winik came up closer to the slab and stood looking at his dead brother who was stretched face upwards on it. The corners of his sunken jaws and his yellow waxen nose stood out sharply, his hands hung at his sides with the fingers spread out as if in despair: the thin beard, frozen seemingly into position, stuck wearily up in the air. It seemed as if the deceased was not yet dead, but had merely shut his eyes in suffering so as not to witness these men mistreating his body so pitilessly. It was as though he had stretched out his neck to the Angel of Death and pleadingly called:

'My soul is weary . . . arise and slaughter me!'

'Why can't I cry?' the doctor wondered—angry with himself.

'It's Shlomke, Shlomke, Shlomke . . .'

He wanted to cry, to moan with tears, as the young orphan had just done at the sight of the black-draped coffin. But a heavy mist seemed to numb his every feeling. For a moment he felt as though a spark were flickering in his heart and he was about to shed a tear, but this lone gleam was soon extinguished and eclipsed by the thick mist that engulfed him. 'Shlomke . . . Shlomke . . .' All he saw was the remote, cold corpse which, with the departure of its soul, had lost every facial expression and individual feature, every characteristic that had once typified it and had made it human. His head . . . his thin neck . . . his hairy chest . . . his sunken stomach . . . his crooked

16. *Ḥevrah Kadisha* (Holy Society). The burial society.

legs . . . his dirty, black, long nails . . . how many such cadavers had he handled in the anatomy classes at the university!

The wailing of the women who had been sent into the adjacent room became ever louder as if it were approaching the edge of despair. Above the din rose Aunt Malkah's hoarse, resolute voice, as she laid bare her claims before the Holy-One-Praised-Be-He with passion, reason, and conviction. 'Avram'l, Avram'l, my good brother, my saintly brother! Oh innocent soul, pure soul! Woe unto me! Come out to greet your righteous son, the son of your old age whom you loved, Shlomele, the virtuous and the chaste! The two of you go before the Master of the Universe, stand before his holy throne and present our case. . . . Woe, Master of the Universe, look at what you have done to us. Why do you pour down your wrath upon us? Woe unto us! Who remains? What is left of our family? One is old, disabled, poor and miserable, and going off to try and make a living in America from which no one ever returns . . . the other left us, became estranged from us and is no longer one of us . . . Shlomele, my good, merciful saint, Shlomele, in your lifetime you were a good husband, a considerate husband . . . forgive your brother Leibl . . . perhaps he didn't treat you like a brother . . . he was not obliged to . . . it is our fault that he is like this . . . don't forget that he has repented recently; he sat at your bedside day and night, prepared to give his life for you . . . Oh! forgive your old Aunt Malkah, your good father's only sister . . . for the sins that I may have committed against you by the words of my mouth . . .[17] You know better than anyone that I had no evil intentions, but had only your best interests in mind . . . Oh, my unbearable misfortunes!'

Winik stood among the dense crowd and listened closely and with fascination to Aunt Malkah's eloquent lament. He noticed for the first time the similarity between her gruff voice and that of his dead father. It was amazing—in the course of time he had forgotten his father's voice! He felt compassion for his bent old aunt, bitterly

17. Based on the verse in the confessional recited on the Day of Atonement. 'For the sin we have committed against thee by offensive speech.' On this custom of asking forgiveness from the dead and other related subjects see Zborowski and Herzog, *op. cit.*, pp. 376–80.

lamenting her unfortunate, deserted family that was disintegrating about her. At that moment he was prepared to forgive her for the harsh words that she had publicly spoken against him before these strangers. With that he turned to Moshe Aharon who was standing against the chest-of-drawers with his face to the wall. Winik stood next to him and he too leaned against the chest-of-drawers, hiding his face in his hands. The two brothers thus stood side by side for several moments bound to each other by invisible bonds of grief. Winik stretched out his hand and placed it on his elder brother's shoulder, as if to embrace him. Moshe Aharon lifted his head in surprise—a single, heavy tear fell on his nose and rolled on to his beard.

'Moshe Aharon,' Winik began in a tender whisper as he felt the thick mist that had enveloped him dissolving before the warmth that was now flooding over him. He tried to say something, but could not utter a word. He felt a torrent of tears welling up in his throat. Quickly, he pushed his way out of the house, staggered blindly through the yard, ran into the barn, buried his face in the small straw-filled wagon and burst into tears.

Dr Winik wept like a baby: he would cry and then pause as if to listen to his heart-beat and would then start again in even greater despair. He was ashamed of his pathetic sobbing and felt that it was weak and indecisive; the private confession and lament of a lonely and deserted man rejected and confused, who has torn himself away from his natural habitat, from his native ground and has gone seeking foreign fields in which to sink roots—only to stray into a wasteland. He now returned, ashamedly, to his poor brothers. He was aware of their poverty and wretchedness which now as always aroused in him horror and dismay; but reluctantly he acknowledged that he was one of them, that he had fled from the battle in weakness and now he, like the others, was too weak to fight. . . .

5

When the funeral procession passed the Berger residence in the heart of the city, Winik noticed the elder Mr Berger and his daughter standing on their balcony on the top floor looking at him. The old man nodded his head as if sympathizing with Winik's position—his need to fulfil that unpleasant obligation of acting kindly towards his poor relatives—dead and living. His daughter looked at Winik with kind, intimate eyes, full of grief and compassion. At that moment the lovely girl's delicate face was radiant and Winik felt his heart beating faster, almost as if he had discovered a haven in which he might soothe his soul after the formidable experiences he had recently endured. When he could no longer see her he lowered his head and woefully followed the coffin, aware now that he would always be torn between the two forces and would never know to which he belonged or in which of them his destiny lay.

A Proud Father

LEIZER, one of the poor boys in town, was the son of Moshe-Yosi-Simpleton.[1] He had begun preparing himself for the *gymnasium*[2] entrance examinations with the help of some rich friends.

From the beginning the whole matter had been far from clear to Moshe Yosi. He could see that his son, Leizer, was busy with all sorts of studies and readying himself for some wonderful event the like of which did not befall the average young man. But the event itself was way above Moshe Yosi's head, and he could not bring himself to inquire of his other children precisely what it was all about. Frequently, Moshe Yosi would see well-dressed young men coming to his house, some of them the children of the town's notables. They were very friendly with Leizer, his son, and would guide his reading, and discuss, like noblemen, all sorts of matters in Russian. They were Leizer's truest friends. Leizer was constantly busy with his books—reading, writing, and memorizing strange, foreign words. Moreover he would write, with incredible speed, the addresses for those neighbouring women whose husbands were in America; he even received a penny in cash for each envelope addressed.

At night, Moshe Yosi would lie awake in bed listening attentively to Leizer struggling with his studies, pacing back and forth through the house, repeating the difficult vocabulary over and over again. At times Leizer would lower his voice as if pleading for life, at other times he would become excited and shout. Moshe Yosi was still not certain about the purpose of these difficult studies to which Leizer was devoting his life, nor did he know why Leizer needed them. But so much was clear: his Leizer, God willing, would be a man among men, a very important person, even though he was his son.

1. It was common for adult men and women to be called by 'nicknames' or surnames based on some personal attribute. See Zborowski and Herzog, *op. cit.*, p. 150.   2. See *Severed*, note 5.

2

Moshe Yosi the Simpleton was a poor, unassuming man whom
people mistook for a fool. For most of his life he had been under the
domination of his wife, Sarah Leah, an overbearing, irritable woman
who ran a grocery shop and supported her family and ruled over it
with a rod of iron. In the summer, during the gardening season,
Moshe Yosi would earn some money as a night watchman in the
orchards of Hayyim-with-the-Short-Sideburns. The nights during
which he served as watchman he spent in a log-hut. His wife, Sarah
Leah, came to receive his wages every Sabbath eve. The rest of the
year he helped out in the store, bowing to her wishes, meekly
listening to her abuse, obediently and affectionately accepting her
rule. The other members of the family also treated him scornfully
and addressed him in an insolent manner which is unusual, since
children generally obey their fathers and respect them. In his heart
of hearts, Moshe Yosi was sometimes hurt by this, but would bear
it in silence, for he was a quiet man who seldom expressed his
thoughts aloud. In short, he was a meek and humble person, ignored
by everyone. He stammered and would usually get by with nasal
grunts. When asked, he would answer 'Yes' or 'No'. But he never
attempted to initiate a conversation. He was always afraid to start
a conversation in case he should not be able to conclude it. He found
that silence served him best.

His older sons were craftsmen, tailors, and shoemakers who paid
their mother for their board and wasted the rest of their money on
fine clothes, patent leather shoes, collars, ties, and, some said, on
eating salami and drinking beer in Eli-the-Red-Head's bar. Leizer,
his youngest son, followed a course different from theirs. He wanted
to make a name for himself and had not the slightest intention of
becoming a craftsman. First he studied *Torah* in the *Talmud Torah*[3]
and then in the *yeshivah*;[4] he was liked and encouraged by his

3. See *Severed*, note 2.
4. *Yeshivah*—rabbinical seminary in which students who had completed the
   Gemara ḥeder began studying at about the age of eleven. See Zborowski
   and Herzog, pp. 97–102.

teachers. Then, one day he announced his desire to study 'secular' subjects.[5] From that day on, something new happened to Moshe-Yosi-Simpleton's family: Sarah Leah ordered that the house be kept clean, and that it be broom-swept every day. Zlota, the oldest daughter, also began to fuss about cleanliness and neatness: she would scrub the floor down with red sand every Friday afternoon, wash and polish the little windows, and decorate them from time to time with coloured cloth and red paper. She did not rest content until two beautifully painted chairs were set up near the table and a gleaming mirror hung behind them. Seeing all this, Moshe Yosi also became excited.

When no one else was in the house he would stand alone for a long while admiring the new furniture, touching it carefully and respectfully, patting it with great affection and laughing to himself with satisfaction.

During the winter evenings, when the wealthy young lads came to teach Leizer and study together, Moshe Yosi would hide away. He would climb up on to the warm stove where his bed was made and listen to them from his hideout. The spectacle of these marvellous boys with their plump, smooth faces, sitting bare-headed and unafraid, the sound of their gay, ringing voices and their rapid foreign speech and, above all, the delightful knowledge that Leizer, the son of his old age, was privileged to be among them, would cast a deep spell over him, and Moshe Yosi would fall asleep content.

One thing was very puzzling: Sarah Leah, his wife, who was a simple woman and ignorant of all scholarly matters—where did she muster the confidence and temerity to participate occasionally in the conversation with these learned young men and offer her advice? Apparently, then, the neighbours' estimate of her must be correct. They praised his Sarah Leah and claimed that she was really a very fine woman indeed. Consequently, Moshe Yosi decided, he would no longer object to his wife's remarks nor contradict her as he was prone

5. 'Secular' subjects—the subjects included in a curriculum of colleges and high schools. The student of the period depicted studied these western disciplines either independently or in the *gymnasium*. They were, obviously, not taught in any *Talmud Torah* or *yeshivah*, and were opposed by the majority.

to do when she insulted him in public. One should remember that
—in the case of a wise woman like her—everything is permitted and
all is forgiven!

3

Years passed and finally Leizer's judgment day arrived—the day he
was to take his *gymnasium* examinations. That day Moshe Yosi was
very upset and excited. All night he was unable to sleep. Lying awake
on the stove, he listened apprehensively to Leizer's heavy steps as he
paced back and forth, spouting words like a fountain. By now
Moshe Yosi had concluded that what Leizer wanted was to become
a purveyor in Shkolnikoff's pharmacy. This was the Shkolnikoff
who rode about the main street on his bicycle with a gold chain
hanging from his spectacles.

From early morning on, Moshe Yosi was assailed by all sorts of
fantasies and visions that crowded together in his mind like summer
flies around honey. In truth, he would soon be involved in something sweeter than honey. How could this have ever happened to
him? To this day he had never spoken to anyone about Leizer's
achievement, because no-one had ever asked him or even mentioned
the subject. But today, it would be known: it would cause a stir
along the whole street. He could imagine the commotion: what a
to-do in the *Beit-Midrash*! The congregants would stand around in
groups—excited and amazed, murmuring: 'Did you hear? . . . Is it
possible? . . . Moshe Yosi's youngest son! . . . That little baby! . . .
Who would have thought? . . . That's true happiness, that's real
luck . . . !' This is what they would say in the *Beit-Midrash*[6] as they
made room for him among them and showered him with honour.
'Treat the whole thing more seriously! This is Leizer the purveyor's
father!' Gabriel, the bad-tempered old sexton, would greet him
graciously and offer him the communal snuff box.

6. The *Beit-Midrash* (House of Study) was the central institution of Jewish
communal life to which people would come after a day's work to study,
pray, and, at intervals, chat about various matters. See Zborowski and
Herzog, *op. cit.*, pp. 100–1. For a poetic description of the unrivalled
place of the *Beit-Midrash* see *Complete Poetic Works of H. N. Bialik*, I.
Efros (ed.) (New York, 1948), pp. 29–57, 76–8.

And Michael-the-Mad's children who sat near Moshe Yosi behind the central platform and annoyed him during services by pouring water on his seat, what would they do now? 'They'll turn green with envy!'

These rather harsh words had first been spoken, not by Moshe Yosi, but by his wife Sarah Leah in a moment of excitement. Savouring the words, Moshe Yosi turned them over and over in his mind:

'They'll turn green with envy!'

Moshe Yosi began to find the little shop oppressive. His hands shook uncontrollably as he passed goods over the counter. Sarah Leah had been cursing him all morning. But the curses now seemed like endearments: a woman like her, whose wisdom and understanding had served her well enough to raise her son to such heights, was entitled to insult her husband at will. Everything is permitted and all is forgiven! Sarah Leah was afraid lest, God forbid, Leizer's courage would fail him in the oral exams when he came before his examiners, and all his efforts would have proved in vain. Consequently she was irritable all day. Could such a thing really happen? Was it possible that his Leizer, this diligent lad, who copied addresses to America with such speed, could fail? Yes, Moshe Yosi's great hour had arrived. Now he would be able to demonstrate clearly that he, too, was a father who worried about his children. The best he could do now was to recite a few chapters from the Book of Psalms with supreme devotion and pray for his youngest son Leizer's success and prosperity.[7] Maybe God would listen to him and show mercy.

But this was most difficult. He had never prayed for any personal benefits in his prayers. He had always been extremely humble and had never demanded anything. How could he now approach God with such arrogance?

4

Finally, Leizer arrived home surrounded by his friends. They were overcome with elation and were all talking at once. A radiant Sarah

7. At moments of crisis the Jew would recite chapters from the Book of Psalms.

Leah straightened her head-scarf, and Leizer enthusiastically began relating all that had befallen him in the *gymnasium*, how the instructors had tried to trap him with their questions and how he had managed to answer them all correctly. At that moment Moshe Yosi, unnoticed, left the house and went to the empty store to be alone with his joy. Unable to bear the loud noise and merriment in the house, he preferred to be alone in the store, to blink at the ceiling and listen to his heart labouring beneath the weight of such happiness.

'Can I help you, young lady?' he asked, turning jubilantly to a young girl who had just entered the store with a bottle in her hand. He was surprised at the opportunity that was granted him and the unusual eloquence which he had acquired. 'Perhaps you came to see . . . my Leizer, do you want to see him?'

'Oil for two kopeks. My mother wants two kopeks' worth of oil,' the young girl replied, raising her black eyes wonderingly at Moshe Yosi.

'Two kopeks' worth of oil?' Moshe Yosi was appalled at some people's petty needs at such a time as this. 'And you don't want to see my Leizer at all? . . . I'll give you the oil right away. I'll give you oil for three kopeks. You'll pay me two kopeks and I'll give you three kopeks' worth. But don't tell anyone . . . !'

As the girl left the store Moshe Yosi blushed deeply. His heart pounded because of the odd transaction he had just completed. If ever Sarah Leah got to know of it, his life wouldn't be worth living. A really stupid thing to do! In a little while all the residents of the street would be talking about him—saying 'Moshe Yosi has gone mad!'

Are all the neighbours only thinking of oil today? All of them must surely be concerned with Leizer's great event—the pharmacist's new purveyor. Everyone must be talking about him and praising him. This evening, at late afternoon prayers, there'll be a great commotion, as he goes into the synagogue. Everyone, from the youngest to the oldest, will rise to greet him and cry in unison: 'Moshe Yosi himself! Leizer the purveyor's father! Here he comes!'

5

When Moshe Yosi arrived at the *Beit-Midrash*, the worshippers neither rose to greet him, nor made any reference to the event. The *Beit-Midrash* was the same as usual, blackened and dreary, the air filled with cigarette smoke. A cold wind was blowing outdoors, and the window panes rattled in the cold. Many of the congregants gathered about the stove to warm their limbs that had been freezing in the market place. Moshe Yosi silently went off to his dark corner behind the reading desk, and looked around amazed and disappointed. Nobody saw him. No one paid any attention to him. As if he were nothing. . . .

Having finished their prayers, a group of Jews assembled, as they did each day, in the north-east corner of the synagogue and stood about Avram-Itze, the flax salesman. Each winter evening between the afternoon and evening prayers Avram-Itze the flax merchant would gather about him a group of idlers who would sit around, as is the custom in humble synagogues, and listen to him relate at length the many adventures he had experienced in the good old days when he was a young man and used to trade in flax. Avram-Itze's speech was deliberate and pleasant, soothing and yet captivating; his tales were entertaining and compelling.

Moshe Yosi decided to leave his seat behind the reading desk and join Avram-Itze's circle so that he might tell them all that had happened today to his youngest son Leizer. But as he was walking over, he hesitated, blushing with shame. In great confusion, he stopped and had second thoughts. He looked at the Holy Ark: From whence cometh help?[8]

The members of the circle crowded about Avram-Itze the flax-merchant's lectern without noticing Moshe Yosi, who was standing behind them quietly, like an unseen shadow listening to the tale, timid and dispirited.

Avram-Itze the flax merchant was in an expansive mood, and was relating in great detail the hardships that he had suffered many, many years ago when he was travelling in his winter coach to

8. Based on Psalms 121:1

the castle of the Lord of Koslov with Prokop, his faithful coach-man.

'That night,' Avram-Itze the flax merchant recounted in honeyed tones, 'there was a violent storm the likes of which are unknown in these times. It was as dark as Egypt during the plague.[9] The snow beat against our faces. The storm whipped the snow until it covered everything, the wagon, the horse, my face, my beard, the horizon. . . . I'm sitting all wrapped up in my fur coat—not in a modern fur coat, but in a real fur coat—in short, I'm bundled up in my fur coat and thinking: Bad business! "Prokop," I say to my uncircumcised coachman, "don't you have eyes," I say, "can't you see," I say, "that we've strayed off the road?" I say . . . I'm still sitting in my coach talking to my Prokop when I hear the sound of barking in the distance. It was a dog barking on the road in the darkness of the night. "Ruff, ruff, ruff!"'

Avram-Itze's tale was long and drawn out. That storm lasted for three consecutive days and nights, no more and no less. Moshe Yosi was trembling in the audience as he looked about at the people. But no one knew that Moshe Yosi was not interested in a tale about a snow-storm or about Avram-Itze's barking dog. Moshe Yosi's heart was aflame. He was desperate to tell his story: the story of Leizer's greatness and of the miracles that had befallen him this day at the *gymnasium*, that he had been examined and had become a purveyor. Would that they might hear and know how great this day was for Moshe Yosi, a great day of rejoicing and exaltation!

However, the men were crowding around, standing open-mouthed and enthralled by Avram-Itze the flax merchant's tale. Avram-Itze went on and on, without the slightest sign of tiring. Moshe Yosi turned red and began to sweat in torment: when would the hard-hearted Avram-Itze end this boring tale that everyone loathed?

A miracle happened, the Heavens took pity on Moshe Yosi. Avram-Itze paused for a minute to take out a red handkerchief with which to wipe his nose. Moshe Yosi seized the opportunity, and summoning all his courage, hurried over and pushed through until he stood right next to Avram-Itze's lectern. He coughed and began:

9. See Exodus 10:21–3.

'I'm also . . . happy today, hah, hah . . . that is, I'm speaking about my son, I'll tell you about my Leizer . . . you won't believe it . . .'

'What,' asks Avram-Itze the flax merchant, slowly wiping his nose, his eyes still glazed with memories . . .

'The simpleton, what does he say?' one of the crowd joked using the words of the Passover *Haggadah*[10] and acting as if he were listening to Moshe Yosi's tale.

'I swear by my life, it's true . . .', Moshe Yosi stuttered as he stretched his hands out towards the audience as though seeking pity. 'He studied and studied and studied . . . all day and all night he pored over the books . . . and now . . .'

'Why are you listening to such prattle?' one of the younger listeners blurted out impatiently and turned to Avram-Itze exclaiming, 'And so tell us, Avram-Itze, what was that dog like?'

Avram-Itze blew his nose a second time just to be doubly sure, carefully replaced his handkerchief in his pocket, surveyed his audience like a commander reviewing his troops, and continued spinning his endless yarn that seemed to unwind so laboriously. Moshe Yosi walked away in silence and stood in the centre of the *Beit-Midrash*, heartbroken and ashamed: he groaned,

'They don't want to listen . . .!'

Moshe Yosi stood alone and forlorn in the *Beit-Midrash*, his eyes roving about in despair. Perhaps God would send a merciful man who would be willing to listen to his tale about Leizer, his youngest son. Several men were sitting at the table near the warm stove and studying. Among them was Nahum the *Gemara*[11] teacher in the *Talmud Torah*, who had once been Leizer's instructor. Moshe Yosi haltingly approached him at the table.

'Reb Nahum, heh, heh . . . have you heard? I'm celebrating today.

10. In the Passover *Haggadah*—the anthology of selections from rabbinic literature and mediaeval songs recited on Passover Eve—there is a rabbinic homily about 'The Four Sons'—a wise son, a wicked son, *a simple son*, and one who knows not how to ask.

11. *Gemara*—discussions of the *Mishnah*. The study of the Babylonian Talmud (*Mishnah* and *Gemara*) and its commentaries constituted the highest level of instruction and was the core of the curriculum in the East European *yeshivah*.

I mean, I'm referring to my youngest son . . . I'm talking about my
Leizer. Upon my soul, you won't believe it . . . hah, hah . . .'

'What?' Nahum the *melammed* asks as he raises his glasses from
the book.

'He'll be a purveyor . . . my Leizer . . . have you heard about it?'

'I heard all about it!' Nahum the *melammed* angrily retorts . . .'I
heard that your precious son has strayed into wicked paths and is
studying evil subjects and most probably already desecrates the
Sabbath!'

'God forbid!' Moshe Yosi was shocked and his eyes looked be-
seechingly at Nahum the *melammed*.

'God forbid, he says to me,' Nahum continued. 'Your Leizer was
a fine lad, he was already able to prepare a page of Talmud by himself, and now he goes off to study foreign subjects and ape the ways
of the Gentiles . . . What's the point of talking to you . . . Are you
a father like other fathers? You're nothing but a simpleton! His son
is about to convert and he walks about celebrating . . .'

Nahum the *melammed*, a cantankerous old man, lowered his
glasses to his book and turned away from the shocked and confused
Moshe Yosi.

6

Moshe Yosi, saddened and embittered, left the *Beit-Midrash*. A
stormy wind was blowing up outside, howling across the open fields,
and billowing under Moshe Yosi's coat-tails. While he was standing
in the street straining to keep his coat down a young boy ran by.

'Hershl, wait a minute,' Moshe Yosi called hopefully to the young
boy, 'are you Hershl?'

'Yes.'

'Where are you headed?'

'Home,' Hershl replied and started running again.

'Wait a minute and I'll tell you something. I have something very
wonderful to tell you. I'm celebrating today . . .'

Hershl stopped running and looked curiously at Moshe Yosi.

'Tell me, Hershl, do you want to be a purveyor?' Moshe Yosi
craftily began his remarks with a tangential question.

'A purveyor, what's that?' Hershl inquired.

'Don't you know what a purveyor is? Hah . . . hah . . . My Leizer has become a purveyor today. I really mean it . . . Did you hear about it . . .?'

'What?'

'About my Leizer. Today he went to the *gymnasium* and tomorrow he'll be a purveyor at Shkolnikoff's. I swear. That's what Sarah Leah says . . .'

'Is it true that Sarah Leah slaps your face?' Hershl asked shyly, changing the subject.

'Ha, ha, ha . . . you're a mischievous lad, you are!' Moshe Yosi laughed aloud since, at last, he had found a pair of attentive ears. 'You're a rascal, young man, but my Leizer isn't. My Leizer reads many books and writes with stupendous speed. He writes addresses to America and receives a few pennies, I swear. . . . Did you ever see the mirror in our house? My Zlota also bought two red chairs. We'll buy a wardrobe soon; we'll soon own a cow, too. If you don't believe me, come home with me and you'll see for yourself. Many young men come to our house. Handsome, rich young boys sit until midnight with my Leizer and study and study. When my Leizer grows up they'll give him a wealthy bride and a gold watch, God willing. I swear, you'll see for yourself.'

For a moment the strong wind stopped howling over the fields. The whole world stood by in silence while Moshe Yosi the Simpleton poured out his heart to little Hershl.

A Barbarian

THE farmer who came to inspect Hershl, Hayyim Mayer the oven-maker's son, was a heavy-set man, short and stout, with a sparse red beard and wavy red hair which adorned the greasy brim of his hat with flaming curls. His tiny eyes, with their white eyelids hidden by folds of fat, were sleepy and smiling. He came in carrying his whip, all bundled up in a thick fur coat with a red sash wrapped round it, and wearing heavy, well-oiled boots. The house was filled at once with the curious, pungent odour of resin, kerosene, and salted fish.

Hershl, a fifteen-year-old boy with a pale face and sharp, black eyes, was eating his breakfast. He had absent-mindedly dipped a piece of black bread into the juice of the pickled cucumbers and was chewing his meagre food slowly and without much pleasure, while devouring the pages of *Kevurat Hamor*.[1] In order that his eating and reading should not interfere with each other, he had propped his book against the plate and set it up as a sort of barrier between him and the rest of the world. Cramped and bent over, he concentrated on every line, completely absorbed in his reading. 'So this is what we're talking about?' the yokel asked Hershl's father pointing at Hershl with his whip. His father had brought the yokel to his house from the *Beit-Midrash* and he was still carrying his *tallit* bag.[2] The yokel had a gruff voice which seemed to come straight out of his stomach. His speech was slow and faltering, with a sing-song inflection typical of Jewish villagers.

1. *Kevurat Hamor* (A Donkey's Burial), a novel by Peretz Smolenskin (1840–85). On the Hebrew novel during this period see D. Patterson, *The Hebrew Novel in Czarist Russia* (Edinburgh, 1964). See particularly pp. 203–4 for a reference to this novel.
2. *Tallit* A full-length prayer shawl worn by married male Jews during religious services. When a man dies his *tallit* is buried with him and is wrapped about him as part of his shroud.

'That's him.'

'So that's the story, then.'

His father stepped aside and looked at the guest with a triumphant smile, as if certain that his prize treasure now being presented to the stranger would speak for itself. Standing erect, whip in hand, the yokel pushed his hat back on his head, spread his legs and from a distance examined with benign and sleepy eyes the young man who was sitting at the table slouched over his book and plate. The slight smile playing on the yokel's lips and over his narrow, wrinkled forehead seemed to indicate that he was about to utter some clever remark, but for the moment was restraining himself and suppressing it.

Hershl pushed aside the plate with the juice from the pickled cucumbers, put the book in front of him and concentrated on a single line. He tried to go on reading, attempting to fathom the meaning of the line, but felt compelled to re-read it several times. The line grew dim before his eyes and became blurred with the other lines on the page. All the while he was considering whether it was worth his while to lift his head and take a look at this stranger. He decided against it. It would be better to remain seated and not remove his eyes from the page. What had he to do with this foul-smelling red-headed peasant? What connection could this flabby yokel have with Yaakov Hayyim, the hero of Peretz Smolenskin's marvellous novel?

From the dark bedroom behind a thin screen came the sound of someone rocking a cradle. The heavy cradle scraped against the floor in a subdued rhythm which was accompanied by the melodious, motherly voice of a younger sister who was lulling the baby to sleep.

'Ay, ya, ya, ya . . .'

His mother with her yellowing, wrinkled face had grown old before her time. She had been sitting in a dark corner near the stove hurriedly peeling potatoes and throwing them into the pot at her feet. When the stranger entered her house, she rose, shook the peelings from her apron into the dustbin, fixed the kerchief on her head, and stepped out of her retreat, peering modestly and shyly at the farmer and saying:

'I expect you've come to look our Hershl over?'

In the meantime his father approached the table, and with a soft, appeasing smile leaned over his son to ask in a cautious and diplomatic manner:

'Are you reading another new book? In what language—Hebrew or Russian? Hershl, did you notice this man . . . Reb. . . Reb . . .?[3]

'Reb Yonah,' the farmer prompted him with a relaxed smile that augured well.

'Yes, Reb Yonah, pardon me . . . he, that is, Reb Yonah wants to look at you, to take you with him to his children.'

At this point the farmer shuffled his boots, and with heavy steps came over to the table, winking at the father as if to say, 'Wait and you'll hear something!'; the suppressed remark was finally uttered:

'That's the whole story, I suppose you know, young man. I have for your information, three brats at home and one daughter, may she be guarded from the evil eye. Well, you know, we have to make them a bit Jewish. Your father told me there's no more capable imp than you for that and he dragged me over here to have a look. Well, looking doesn't cost anything—so I'm looking . . .'

The farmer, with beaming face, inclined his head to one side and looked at Hershl with squinting eyes; Hershl blushed but did not stir; he kept his eyes glued to the book.

'Well, my lad,' the farmer continued, 'what do you think? Your father's not fooling me, is he? . . . You know, when I buy groats, I expect them to be groats! Without any sand, and without any gravel, you know! . . . A good chunk of the Pentateuch and Rashi,[4] correct Hebrew reading, and all the odds and ends that go with it . . . what are you studying there? *Mishnah* or "Verses"?'[5]

3. See note 12 to *Severed*.
4. *Ḥumash* (Pentateuch) and the commentary of Rashi (Rabbi Solomon ben Isaac 1040–1105) were the subjects taught immediately after the student had mastered the elements of Hebrew reading. Therefore, they represented an elementary and, for many, final phase of formal instruction. See C. Pearl, *Rashi* (New York, 1970).
5. *Mishnah*—A collection of the Oral Law, edited, *ca.* 200 C.E., the later discussions of which constitute *Gemara*, and together make up the Talmud. 'Verses' was the popular way of referring to the books of the Prophets and 'The Writings' and usually implied that the person was 'enlightened'.

'This is a bit out of the ordinary,' the father explained, 'it's one of those "printed books".'

'What does that signify?' the villager asked, using a scholarly idiom and shutting one eye as though deep in thought.

'It simply means—it has to do with literary matters.'

'With literary matters? Really? Very well . . . That's just fine. I like that very much. I swear I do.'

He slouched over the table, thereby bringing the hybrid stench of resin, kerosene, and salted herring even closer to Hershl. Hershl coloured and began sweating. He removed his hands from the table and so released the book into the yokel's grasp. The stranger's sparse red beard was now close to his face. Hershl was afraid he would be tempted to tweak it. He turned away and visualized a god-forsaken village somewhere in the swamps of Poliesia, a squalid house with the characteristic little windows, half-witted boys playing with their red curls over an open Pentateuch with Rashi's commentary, and the endless, miserable, cold winter nights sinking in the mud outside—a black, bleak abyss in place of his golden, summery dreams.

The farmer was toying with *Kevurat Ḥamor*. First he examined the binding, then touched the edges of the pages as if he were trying to estimate its worth; then he ran his fat little finger over the top line as he proudly read it to himself. Having finished the top line, he returned the book to its place, sighed deeply and said,

'Happy is the man who has knowledge . . . You see, my boy, I like this. You've hit it right. Teach this to my boys so that they'll also know how to read a short note.'

His father who had been standing to one side, smiling confidently to himself, now realized that he must say something and exclaimed,

'What are you talking about, Reb Yonah? Do you have any notion with whom you're dealing? I don't want to praise my son in his presence, but since we're telling the truth, I guess there's nothing wrong. He has been through every book in town. Not only that, but as true as you see him here, he already writes addresses to America for the neighbours. I swear it as I'm a Jew!'

'Eh!' the villager exclaimed as he looked at Hershl with one eye open and the other shut as if to say, 'Is it really true or are they fooling me?'

'I swear as I'm a Jew!' his father repeated his oath for greater emphasis.

'Well, what's so fantastic about that?' his mother interjected in order to strengthen their case. 'Books have always been the most important thing in his life! Night and day he sits alone with his books! He doesn't eat or sleep—just reads and reads. I'm always pleading with him—I'm a mother, aren't I—spare your eyes! Let Israel's enemies go blind! . . . but he won't leave his books! A madness has entered his bones! He has to become a scholar! . . . True enough, a scholar is a fine thing. Don't I know it? But who are we and how can we afford it? Burning the kerosene at night costs money, eight kopeks a jug, and his father is only an oven-maker. There's been no work, may God be praised, for a long time; nobody has ordered new stoves; they don't care if the old ones belch smoke. . . .'

'What wind blew you in?' her husband shouted at her and pushed her away from the table. 'Who's talking about stoves? What do you know about it? Mind your own business! . . . The main thing, Reb Yonah, is this: remember, I'm not a boastful father, but we can't ignore the facts. I'm telling you he's first-rate! Such treasures can't be picked up in the streets nowadays, and as for the rest, you must do as you please!'

The farmer stood near the table whip in hand and listened to the talk with a thoughtful smile. His low forehead wrinkled shrewdly and his little eyes were glinting. He was, apparently, getting ready to emit another verbal gem.

'Well, what do you say, young man?' he asked as he turned towards the blushing Hershl who was sitting quietly at the table, never lifting his eyes from his book. 'Do you want to come to the village with me? Don't be bashful, let's have the truth! I'm a simple man, you know—a farmer. I like to call a spade a spade! I promise you now that, with God's help, all winter long you'll never lack for boiled potatoes in their jackets with good cold sour milk straight from the cows in my barn. I swear! But, you must be man enough to be able to control the reins in your hands. Without the strap, you know, my boys will most certainly stray from the straight and narrow. I suspect they'll never become rabbis. Nevertheless, my fine lad, I want them to get the best sort of proper prayers and blessings, and a good bit of Pentateuch and Rashi. For rotten merchandise, you understand, I don't pay good money.'

After this sermon which the farmer delivered to his prospective teacher, Hershl looked up from his book. White-faced, the young man stared contemptuously straight into the stranger's eyes.

'Well, why are you gaping at me like that? Say something, so I'll hear. At least I'll discover that you know how to talk. After all, you know, I want to hire you as my sons' *melammed*'![6]

'I'm not a *melammed*!' Hershl retorted sharply.

His father, startled at his son's audacity, immediately started to laugh indulgently and, with a knowing look, quickly began to explain matters to the shocked farmer:

'Ha, ha . . . boys will be boys . . . You realize, of course, that he objects to our calling him *melammed*. They, that is the moderns, refer to this type of lad as a "pedagogue": that's the custom these days.'

The farmer's forehead again wrinkled with shrewdness.

'How do you pronounce that? A pedagogue? I'll accept that—let it be a pedagogue! What's the difference? So long as it doesn't cost me any more money! In our village we don't know anything about these new-fangled ideas. I'm a simple man, a farmer, you know. I say—what's in the can put in the pan! That's simple logic. You, my fine lad, know how to get through a chapter of Pentateuch and Rashi and all the other paraphernalia—so hop on to the wagon and let's hope for the best! In return you'll receive, besides wholesome meals, twenty-five silver coins for the term, and you can call yourself what you like, *melammed*, "pedagogue," or "cow-herd".'

'Now, now, Reb Yonah,' his father exclaimed as if insulted, winking the while to his wife as if to say, 'You see it is a serious matter, indeed.' She smiled shyly and a dull red blotch spread over her left cheek.

Hershl jumped up furiously from the table and protestingly ran off to a corner. Hershl's chair was immediately taken by the farmer

6. *Melammed* (teacher), especially the *dardeki melammed* or little children's teacher, was not a very respected title. It was generally assumed that such a person, neither well educated nor professionally trained, became a *melammed* only after he had failed at other occupations, by default. See Zborowski and Herzog, *op. cit.*, pp. 88–96.

who settled his massive bulk heavily on the chair and placed his whip on top of the *Kevurat Ḥamor* that Hershl had left open. He rolled up the sleeves of his fur coat, while his tiny, sleepy-looking eyes lit up with confidence.

'Well,' he said, 'it's your merchandise, so let's hear your price!'

'What are you talking about, Reb Yonah, really, now?' his father answered prudently. 'That's quite impossible. Are you looking for a bargain? Do you think you can properly evaluate something like this? I don't generally talk about him in his presence . . . God forbid! But if that's the case it would be better he sat home and read his books.'

'Are you serious?' chimed in his wife, blushing furiously. 'Do you imagine we would send off a young child to a strange place for nothing? Do you think we have reached a decision lightly? What can we do if we've had bad lack? When I consider that winter is coming and the lad needs boots, a coat, a shirt . . . I'm not ashamed . . . do you hear me, my friend? If a person's shoe is too tight on him he alone can feel the pinch . . . Oh—if only I could express myself better!'

'What wind blew you in?' scolded her husband. 'Who's asking you to express yourself!'

The farmer listened to both of them and mockingly replied:

'Do you expect me to open my belt and give all my money for this meagre piece of merchandise? Look at him—a mere baby, I swear! . . . It's daylight robbery! . . . Last year I also engaged a teacher, but he was twice as big as this one, and how much do you think I gave for him . . .?'

'Look here, Reb Yonah,' the father responded as if insulted, 'I'm sorry, but you're talking nonsense, really. Can you measure such things with a yardstick! . . . I thought you understood such matters, so I brought you to look the boy over. But I see now . . . it's all for nothing!'

As the haggling progressed both sides became suitably enraged. Hershl, furious now, went silently to the table, pulled the *Kevurat Ḥamor* from under the villager's whip and placed it on the rickety chest of drawers which stood in the corner. On seeing his subject's show of strength the farmer was pleased and added five coins, swearing by his Jewishness that he had just thrown five roubles to the dogs. Yes, this merchandise was the real stuff. Why should he lie? He liked the boy. He was a simple man, a farmer: what's in the can put in the pan . . . the father, for his part, agreed to forty. The villager sprang from his seat and grabbed his whip from the table.

'Let's get this over with—thirty-two—I won't give any more even if you dance in front of me.'

To show that he was not fooling he started to wrap his red sash around his waist. The father was startled and seemed ready to capitulate. Just then Hershl leaped from the corner and shouted, 'Father, I'm not going for less than fifty!'

'You're talking like a child; what do you mean? Nonsense!'

The yokel stood at the door but, in order not to look as if he were waiting, stared at the ceiling and scratched his beard.

'Well, is the deal on or not?' he inquired.

His father looked pathetically at Hershl. Hershl was adamant and replied defiantly, 'No!'

After the farmer had left, a heavy silence fell over the house and everyone hesitated to look at each other. His mother sighed quietly, and sadly returned to her dark corner—and again one could hear the sound of potatoes dropping into a pot of water. Hershl, utterly depressed, took his book and sat down at the table. But he found he could not read. He got up again, turned round and went to peer out of the window. It was a dreary, gloomy day. A raging autumn wind was howling as it drove low clouds above the shiny wet, wooden roofs, lashing the wet earth with slanting sheets of rain, and stirring up the sewage in the open drains. On the edge of the rickety fence of the neighbour's garden was perched a lonely rooster, blown by the wind and rain. Its reddish-green plumage puffed up, it stood on one leg, trembling and dazed by its solitude, staring bleakly at its surroundings. Hershl sensed a comparable feeling of isolation engulfing him and casting a damp chill over his entire being. Gloomy and dejected, he appeared to have aged suddenly; he bowed before his father's cautious words of reproof. 'You must admit you are a barbarian after all. You let yourself become upset with the lies a yokel blurts out? And if, indeed, he doesn't know what a pedagogue is—is that the end of the world? You can't expect the whole world to run according to your books. I'm also a simple Jew, I don't know much about grammar and suchlike; yet, nonetheless I'll tell you openly, Hershl—are you listening?—this time you made a mistake! . . . An intelligent man doesn't do such things. You don't let such an opportunity slip away. Money, no matter what, is still money. A farmer, may no harm befall him, with cows in the barn, with dairy products and the rest, will always have food for you. Moreover, thirty-two roubles don't fall from the skies these days—thirty-two roubles are thirty-two roubles! . . . I know what you're thinking. Most likely you're thinking that your father is an evil man who is chasing you out of his house. . . . Well, what can I say, son? Certainly, if I were healthy and rich, there'd be no problem . . . God knows I give the dry bread that you eat at my table with all my heart . . . But can you call this proper living? Is this the sort of life you want?'

Calmly but persuasively the father produced these and similar arguments. At the same time the arguments were tinged with a barely concealed note of grief, of forgiveness begged of a son, young in years and experience. Hershl lowered his head as though accepting an unavoidable burden. He gazed mutely through the window and pictured the bitter winter and the bleak poverty that would descend upon these blackened walls. His father was standing in the corner, stretching his thin hand for a towel, coughing feebly and without hope. His cough was the cold, sullen response to the bright, fanciful dreams of Hershl's youthful imagination.

2

As the sun set, the villager's wagon was standing in front of Hayyim Mayer the oven-maker's home. Inside the house confusion reigned. The father submissively followed his son about rummaging nervously through his empty pockets. His anxious mother was sobbing as she packed some small hard apples into his sack. Hershl tried with all his might to prevent his jaw from quivering.

'Well, my son, go in peace,' his father said in a strangely feeble voice as he bent down to Hershl. In his confusion he kissed him on the side of his nose.

A few minutes later Hershl was sitting with the farmer on his little wagon which was laden with food, vats, and large bottles wrapped in straw. The sun was setting as the neighbours came out to see Hershl off and stood on their porches. They were shivering in the cold and smiling enviously at the young breadwinner who was leaving his nest for the wide world. One woman dressed in a long yellow woollen coat expressed her feelings with a deep sigh as she said, 'Happy the parents who have raised such a son . . .' These words together with the clear evening air, invigorated Hershl, and blunted the edge of his anger. The wagon rolled ponderously through the street, its rattling bottles banging and clanging and attracting the attention of passers-by. Hershl sat alongside the ungainly villager who towered above him like a fortress. He still sensed the warm touch of his father's thick beard on his face. Peering bravely at the small, familiar houses fading behind them, he brooded over the statement 'Happy the parents who have raised such a son . . . .'

The setting sun was dipping behind soft, red clouds and chilly shadows were spreading over houses and fields. From one of the barns came the eager sound of geese screeching at the first sign of nightfall. A lonely cow, abandoned outside the barn, straightened its sombre face and lowed at the heavens as though protesting that the days were so short, the nights too long and the fields barren and desolate. When the wagon reached the bridge that marked the end of the town, Hershl cast a shy glance at the last little houses, their windows facing the open fields, and recalled a poem he had read:

Ah, my birthplace,
Cradle of my childhood
The warm nest of my youth
I am one of your wretched sons . . .

But when, on the other side of the bridge, he saw the level road that stretched into the distance and then disappeared into the haze of the open fields, the poem faded from his mind and he was overcome with fear of the harsh, alien life that awaited him in an unknown place.

The wagon crossed a hillock sheltered by a small yellowing copse. The sunset cast a bright glow over the tall trees, that stood stark and exposed against the red banks of clouds. Hershl was sure that this must be that majestic Nature which had been so celebrated in his books and of which he had always dreamed. Then he remembered that, from this day on, for the duration of a whole long winter, he would be cut off from his beloved books. He had been uprooted from a world full of wonders to be banished to a solitary and deserted country among a pack of savages. He covertly examined the gloomy yokel who was sitting quietly at his side. He looked at his red beard and the unruly red curls that adorned the brim of his hat. Hershl felt even more depressed. He turned round and looked behind him. Now his village was far away. All he could see was the green roof of the 'cold synagogue',[7] and the tall poplar tree in the priest's garden. Everything else was blurred and fused into one dim, shapeless mass. Suddenly, at a distance, a grey shape appeared on the road, and seemed to be pursuing them. Gradually, the shape grew larger and eventually could be identified as a farmer's wagon.

'Perhaps it's my father coming to take me home?'

Hershl knew well enough that this was a foolish thought. He did not, however, abandon it but continued to toy with the idea until the lonely figure of a Jew materialized—it was a farmer in a black fur coat, returning home from the city. His wagon overtook theirs, and then the two continued side by side. The farmers, who were old friends, began to converse. They discussed the extortionate ways of the city shop-keepers and their attempts to exploit the villagers. They then went on to other village concerns, spoke about logging, wool manufacturing, the leather trade, and about a certain Gentile with the odd name of Anuferi. Anuferi was a bad man, an antisemite. There was no escape from him. Matters had reached the point where the Jews were ready to abandon the village. Everyone knew that he had started the fire in the Novodevortz mill. Yet they were all afraid to say anything against him. The village Jews were in a two-fold exile . . . Hershl tried to picture this Anuferi: a tall, strong farmer with a crooked nose and vicious eyes ablaze with all the seven deadly sins. While speculating about Anuferi, he recalled the cruel farmer in *Kevurat Ḥamor*, who had attacked Yaakov Hayyim at night

7. In *Slutzk* and *Vicinity: Memorial Book*, Chinitz, N. and Nachman, Sh. eds. (New York, 1962), p. 275, there is a photograph of the 'cold synagogue' in Slutzk, so called because services were held there even during the winter.

brandishing an axe over the poor man's head and ordered him to hand over his ring. He shuddered and sank into a mood of depression as he thought about his harsh fate. He began to realize the complications of life; the longer one lives the more intricate life becomes. The only one who could be considered fortunate was his baby brother who lay cuddled in blankets and pillows in his cradle tended by their sister, whose soft pleasant voice would be lulling him to sleep. He knew no pain; no one disturbed him. Hershl remembered how fidgety his father had been all morning—unable to sit still until he had seen him off on the farmer's wagon . . . what a strange farewell, he had kissed him on the side of his nose . . . He felt outraged because, despite his youth and innocence, he was already alone and abandoned, without father or mother. . . .

'Who is this young man?' the other farmer suddenly asked.

Hershl was roused from his distressing thoughts, and his heart began to pound.

'This?' the yokel replied pointing to Hershl, 'I hired him in town to be my children's *melammed*.'

'A *melammed*?' the cheerless man retorted, 'this pipsqueak?'

'This little fellow,' the villager boasted, 'exactly as you see him now, has already read and devoured every book in print!'

'Really?' the gloomy man replied, glancing at Hershl from his wagon with a trace of respect.

'As a matter of fact he's a pedagogue!'

'Fine, may God be with you,' the morose farmer sighed, 'but I'm afraid your brats will band together against him and beat him down . . . how much are you paying?'

'How much am I paying!' the villager replied unwillingly, 'I'm ashamed to tell you; for that price he should have been a bit bigger —thirty-two roubles. . . .'

'Thirty-two?' the dark man shouted in disbelief, 'what did you see in him?'

At that moment something strange happened. Hershl seized his belongings and leaped down from the wagon. In jumping he slipped and fell. Then he was on his feet again—pale, shivering, and on the verge of tears; and without a word he hurried off in the direction of the town.

'What's all this about?' the farmer asked in astonishment, 'Where are you going?'

Hershl turned his contorted face around and replied with trembling lips:

'I'm going home.'

Both farmers stopped their horses and looked at each other in bewilderment.

'Are you crazy or just an idiot?' the red-headed farmer shouted as he leaped from the wagon. 'What kind of a trick is this? Get back into the cart this minute! Well?'

Hershl, adamant, made no reply but continued walking briskly.

'Young man, don't be silly, really now. Have you lost your mind or are you just a fool?'

'A barbarian,' the gloomy farmer grunted out of the depths of his black fur coat; 'where did you get hold of him?' he added as he scratched his side curls. 'Nobody did anything to annoy him . . .'

'No matter, you'll get another teacher. You can find this kind of merchandise anywhere! Let's get going, it'll soon be nightfall.'

But the red-headed farmer was very upset about the young man who had run away. For a few minutes he stood near his wagon holding his whip, staring after Hershl and yelling into the darkening fields.

'Young man!'

But Hershl obstinately continued on his way with quick angry steps. Behind him he heard the grinding wheels of the wagons roll off into the distance; he did not turn around. Eventually the sound of the wagons faded until it could no longer be heard. A strange, eerie quiet descended upon the fields and then Hershl realized what he had done. . . .

The sun had set and the reddening clouds had changed colour and were fused into one black mass on the horizon. The town was wrapped in mist and hidden from sight. The trees in the distance looked different—they seemed bigger and more forbidding than before. Hershl felt alone and forlorn in a world full of wretched fear—abandoned by God and man. Who would take pity on him, a young vagrant; who would watch over him in these open fields? He set his belongings on the damp ground and sat down on them.

Like a child, his face contorted, he began tearing at his hair with both hands. Then, remembering that night was about to fall, he jumped up and began to walk back home. When he reached the forest at the foot of the valley, he suddenly felt a heavy fog engulfing everything. A cold, wet wind was blowing on his back from secret distant haunts; the black forest began to stir with the sound of leaves rustling and a hushed, tense moaning. Great shadows rolled back and forth as they slid down the hill into the valley—a tall, terrifying farmer was lurking behind the trees, waiting to leap from his hideout with an axe in his hand . . .

In a cold sweat, and tormented by the fear of death, Hershl began running with difficulty into the darkness of the night sobbing rhythmically,

'Mother, Mother . . . Mother!'

Faivke's Judgement Day

FAIVKE was a wild nine-year-old village lad, who had grown up among the unruly village children. His father, Matis the Blacksmith, was the only Jew in Starodubov[1] among his Gentile neighbours, and Faivke was the only Jewish lad in the crowd of Gentile village children. He had neither seen nor heard of any other kind of children but them. Were it not for his two dark eyes that sparkled brilliantly and resolutely from beneath his faded, old peasant's cap, it would have been difficult to identify him as Jewish. Where would a Jewish boy get such odd bruises on his face, or that upper lip with its blood-red scar, or those bare, flat, calloused feet? The dark eyes that glowed with such tenacity he had inherited from his mother.

Faivke spent most of the autumn and winter in the woods near the village with his Gentile friends. They would gather truffles and mushrooms, climb trees, and frighten storks roosting calmly in their nests. Or else he would wade in the ponds up to his knees searching for black eels, trout, and other fish. At harvest time, like a calf at liberty, he would run over the open fields, climb on a wagon packed high with hay and jump about under the scorching summer skies shouting wildly and hoarsely to his friends. Often, in the heat of the day, he would go off alone to some cool dark barn and swing on one of the rafters, or peel the dried pears he had filched from the sack hidden under his mother's bed. He would gaze at the sunbeams which filtered into the barn through the holes and cracks and which cast a film of gold dust over the gloom of the barn, and he would pleasantly laze away his time in idle reverie. While sitting alone he would think about Mikita, Avedor's son; he was Mikita the soldier, who had won glory in far-off places and become a train conductor. Recently he had returned home and shown off a purse stuffed full

1. Starodubov. A town some seventy-five miles south-west of Bryansk in the Russian province of that name.

with gold coins. He would often sit on the doorstep of his father's house, telling boastful yarns and twisting his moustache, with groups of young boys and girls crowding around him. When he was in a good mood he would play tunes on his flute.

Faivke would often disappear for days and nights with no one knowing his whereabouts. But his father and mother, Matis the smith and his wife, paid no heed and made no attempt to rebuke him. They felt that God's curse hung over this unfettered lad who was growing up untutored and unmannered, as carefree as a wild young desert ass.

Faivke was a fearless young boy. Only two things frightened him and made him tremble—God and prayers. Faivke had never seen God's face, but he had often heard His name on Sabbaths when Matis and his wife would reprimand him in God's name and would assure him of dire punishments in the world to come. Afterwards they would look up at the ceiling and sigh bitterly. These were always dreadful occasions which would worry him for days after. He knew full well that as he grew older the awful day of retribution was gradually drawing closer. Then he would have to present himself before the mighty, awesome God who dwells in a secret abode. One day Faivke experienced something of that peril. On a cold, winter morning, when the whole world was miserable and a snowstorm was blowing outside, the dark figure of a Jew dressed in a black fur coat tied with a red cotton sash appeared unexpectedly at Matis's house. He had a long beard and thick, forbidding eyebrows. He had a sacred duty to fulfil in Matis's house—he had come from the city to empty the whitewashed charity box that was nailed to a beam above the door. Matis's wife offered her guest, the man of God, a meal: a bowl of boiled potatoes and a bowl of sour milk. The man rubbed his thin white hands together, and fervently shut his eyes which had been fixed on the two full bowls in front of him. Upon opening his eyes, he spied, through the dense steam that rose from the boiled potatoes, a frightened young boy standing in the corner and hiding near the beds. The man of God motioned to Faivke.

'Have you studied Torah, son?' he asked stretching out his hand and pinching Faivke's cheek with two cold yellow-stained fingers which stank of snuff. His mother stood nervously by the stove blushing to the roots of her hair. Haltingly she came closer to try to explain the reasons for her son's wildness before this saintly guest who lifted his head from between the two bowls, raised his eyes and nodded with his beard. The gestures made by the man of God were ominous. Faivke trembled and felt a strange chill grip his heart. Afterwards he had nightmares. He saw hundreds of thin icy, yellow fingers pointing maliciously at him and choking him with their pungent, bitter-sweet smell.

Faivke had never been taught to pray. Starodubov was a remote village, far from any Jewish community. Every Saturday at dawn, Faivke would lie awake in bed and watch his father go through all sorts of motions that he never performed during the week. He would put on a ragged black coat, don his yellowing *tallit*,[2] shut his eyes and stand facing the wall as he bowed and said his prayers in a whisper. Faivke sensed that these bowings and mumblings were directed to God, and he became restive. It frightened him to think that his father would venture so willingly into such danger. If it were up to him, he would never bother God—neither for good nor for evil. Hiding under his blankets, Faivke would brood over these thoughts as he lay awake in bed. He would not stir until he heard the clatter of pots and pans as his mother began to potter about the stove and basin and he could smell the special Sabbath aroma of chopped radishes, onions and chicken fat.

2

Years passed by, summer following winter, winter following summer; Faivke was now a nine-year-old lad with a scratched face, a bright blood-red scar on his upper lip and bare calloused feet unlike the feet of other children, a wild, carefree lad, over whom a divine curse hovered. The last days of summer had passed and autumn had now arrived.

That autumn Matis's wife was due to give birth for the seventh time. While she was in pain and weak, the high holydays arrived.[3]

2. *Tallit*—see *A Barbarian*, note 2.
3. 'High Holydays' or 'Days of Awe'—*Rosh Hashanah* (New Year) and *Yom Kippur* (Day of Atonement). The latter, a fast day, concludes this

The air outside was cold, the mornings misty, and even the fish in the sea shivered. To the lonely woman it seemed that her painful pregnancy blended well with the awesome days of judgement to create a sorrowful time of contrition and penitence. She walked about stealthily as if carrying a heavy burden, trembling like a shadow in hopeless dismay. The last few years had been difficult. Her grown-up daughters had left the village and gone to serve as domestics in strange households in neighbouring towns. The farmer from whom they got their flour had become more worldly-wise and craftier than ever. And her days of youth and vigour had gone for good. For *Yom Kippur* this year the smith's wife had decided to send off her two men, Matis and Faivke, to the synagogue in the large village. Who knows, perhaps the good Lord in his abode on high would listen to their prayers and have mercy on them.

One morning Matis arose, washed his sooty face, put on his well-worn Sabbath coat, stood near the window and blinked his swollen eyes in the bright sunlight. It was *Yom Kippur* eve. In the small, low-ceilinged house smoke billowed from the stove and the sweet smell of sugared carrots filled the air. Matis's wife went to the village to look for Faivke and brought him home. He looked wild, excited and bewildered. He had been dragged away from the village at an exciting and joyful moment that would never return. Mikita, Avedor's son, had harnessed his father's colt to a wagon for the first time. This high-spirited colt was widely admired, and all the village boys were there to watch. The colt reared up at its owner, and kicking out with its hind legs, pulled violently against the reins and snorted hotly through wide, quivering nostrils. In a rage, it glared at the children who had gathered around, and pawed the ground wildly as if to shake the very foundations of the earth. Suddenly it sprang forward with all its might, took a stupendous leap and, with the wagon behind it, flew through the village streets. There was a tremendous commotion. Faivke had been one of the first to chase after the colt through the dust clouds and at risk to his life had seized hold of its reins.

period of penitence, during which it is believed the fate of the world and each individual is determined. See Zborowski and Herzog, *op. cit.*, pp. 391–7 and S. J. Agnon, *Days of Awe* (New York, 1948).

His mother washed his face, looked him over from his bare calloused feet to his head covered with the worn-out peasant's cap,
gave him a little bag with some food in it and said to him, 'Off you
go! Try to be a pious lad, and may God forgive you.'

Then she stood on the threshold and watched her two men walking off to pray on the Day of Judgement with the congregation in a
distant village. The seven children she had borne had aged and weak-
ened this tough and vigorous woman, so that when she stood alone
at the door watching her wild, young, barefoot son walking off to
stand before God for the first time in his life, she could not refrain
from pressing her face against the *mezuzah*[4] and bursting into tears.

Faivke followed his father as quietly as a docile lamb. The sandy
path wound its way through bare harvested fields. The big village
was some hours away. Faivke was fearful and anxious. He did not
fully comprehend where he was being led, or precisely what would
be done to him there, in that unfamiliar place. The fervour with
which Mikita's young colt had bolted off through the village had
not yet receded from his mind. Why had his father put on his ragged,
Sabbath coat on a day that was not Sabbath? Why was he carrying
his *tallit* and that wide, white smock? The awesome, fateful, ominous
hour from which no one escapes had apparently arrived.

They approached the huge Starodubov forest. The trees stood
motionless and sad amidst their falling, yellow leaves. Faivke left his
father and walked towards the forest. An idea flashed through his
mind—should he perhaps run away into the heart of the forest and
save himself? It might be better to remain there for the rest of his
life! He could join Stiopa, Mikhaelena-the-drunkard's one-eyed
son. They could both roast potatoes in the ashes of wood fires, and
lie in wait for the cows grazing in the meadows and drink milk
straight from their udders. Let them come and beat him or kill him
—he'd never leave the forest!

However, Faivke did not carry out his plan. Scarcely had he
stepped among the trees in the silent forest and over the dried leaves,
than he imagined that the entire forest had become bathed in a
wondrous pale light which seemed to emanate from the bowels of
the earth. He heard strange echoes—the sound of falling leaves—

4. *Mezuzah*, see page 69, note 8.

and then the sound of leaves rustling under his feet. He was over-come with fear—the fear of silence and solitude.

Puzzled, Matis the smith stopped walking and looked about with his swollen eyes.

'Faivi, where are you?'

Faivke came out of the forest.

'Faivi, you must understand that you're not allowed to go into the forest today. God will be angry. Try to be a pious lad today,' Matis repeated his wife's words, 'and you'll have to say "Amen".'

Faivke stared at his feet.

'But I can't,' he responded angrily.

'Is it so difficult to say "Amen"?' his father pacified him and a worried smile appeared on his meek, hairy face, 'When you hear them all say "Amen" you'll say it too. And may God forgive you,' Matis once again recalled his wife's words.

Faivke was quiet and continued following his father as obedient as a lamb. What would they ask him there, in that strange place, and what would he answer? Faivke gazed straight ahead and imagined they were walking towards some distant destination where the edge of the pale heavens shines with pure light. There, on a high mound, sits God—a white-haired old man wrapped in a great, wide fur coat. Everyone comes up to him. He questions them all and they have to reply. God nods his long beard which rests on his great, wide fur coat. But how will he, a wild young boy, begin to talk and what can he answer the mighty, awesome Lord from whom no one escapes?

In his short life Faivke had already committed some grave and some lesser sins, of which his mother constantly reminded him and for which she often reprimanded him on the Sabbath. But now Faivke was thinking only about two sins which he had committed recently and of which his mother knew nothing. One sin concerned Aniska, a blind beggar, who felt his way through the villages by tapping with a stick. Several days ago, Faivke with another boy had planned to trick Aniska and to trip him up. They had placed a ladder down on the ground and Aniska had tripped over it and had fallen heavily, injuring his nose. The farmers banded together and caught Faivke. Aniska the blind beggar sat in the village square, blood gushing from his nose. He was crying bitterly and he swore that God would avenge his spilt blood. The farmers beat the young boy in full measure for his crime. Faivke, however, felt that he had not yet fully atoned for his sin. God would not forgive him for Aniska's spilt blood!

The second incident occurred outside the village in a place near the farmers' cemetery. At the time, a group of village children, Faivke among them, were chasing a flock of pigeons and throwing pebbles at them. Faivke also threw some pebbles into the air. As luck would have it, one pebble hit the naked figure of Jesus on the cross that stood on the small hill at the entrance to the cemetery. When the Gentile children saw this they were horrified, but a group of Faivke's closest friends defended him from the zealots. Faivke's friends told him that he had committed a mortal sin for which there was no atonement—he had struck the son of God. Anyone who struck the son of God would hang and be condemned to Hell.

Faivke was now considering these two grievous sins, and his heart was beating heavily. It was clear to him that in a little while he would be brought to trial and punished for the sins which he had committed against Aniska the beggar and against the son of God. He did not know what he could say or how he would defend himself.

3

By the time they arrived some hours later at the windmill of the large, unfamiliar village, the sun had begun to set. In the distance, one could see the river in between the drooping willows. A high, rickety, wooden bridge spanned the river.

'That's where the congregation is,' Matis asserted, pointing to the thatched roofs shining some way off in the setting sun. As they stepped on to the shaky bridge Faivke looked down into the deep murky waters flowing quietly and calmly in the shadows of the bent willows. How high the bridge was, and how deep the waters below! Faivke was in great distress and felt faint. He pulled at his father's coat and muttered through parched lips, 'But, Daddy, I can't answer!'

'What, "Amen?" You silly child! It's not hard at all. Is it really

such a difficult task? When everybody else responds you say it too!'
Matis spoke in a gentle pleading tone. But Faivke sensed a tremor in
his father's voice.

On the other side of the river they arrived at a large inn with a
wide porch that faced the street. In front of the porch they found a
group of village Jews dressed in their black holiday coats, several
women with their heads covered with yellow silk kerchiefs, and a
number of young boys walking about in stocking-feet and clutching
small prayer books.[5] Insisting that he did not want to follow his
father into the inn, Faivke remained outside. He walked over to a
corner between the stable and the wood shed, his black fiery eyes
shooting glances from under his large hat. But he was not to stand
alone for long. Soon one of the boys came up to him. He was a
young red-headed imp, who had freckles on his tiny bird-like face
and small, pale, darting eyes. The young boy, in his bright new
clothes, at first simply stood in front of Faivke. Then he took out
of his pocket a small bottle full of some liquid, waved it back and
forth through the air, and then pushed it against the young guest's
nose. Finally, he asked, 'Whose son are you?' Faivke grew pale and
lowered his eyes.

'Say, listen now, you chicken-hearted little rascal, why are you
standing outside? Go in and join the afternoon service. Have you
said your prayers already?'

'N-no . . .'

'Did you bring a candle along?'

'N-no . . .'

'Is that man with the torn coat your father?'

'My f-father . . .'

The red-head grabbed Faivke's hand.

'Come and see what they're going to do to your father in there.'

The air was hot and stifling in the building into which the red-head
had pushed Faivke, and there was a strange commotion. Men with
black caftans were swaying next to the walls, pounding their breasts
with their fists, reading aloud from their prayer books, and blowing
their noses with red handkerchiefs. From behind the partition came

5. On not wearing shoes or sandals on *Yom Kippur* see *Mishnah Yoma*
VIII.

the wail of women who were weeping aloud as they prayed. There was also the clatter of cutlery and the sound of an infant crying with all its might.

Faivke saw his father, looking meek and contrite, standing near a bale of hay in a corner glancing about him with his swollen eyes. A group of curious boys who were waiting for some excitement winked at each other slyly as they gathered around Matis the smith.

'That's his kid—the one with the stupid hat and funny lip!' the red-head blurted out and pushed Faivke into the centre of the ring.

A young man wearing a white collar and no tie and a shiny polished brass buckle came up to Matis. The young man was holding a whip and snapping it in the air like a coachman when he approaches his horses.

'Well now, Reb smith, I'm ready to flog you!'

'What? I mean . . . I suppose you want me to lie down?' Matis hesitated, smiling ruefully at the group of boys who were standing about impatiently.

'Yes. Do me a favour and lie down. Quickly now, don't just stand there! It'll soon be dark.' The young man with the collar winked at the boys in the crowd, raised the whip, and snapped it through the air.

Matis pulled his coat tails together, bent low and slowly lowered himself on to the straw pad in front of him. The young man waved the whip above him and rhythmically, soberly, and, with much apparent delight, flogged him.

'One, two, three,' the boys counted the number of strokes loudly and gleefully. 'Beat him, flog him well!'

Faivke, frightened and shocked at what he was witnessing, was about to rush to his father and help him up so that he could run away. But Matis, humbled and embarrassed, rose up by himself, and rubbed his blood-shot eyes.

'Now then, sir, take the whip and beat his son,' the red-head called to the flogger and pulled Faivke over the the heap of straw. Enraged Faivke struggled silently and furiously to escape, but the boy would not let go. The two boys wrestled until they reached the door. Then Faivke with his fiery, black eyes stared into the boy's tiny, bird-like face and said with suppressed rage:

'I'll knock your teeth out!'

'Who? You? A little brat like you? This is our place! Do you realize that on *Rosh Hashanah* eve I went with my grandfather to the city? . . . I'll call Leibritz over, then you'll hear all about it!'

Leibritz appeared at once. This was Leibke the coachman who tended the innkeeper's horses. He was a short, large-boned sixteen-year-old, who was now dressed in a new peasant's shirt with a red pattern embroidered on it. The young man was ready for the Day of Judgement—he was wearing white linen stockings and holding a large bottle of smelling salts. As he came closer he pushed his way through the group of boys and walked directly towards Faivke—as though coming out to battle. With one eye he stared at him disparagingly and with the other winked at the hotel-keeper's grandson, the freckle-faced red-head.

'Who is this creature?'

'How do I know? Some kind of rascal! He belongs to the smith from Starodubov. He's bragging that he'll knock my teeth out.'

'So that's the story, my good friend.' Leibritz intoned with satisfaction and casually slapped Faivke's face. 'In that case, perhaps we should give him a sniff of these salts and then watch his eyes light up! . . . Listen, my warrior from Starodubov, you'd best keep your hands in your pockets, because Leibke's here! Do you know who Leibke is? You're lucky that I have a Jewish heart and that it is *Yom Kippur* today . . .'

But the red-head was not satisfied.

'Did you ever see a brat like this? He comes here from Starodubov without any shoes on and wants to hit me in our building!' The group of boys encircled Faivke on the porch. They sneered at him and insulted him. He stood on his bare calloused feet in the midst of this hostile crowd, silent and not daring to look up, just like a small angry animal that has fallen into a trap.

4

Night fell. A number of tall memorial candles were already burning on the long tables in the inn. The large dining-room was filled to capacity with worshippers who were flushed and sweating from the heat of the candles. They were wrapped in their *tallits* and broad, white *kittels*. The *Tefillah Zakkah*[6] was being recited with passion. They all gathered around the tables and swayed fervently over the prayer books lying open before them. A torrent of deafening noises filled the building. Each one tried to pray louder than his neighbour. These yokels were simple folk and did not know the beauty of silent devotion. Throughout the rest of the year they were unaccustomed to public worship and were far removed from the Lord of the Universe and sacred duties. When, however, the Day of Judgement arrived they would rush around fervently trying to compensate for what they had missed throughout the year. Individually and in unison, they tried to placate the Lord energetically so as to gain God's favour with their joint strength. Their prayers swelled furiously. The cantor, the young man with the white collar and brass buckle, sang with fervour and passion, his voice rising above the rest. This *yeshiva* boy came from the city, and tried to demonstrate his ritual prowess to these yokels, so that they might have good cause to trust in his services. The temperature rose, and the lonely Faivke began to see stars flashing before his smarting eyes. As he was standing, stunned and lost among the worshippers, expecting something extraordinary to happen, there was a stir in one of the corners. The Ark, covered with a white velvet curtain, was opened. A stately old man walked slowly hugging something white and round wrapped in cloth and decorated with gold ornaments—it looked like a baby in diapers. The gold ornaments sparkled in the candlelight and shone on the old man's silver beard, clothing him in majesty. A tremor shot through Faivke. 'The hour has arrived . . .' Everything now appeared dimly through a pale, distant haze, above the tumultuous sound of the unfamiliar songs. That magnificent, round, white object had vanished along with the mysterious old man who melted into the crowd. Faivke's face was ablaze, his flesh was prickly, his hands and feet shivered with cold as if they had been skinned.

At one point, standing near a long table opposite the bright

6. *Tefillah Zakkah* (Pristine Prayer) composed by Rabbi Abraham Danzig 1747/8–1820. For an English translation of this elaborate confessional, see *Prayer Book for the Day of Atonement*, trans. by A. T. Philips (New York, 1931), pp. 17–21.

lights, he felt exhausted with excitement and closed his eyes. He heard a deafening tolling of bells in his ears. Suddenly, someone banged on the table, and immediately all was still. Faivke awoke and opened his eyes. He was suddenly terrified. He tried to move away; but there were many worshippers in their *tallits* and white *kittels* surrounding him, bowing and praying over his head. One of them pressed Faivke to a big, open book with large and small black letters that covered its stained pages like a flock of flying birds. Faivke trembled. The angry worshippers rebuked him in whispers: 'Well, well . . .!' Faivke stood motionless in his place in front of the open book, with all the tall men swaying fervently above his head as they prayed to God in an ardent whisper. By the time he could escape he was weak, dizzy, and exhausted. He made his way into the corner where his father was standing. There he dropped to the floor and fell asleep.

That night Faivke had an odd dream. He had been turned into a tree rising out of the ground like the other trees of the forest. The trees had human faces. Then he saw Aniska, the blind beggar, beaten and bruised, with blood spurting over his face, coming towards him. In one hand Aniska held his big staff, and in the other a pebble (Faivke immediately recognized it as the one with which he had struck the son of God). Aniska kept turning his face around, motioning with his stick and calling out to someone to come to him. Faivke looked straight in front of him. Over there, in the centre of the forest, stood God himself, as white as falling snow, amid sparks of fire, clutching his son to his heart—but whether it was a baby in diapers or a statue of a naked Jesus he could not make out. Then, carrying the infant in his arms, God began to ascend out of the forest. The higher he rose above the forest the more piercing his eyes became. Faivke sensed this very vividly but could not behold God, who was enveloped in a thick cloud. Faivke could see only Aniska the blind beggar with a stick, who was getting closer and closer to him. Faivke wanted to cry out—but could utter no sound. He wanted to uproot his feet from the earth and run for his life but he was too weak. He was a tree growing out of the earth among the other trees of the forest.

When Faivke woke up he found himself surrounded by the other worshippers who were sleeping on the floor. He was drenched in perspiration. Looking up, he saw in the candle-light a tall pale Jew, standing over the sleeping Jews and looking as if bent on some mischief. The tall man fell on his knees, crept silently up to Matis the smith who was snoring loudly, and tickled his nose with a small bottle. Trembling, Matis cried aloud and sat bolt upright.

'What, who is it?' he cried in fright.

The tall, pale Jew was the *yeshiva* boy with the white collar who had served as cantor.

'It's me!' the young man replied with a smirk. 'Now there's nothing to be afraid of, smith, these drops are like medicine.' 'But why me', Matis pleaded as he blinked his red eyes in the light, 'why me?'

Outside, dawn was breaking. The heat in the building had given way to the chill of an autumn morning. The flickering candles were reflected in the windows that had misted over. The reflections seemed as distant as another planet. Several men arose from the straw-strewn floor and looked around with surprise at those already upright. Faivke leaped up and stood by with open mouth and piercing eyes. The young man with the bottle turned to him and tried to grab him.

'What's up with you, you little runt? Why are you staring at me with those eyes? Do you want a whiff of this? Here, smell it!'

Faivke turned round and hurried away to another corner, for all the world like a little animal disturbed in its lair.

5

At daybreak the congregation resumed its fervent prayers and again the building resounded with the din of village worshippers competing in prayer. But by the light of day the magic of the scene was gone; Faivke felt naked in the clouds that surrounded him. Even the image of Aniska the blind beggar with the pebble in hand no longer frightened him—it was only a fleeting nightmare. When they took out the infant-like Torah scroll wrapped in its white coverings from the Ark, Faivke stood near the table and stared without emotion at the unveiled parchment with its clear black letters. Faivke watched the young cantor with the white collar, bending his head over the open scroll and chanting aloud as he swayed in the manner of a practised, professional reader. Faivke walked away dispirited and dejected.

The younger boys wandered around the building in stocking-feet holding bottles in their hands, and yawned into their prayer books. Dust billowed from the straw-strewn floors. Sunlight burst into the room: the candles were guttering in the rising dust. Faivke felt as if he had been in this strange place for a very long time—here his life had become entangled and veiled in darkness. His former, carefree, unclouded life now seemed like a remote dream that would never return. Stark desperation gripped him, his feet shook with cold as if they had been skinned and left exposed. He went outside and sat alone on a ledge behind the building. There, cramped be-tween the briars and weeds, he dozed for a long while in the sun. He dreamt of raging red rivers that spewed up mighty waves. A strange, tall, dark figure was standing in front of him, sheltering him with his *tallit*, swaying solemnly and praying with hushed devotion.

Then Matis, looking dazed and surprised, came out and went over to him. He tapped Faivke and implored him with a peculiar tender-ness.

'Well, Faivi? Why are you sleeping here? What makes you sleep all day, Faivi? You didn't eat yet, did you?'

'I don't want to.'

With stumbling steps Faivke followed his father into the inn. Here they saw exhausted men with red handkerchiefs in their hands and chafed noses, lounging about on the porches and on the benches. The sun was beginning to set behind the village, drenching the win-dows with its reddish rays. Faivke and his father stood near a window in a corner of the building. Faivke felt dizzy with the bright sunshine. Matis blinked as he pulled at his tangled beard with trembling fingers. Soon the prayers began again. After a thunderous bang on the table, the silent prayer began. Afterwards the young cantor chanted away with a now faltering voice and waning strength. It seemed as if the whole thing had become burdensome; he was now merely completing his obligations and putting the interests of the majority before his own. For a moment Matis the smith, standing

near the window, forgot where he was; he forgot about the open
prayer book, and stared out at the tops of the trees aglow in the setting sun. Then something happened that startled the worshippers.
Matis dropped his head on to the windowsill, hid his face in the prayer
book and wept bitterly. Everyone turned towards him. Some burst
out laughing. The words that the cantor had just chanted should,
in no way, have evoked tears. Why should anyone weep at the
words 'Michael praises on the right'[7] in the late afternoon service?
Laughing and joking, several young boys and some men came up to
Matis. The innkeeper's son-in-law tugged at his *tallit*.

'Mister, you made a mistake, no one cries at this place!'

Matis controlled his tears and did not reply: he did not even
acknowledge the man's presence. The red-headed, bird-faced lad
with the freckles also leaped into the fray and pulled at Matis's *tallit*:

'Mister, we don't cry here!'

Faivke looked in confusion first at his father and then at the
crowd. He leaped up impetuously and glued his piercing, black eyes
on the red-head's face:

'You, you . . . may wolves devour you!'

Boisterous laughter exploded in the room and in the confusion
that followed someone yelled out, 'Brat! In a holy place?' One of
the worshippers responded with 'Ha, ha, the lad from Starodubov
must be a fully-fledged Goy.'

The young man in the white collar standing on the podium
slapped his hand down on the prayer book, because no one was
listening to his chanting.

Faivke ran off to his hideaway behind the inn, to the rough ledge
covered with thistles and brambles. He was followed by the gang of
youngsters led by Leibritz the coachman.

'Here's the brat from Starodubov,' the red-head shouted shrilly.
'Did you ever see the likes of him? He wants to punch me? In our
own place . . . Leibritz, what do you say to someone like that?'

7. This is the first verse of a chant recited during the late afternoon service
on *Yom Kippur*. 'Michael praises on the right hand/ Gabriel acclaims on
the left hand saying,/"There is none like God in Heaven!/Who is like
thy people Israel on earth?".' For an explanatory note see *High Holyday
Prayer Book*, P. Birnbaum (trans.) (New York, 1951), pp. 921–2.

Leibritz, a careful and composed person who did everything with a quiet confidence, swayed towards Faivke with relaxed and leisured strides.

'Hold it, men, don't rush! We'll give him a taste of these smelling salts—and then he'll feel better!'

With that, Leibritz grabbed Faivke's hands, twisted them with calm brutality and motioned to the freckled red-head;

'Well, Ahrze,[8] let him have it!'

The red-head quickly took out his bottle, hastily removing the cap and thrust it under Faivke's nose. In absolute frenzy, Faivke tore himself loose from Leibritz, pounced on the red-head and sank his nails into his bird-face. At once he felt Leibritz's heavy hands pounding on his head. Dazed, Faivke fell to the ground. Then, like a tiny animal of prey, he jumped on Leibritz and sunk his sharp teeth into his arm.

Leibritz screamed with pain.

Pandemonium. The worshippers crowded about in their *tallits* and *kittels*. Pale-faced women stood on the porch shouting to their children. Old men scolded the smith from Starodubov for his son's behaviour. Then they returned to the service, and Matis and Faivke remained alone by the dirt ledge that by now was sunk in evening shadow. Matis looked at his son, blinked his red eyes but said nothing. Finally he muttered: 'Faivke, mother's at home ... and you're here?'

Matis left Faivke alone on the ledge and Faivke again fell asleep. Again the red rivers that spewed up mighty waves appeared together with the tall stranger who covered Faivke with his *tallit* as he swayed above him and prayed incessantly. But now the gushing rivers were very red and the prayers battered against his head, and a dreadful wailing grew louder and louder in his ears.

6

When Faivke opened his eyes there was darkness all about. Matis took him by his hand, picked him up and told him, 'We're going home'.

8. Diminutive form of Aharon (Aaron).

The building was transformed. The putrid stench had subsided, holiness had given way to the profane. The candles had disappeared. In their stead, a large crystal lamp brightly illumined the spacious room. Men in hats and unbuttoned black jackets, without *tallit* or *kittel*, were drinking each other's health, eating honey cake, clinking glasses and talking loudly. To Faivke it all sounded as raucous and deafening as bells. He felt he was seeing the place for the first time, and these men, seated around the table, seemed to have come from some other world. The old man at the head of the table near the glasses and bottles, with his quivering yellowish beard and trembling lips, had lost the mystifying spell of the old man who had appeared last evening with the Torah scrolls in his arms. The sudden change sapped Faivke's strength; he felt nauseated and dizzy as if he were falling into a bottomless abyss.

Matis the smith came over to the table, coughed, bowed to all the assembled men and greeted them with: 'A happy New Year!'

The old man looked up at Matis with weak but impatient eyes, and in an abrasive voice that sounded to Faivke like thunder, roared out, 'What!'

'I said . . . I mean, I'm going home, I'm going home . . . A good year, I said.'

'What! A good year! A good year to you too. Don't rush, take a little brandy. You fasted, didn't you?'

Faivke leaned against the table and shut his eyes. The bright glare of the lamp and the old man's voice rolling like thunder troubled him, and he grew faint.

'What!' the old man rumbled, 'Is this your son? He scratched my Ahrze's face. A wild animal! Beat him! Give him a glass of brandy too! A piece of cake! Have him recite the blessing. You say he doesn't know how to recite it? That's awful. Then we ought to beat you! You want to go home—so, go—go in peace! In her old age your wife gave birth to a daughter? . . . then, *Mazal Tov* (Good luck). A good year, a good year. Wait a bit, maybe you need some money for the holydays? *Sukkot* is coming . . .?'[9]

Matis and Faivke left. Once outdoors, Matis gazed at the clear sky

9. *Sukkot* (Booths) the autumn harvest festival that commences five days after *Yom Kippur*. See Zborowski and Herzog, *op. cit.*, pp. 397–400.

that was lit up by the moon and said to his son, 'Mother must be waiting for us.' Then he began to walk more quickly. Faivke followed sluggishly behind.

A cold wind met them on the bridge. After they had crossed the bridge Matis started to walk faster. As he swung along his breath started coming in short gasps and his coat-tails fluttered in the wind. Suddenly he stopped, and realized with a shock that he had left Faivke far behind. He found him on the ground at the side of the road, rolled up in a ball; his body was shaking with cold, his teeth chattering.

'Faivke, what is the matter? Why are you sitting here? Let's go home!'

'I'm not going . . .' Faivke replied trembling all over and staring strangely into his father's face, 'I can't . . .'

'Did they hurt you, Faivi?'

Faivke was silent and continued staring at his father with feverish eyes. Then he blurted out, 'What about you . . . what happened to you? . . . Why did you cry? Tell me, why did you cry there?'

'I didn't really cry, you silly boy,' said Matis. 'I didn't cry at all it's only that today is *Yom Kippur* . . . and mother is at home all alone . . . waiting for us. . . . Get up, Faivke, let's go home! Mother'll put a bandage on your head.'

'No!' Faivke persisted, 'tell me, why did you cry? Why did you cry, when they were all laughing? You shouldn't cry when they laugh. You cried and they laughed . . . we ought to knock their teeth out, slap their faces, bite them, bite them . . . bite them all. May wolves devour them . . .!'

Faivke clenched his fists and beat his hands and feet deliriously on the ground. Helpless, Matis stood near his son and stared into the darkness, as if pleading: From whence cometh my help?[10] In the distance he could hear heavy footsteps on the tall rickety bridge. A few minutes later he was able to recognize in the moonlight a farmer he knew from Starodubov.

'Who is that? Is it you, Motke? What are you doing here all alone at night? Are you performing witchcraft in the light of the moon? Who's lying on the ground over there?'

10. Based on Psalms 121:1.

'I can't figure it out, Trochim, my friend! It's my son, Faivke. He says he doesn't want to go home. I guess he can't. What can I do?' Matis entreated his neighbour.

'What's this? Has he gone crazy? Give him a good wallop . . . Hey, there, little devil, get up!'

Faivke did not get up; he just lay there trembling.

'Oh, you little devil,' the farmer fumed, 'why did you raise such a son, Motke? It's a punishment, a punishment from heaven! Why don't you do what you should—flog him with a wet strap? A few days ago some people reported that . . . Ahapa herself saw it . . .'

'I don't know, myself, Trochim, my friend,' Matis apologized, making a gesture of the most profound despair.

7

Next morning Matis rented a farmer's wagon and took Faivke off to the city clinic. Standing by the *mezuzah*, his wife watched them out of sight.

On a cold bright morning at the end of autumn when the road to town was being repaired and the sun was shining over crumbling mounds of dirt, the news spread among the Gentile urchins that Faivke had died in the city.

Twilight[1]

THE details of the journey from a tranquil Lithuanian village to remote New York floated past Dvorah as in a dream. The swift train ride that went on for several days and nights, the big, bustling stations on the other side of the border with the strident voices of strange people, the rapidly changing scenes and faces, the foreign countries and languages, the confusion and commotion of her fellow Jews—all seemed like some incredible incident which had once occurred in the distant past, some forgotten childhood tale that was being re-enacted before her very eyes. Old scenes from the *Tzena-Urena*[2] were reawakened in her dim old imagination: the legend of the tower of Babel in which men and women called to each other in foreign tongues; Jacob's sons journeying to the land of Egypt and entering the gates of a foreign city; the Judaean exiles, starving men and women led in chains by the commander Nebuzaradan; at night, when the dark fields roared past the train window, Rachel lamented her children at the crossroads.[3] These scenes appeared to

1. In the Yiddish version this story is entitled *Untergang*, and hence the English title.

2. *Tzena Urena*—A Yiddish version of the Pentateuch interwoven with fables and rabbinic homilies and divided into sections parallel with the traditional divisions of the Pentateuch. It was compiled by Jacob ben Isaac Ashkenazi and was the cherished possession of almost every Jewish woman in East Europe. For English translations see N. C. Gore *Tzenah U'Reenah: A Jewish Commentary on the Book of Exodus* (New York, 1965), particularly his introduction pp. 13–28, and P. I. Hershon, *Rabbinical Commentary on Genesis* (London, 1885). See Zborowski and Herzog, *Life Is With People*, pp. 125–6.

3. The Midrashic legend that the matriarch Rachel continues to lament for her dispersed children, the Jewish people, is based on Jeremiah 31:15 'Thus saith the Lord: A voice is heard in Ramah, lamentation and bitter

her through the darkened panes of the train; and the image of her dead daughter raced with outstretched arms to the rhythm of the wheels, her cries blending with the screeching whistle. Then came the voyage over the sea with its dreary uneventful days. Under the low ceiling of her sunless cabin, and to the sound of surging waves and the ship's endless creaking, the old woman tossed on her narrow bunk in mute loneliness, brooding over the dark abyss below her. The little town in which she had lived her seventy years now seemed to her like a solitary, abandoned island, its hills and rocks strangely aglow in the setting sun, which had slipped out of sight as the ship drew away from land. In the distance she seemed to see her five children who had died at an early age, her late husband and a multitude of shadows rising from the abyss of oblivion. They stood gaping at her from the quiet graveyard on the hill, white with its low gravestones; they peered through the green trees and nodded their heads at her as if to say 'Where are you off to? Why are you running away from us?' Behind the ship the sea surged angrily. In the dead of night the old woman lifted her aching head from the pillow, as if rousing herself from another world. She sat up and peered at her sleeping companions. She was unable to understand who they were, what she was doing here, or where her tortuous fate was leading her in these final days of her life. The sole hope that glimmered like a spark in the night was the thought of her son in America—but even he was no more than a vague and disembodied memory.

One morning she was awakened from her reverie by the announcement that the ship was nearing shore. She was roused from bed, led through a long, narrow corridor and brought before several uniformed clerks who asked her questions. With the help of some friendly people she was able to answer the clerks, who recorded the information in a book. Then she was led off the boat. At once a strange new world was unveiled. Tumultuous crowds rushed past excitedly trying to get to their destinations. The sun shone bright and warm over white ships with tall smokestacks glittering in the clear air as they moved to the ocean's swell, belching smoke and

weeping, Rachel weeping for her children, She refuseth to be comforted for her children, because they are not.'

blasting their whistles. The little old lady with her black head-scarf tottered unsurely on her weak feet. Convinced it was all a mistake, she hesitated. As she stepped down the gang plank accom-panied by a porter who was carrying her belongings, she noticed someone pushing his way through the crowd below and rushing towards her waving his hands and smiling with a mouth full of bright, gold teeth. Momentarily, she was attracted to the man whose dark, merry eyes seemed so familiar, but the strange flash of his gold teeth put her off. While she hesitated and moved aside, the man hugged her and embraced her with strong, warm arms.

'Mother, is it really you? . . . Didn't you recognize me, Mother dear?'

'Mr. Rabinowitz?' the clerk inquired.

'Mr Rabinowitz, Mr Robbins—it's all the same, my friend!' he answered gaily. 'I'm the man you want!'

Bent and weak, supported by her tall, broad-shouldered son, the tiny old woman was led through heaps of baggage strewn over the quay-side. She blinked her fading, tearful eyes at the strange, shaven face of the man at her side. Her wrinkled lips quivered alternately with tears and laughter.

'I didn't recognize you . . . honestly, I didn't recognize you, son! It's been such a long time—it's eighteen years since we last saw each other . . . so I stared at you, wondering who is that strange man? But it really was you, Reuvele! I always carry your photograph with me, but you're so different there . . . as you were at home, with a mous-tache . . .'

'The moustache, my dear, went a long time ago!' he replied cheerfully. 'Why do I need a moustache now that I have money?'

'Well if that's so . . . Thank God . . . I didn't mean anything by it, son . . . Where's the trunk? My head is spinning, and my eyes, thank God, don't see so well any more . . . I have just that one trunk. I brought the inheritance your father left you, may he rest in peace—a trunk-load of books. And a special gift for your wife—bless her—a pair of silver candlesticks, my mother's candlesticks. . . .'

She was welcomed into her blond son's home by a tall young woman with short hair and gold-rimmed glasses. She came forward serenely to greet her guest, she removed her spectacles, glanced at her with cold, blue, quizzical eyes, and with a polite movement, forced a smile to her hard, chiselled face and said, 'Hello, Mom!' Then she kissed her nonchalantly on her cheek. Replacing her spectacles she continued to stare curiously at her guest. Apparently shocked by her looks, the old woman turned aside.

'Mother, this is my wife, Florence,' the son proudly introduced her.

'I see, son, I understand,' the old woman said softly, looking at her daughter-in-law in confusion.

'She's a fine wife, a very careful housewife, Lord protect us,' he continued in the same tone, hugging his wife. 'Did you expect to find such a wonderful daughter-in-law with short hair and a pair of spectacles? That's the style now, you know. If you want to use her Jewish name, it's Faige Leah. Her grandmother used to call her that. . . .'

'No, please, not Faige Leah,' Mrs Robbins protested in a jargon that was half Yiddish and half English, pulling herself away from her husband and making a wry face. 'I don't like that at all!'

Mr Robbins's two sons came out of a nearby room and kissed their grandmother. The older one, a fourteen-year-old with blond hair and blue eyes like his mother, came directly over to the old woman. He had just asked his father in the cautious tone of a person who likes to know exactly what is going on, 'Is this our grandma?' and with cold precision he kissed her in the polite manner of one who is aware of his obligations. But the younger boy, a ten-year-old with dark, merry eyes like his father's, was excited, he blushed as he touched the trembling bony hands of his grandmother who had just arrived from Europe.

'They're both Goyim! Pure Goyim!' their father announced exuberantly. 'They don't know a word of Yiddish! Thoroughbred Yankees, you know!'

In the quiet handsomely decorated living-room, the old woman sat down in the company of her new family. As if seeking some support in this strange environment, she clutched at the valise that was lying at her feet. The members of her family stood in front of her gazing curiously at the little old lady with the shrivelled face who seemed so bizarre in her black head-scarf and voluminous old-fashioned black dress. It was as if she were merely a visitor and would shortly gather up her belongings and leave. The older son interrupted the silence. Looking bored to death, he walked away and sauntered about the room for several minutes staring at the ceiling. Suddenly, he strode up to the wall and slapped it with a loud clap.

'A fly,' he shouted in explanation of the incident.

When the old woman and her son were alone in the room, she stared at him with faded eyes. Then her lips quivered and her eyes filled with tears as she asked her son,

'Reuvele, what do you say to my sad plight? Shifrale is dead, too. I had one daughter left, but God took her away, too. Everyone is gone, and I am left alone like a broken vessel. . . . And, alas, my son-in-law didn't even wait a full year before hurrying to re-marry and bring a stepmother to my daughter's orphans. How could I bear it? So I came to you, dear. You invited me, so I came. What else have I got in this world? Look what I've got for my sins! . . . I dragged my old bones to America, though God knows how hard it is for me to be a burden to you and your wife and children, bless them. I don't even understand English . . .'

'Now, now, mother, nothing of the sort!' Mr Robbins responded excitedly, sitting down next to his mother and compassionately patting her bowed shoulders. 'Heaven forbid . . . on the contrary . . . both of us, my wife and I, that is, Florence and I, feel honoured! . . . You'll soon adjust to us, and you'll be very comfortable with us. America's different from Europe. At first many things seem odd here . . . But that's America for you! You know, Mother dear, America's different. She pays out with an open hand. America has more than enough!'

Mr Robbins lit a cigarette, thrust his hands deep into his pockets, straightened himself and looked at his old mother with twinkling eyes as he said softly, 'Do you realize, Mother, that I'm a rich man, thank God? Mother, how much do you think I'm worth? I'll tell you the truth; you couldn't buy me out for one hundred thousand dollars! In European money that would be—how much? And that's excluding the house, the garden, the furniture and the ornaments . . . they're all mine! I did it with my own two hands—with my own ten fingers! But lots of things happened before I got where I am today!'

Triumphantly, Mr Robbins related in detail the trials and tribulations he had gone through. Excited and attentive, the old woman listened eagerly with her slightly deaf ears, not so much to his tale as to the sound of his voice which sounded more and more like his father's, her husband's voice with the same intonations and inflections.

'Eighteen years,' he repeated, blowing smoke at the ceiling . . . 'how many trials did I suffer . . . can you imagine, Mother? How strange it all seems, I swear . . . I recall . . . during those early days when I could only afford bread and herring, and I still thought about returning home, I would lie down at night and think how I'd return home to father and mother, how I would relax a little in front of the stove and tell you what I had seen and experienced in that distant country . . . For years I've kept it a secret. . . . But since then, many years have passed, and everything has changed. Father is dead . . . now you've come to America. Thank God, I could afford to pay for a first-class ticket. You've come to a house with fine furniture, ornaments and . . . with . . . everything good . . . When I try to recall all those things now I can't . . . no, *well nothing doing,*[4] I simply can't . . . I forgot everything . . . even the important details I've forgotten . . .'

Straightening her glasses, Mrs Robbins came to the door and, without looking at either of them, asked coolly but pleasantly, 'Would you like to have something to eat now, Mother? The table is set.'

'Do you want to eat, Mom?' Mr Robbins repeated his wife's invitation.

'No, Daughter, I'm not hungry,' she replied, turning affectionately to her daughter-in-law.

'If Mother wants to eat, she needn't be afraid,' Mrs Robbins lowered her voice, 'we've made everything kosher.'

The old woman looked up in surprise.

'Florence says . . .,' he tried to explain to his mother, winking pathetically at his wife, 'that is, what Florence means is, that in our house everything. . . that is, I mean . . . that we behave like real

4. 'Well nothing doing' is in English in the text, as are all the italicized phrases in this story.

Jews . . . that is—our food is kosher . . . *strictly kosher* . . . you needn't worry at all . . .'

'God forbid . . .' the old woman responded fearfully.

2

The trunk with the books was removed to the old woman's room in a corner of the house near the children's room. Silently and with some embarrassment, the woman fondled the trunk as she opened it in the presence of both grandsons. She fumbled among the old worn volumes and took out two small new prayer books which she shyly presented to the boys. The older boy opened the strange little book, and after examining it, put it back into the trunk as if to say, 'what use is that to anybody?' The younger boy seemed pleased with his grandmother's gift. Upon receiving his prayer book, he at once went to his room. A few minutes later he returned, walked over to her with sparkling eyes, and without a word showed her how he cherished her present—he had covered it with yellow paper. She patted his uncovered head smiling sadly, for she felt towards him as she would to a non-Jewish child.

Mrs Robbins accepted the silver candlesticks from her mother-in-law with a slight nod, commenting 'Gorgeous!' The next day the old woman found them, polished and shining with wax candles in their holders, on the table in her own room. Later, smiling apologetically, Mr Robbins explained that European candlesticks did not match their American furniture. He himself was not much concerned over such matters, but she, Florence, was very fussy about little details. Besides which, she *was* the housewife, and a native-born American, and so she knew more about American styles than any of them. *Nothing doing. . . .*

During her first days in his home, her son conducted her through the whole house—pointing out the beautiful furniture on the second floor and the amazing boilers in the basement, and instructing her in the use of coal for heating and for hot water. At the same time he indicated the price of each object and its value in European terms. Then he escorted her out to the lawn and enumerated every bush and plant that he had planted. As it was the end of the summer,

nothing remained to bear witness to his labours except some young
trees that were beginning to shed their leaves, and a number of
lettuce plants that had not taken and were scattered about haphazardly
in dried-up holes. Mr Robbins soon realized that he had, in fact,
very little to show her here. Instead, he promised that in ten or
twenty years the lawn would have given place to a magnificent
orchard, and that when the subway was extended to his neighbourhood, the value of his house and property would go up tenfold. In
European monetary terms that would be very substantial indeed.

The old woman listened to all this strange talk. Nodding to her
affluent, self-satisfied son and smiling a sad, resigned smile, she surveyed her surroundings with much grief. Mr Robbins's home was
situated in a new suburb, a quiet, secluded neighbourhood. Behind
the lawn, empty fields and dirt tracks stretched away through a
thin haze to a dense forest—distressingly strange surroundings for
a lonely, smarting heart.

When Mr Robbins travelled daily into the city on business, the
old woman would wander aimlessly through the large rooms as if
in search of something; or else she would sit for hours on end at the
table in her room, staring through dimming eyes at the polished
silver candlesticks which shone with the splendour of bygone days.
From the adjacent rooms Mrs Robbins could be heard ordering her
maid about in the sharp voice of a woman who is mistress of her
household. Mrs Robbins's young neighbours were frequent visitors,
and then the house was filled with boisterous laughter that startled
the old woman out of her depressing thoughts and disturbed her
dreams and reveries.

Once as she was walking from room to room she quietly entered
the kitchen where she saw the negro maid working. She stood in
the doorway for a moment like someone who had chanced upon a
strange and dangerous place. The maid smiled kindly, flashing her
glistening white teeth and respectfully offered her a chair. For a few
moments the old woman stared curiously at the fat maid's black,
shining face. Then with equal curiosity she watched her work.
Suddenly she noticed something strange and disturbing that pierced
her to the quick. She left the kitchen in horror. In her distress she
lost her way and instead of reaching her own room, she entered a

room where she found her daughter-in-law standing half undressed
in front of a mirror as she struggled into a girdle. She looked at her
coldly and demanded: 'What are you doing here, Mother?'

That evening, at dinner, the old woman ate nothing. She apologized and complained of a headache. But after she had refused to eat
for a couple of days, Mr Robbins became worried and went to her
room to see what was wrong. She burst into tears and begged him
to permit her to eat only dairy products in his house or to take pity
on her and send her back to her village.

'I can't do it, son,' the old woman sobbed, 'how much longer have
I got to live? I can't change now. . . .'

'But what is the matter?' Mr Robbins asked in confusion, 'I
thought we had made everything kosher . . . we even purchased new
dishes . . . *strictly kosher* . . .'

'Certainly it's kosher, son . . . Did I say it wasn't, God forbid? But
I can't change now, Reuvele . . . I can't . . .'

That evening the argument between Mr and Mrs Robbins could
be heard coming from their bedroom until midnight. Mrs Robbins's
piercing, imperious soprano fused with Mr Robbins's soft, submis-
sive baritone. The next morning Mr Robbins, freshly shaven,
entered his mother's room and happily informed her, 'Well, now,
Mother dear, everything's *all right*. Did you think we'd let you starve
in America? Would that be right? . . . In short, Mother dear, everything is settled, thank God, for the best. From today on you can
cook your own meals as you see fit. We'll buy you the best kosher
cuts of meat, with the kosher stamp on it—and you'll prepare them
as you wish: salt them, wash them, cook them, and eat them with a
hearty appetite!'

From then on the old woman began to cook her own meals.
Embarrassed and guilty, she would stand in a corner of the kitchen
silently preparing her meals. Then she would take her food to her
own room and would sit motionless and silent for hours on end.

When *Rosh Hashanah* came Mr Robbins donned a new top hat
which he had bought in his mother's honour, took along his two
sons and went with his mother to the synagogue.

'Don't think that this synagogue is like the one back in our home
town,' he boasted as he walked in front of his mother, 'you'll soon

see what kind of a synagogue Columbus builds for his Jews in
America. I bet you couldn't buy this synagogue for half a million
dollars!'

The old woman was led into a large congregation of elegantly
dressed people. She was wearing a wide, white polka-dotted holiday
dress with a crocheted silk kerchief over her wig and old-fashioned
earrings. She sat down next to her son, turning her trembling head
to look with amazement at the paunchy, broad-shouldered, fat-
faced, self-satisfied, worldly men and their stout, bejewelled and bare-
necked wives, whose gold teeth flashed as they laughed and chattered
away with carefree abandon. Some distance away, the cantor and
his choir, clad in gowns and black hats, stood drawn up over the congregation like soldiers in battle array. Tediously and without any
expression they chanted uninspiring tunes in unison. Through the
hot stifling atmosphere blew a chill wind of profanity—the brilliant
electric lights seemed to make the air tawdry and tarnished. The old
woman, saddened by what she saw, sat staring silently at the yellowing pages of her prayer book. The awesome fear of the holy that used
to engulf her in her village every year at the approach of the Days of
Awe all at once seemed to disappear. Her soul was empty and
barren. On the verge of fainting she shut her eyes and relapsed into
the darkness of a deep abyss.

'There is no God here,' a stark, shocking awareness seized her
dazed mind, 'No there isn't, there isn't . . .'

Later on, when they were seated for the holiday dinner amid the
clatter of the silverware, the old woman unobtrusively left the dining-
room, pursued by the smell of the hot, fatty pudding that she had
come to loathe. She went to her little room and stood facing the
window that looked out on the dark vacant fields and empty grey
skies. Like a prisoner at the window of his cell, she stood transfixed
in a dumb, wordless prayer to a distant invisible God across the seas
in her far-away village in Europe.

3

The dismal, rainy autumn days arrived with their long, dreary
nights. Now the old woman sensed her loneliness more keenly than

ever. The window in her room looked over a long, narrow, fenced-in yard in which the laundry was hung out to dry on clothes lines. The old woman sat near the window staring at the long lines of clothes blowing in the dull light as she pondered over her remaining days in this remote place, far from her friends, far from God, and far from mercy and compassion. At times she would fall asleep, and images and forgotten shadows of the past would gather around her. Among them she would see her tall, black-bearded husband walking erect to the water bucket in the hallway to wash his hands and then return to chant his prayers in a familiar, sad-sweet melody redolent of eternal peace.

Something new had recently been added to her son's household. Mr Robbins had purchased an automobile, and the whole family seemed to have been rejuvenated by this great event. Everyone who could learned to drive: Mr and Mrs Robbins, her two brothers who lived in the neighbourhood, Mr Robbins's business partner who made a number of visits from the city to see this spectacle for himself. Mr Robbins would walk around it with his sleeves rolled up and an oily face as he busied himself with his new source of happiness. He was like a man for whom success had opened all the well-springs of plenty, but he could not devour them all at once. One day he entered his mother's room with a triumphant smile on his face.

'I nearly killed someone with my car . . . And you, Mother dear, you probably still think that America produces nothing except blouses, women's stockings, and underwear . . . Wait till I really master the coachman's trade . . . and I'll show you what a fine country this is!'

In the evenings, young couples would arrive and sit about drinking tea and playing cards until late at night. Mrs Robbins supervised the card game, completely transformed, her face flushed with excitement, her blue eyes sparkling with an odd light, and her glasses steamed-up. When the tea was served, they would call the old woman to join them. In order to please his mother, Mr Robbins would play Jewish records on his phonograph. They would listen to recordings of Jewish comedians, wedding tunes, Jewish theatrical music, and the *Kol Nidrei* prayer.[5] The old woman would sit among

5. *Kol Nidrei* (All Vows) the prayer that ushers in the *Yom Kippur* fast day;

the company, awkward and embarrassed, listening dumbfounded to the familiar songs which came wailing out of this magic box in hoarse whispered tones. She would think of the unfortunate man who had sold his soul for gold and transformed this most sacred prayer into a ditty for a pack of scoffers.

At night she tossed restlessly on her bed. In one of her dreams she saw her townlet transformed: it was rebuilt with new houses that stretched away for miles. Looking for her home, she wandered through the long, narrow streets. There she saw her husband sitting and waiting for her, but from every side, wet laundry was billowing on the drying lines and blocked the sun from her face. As it grew dark, her daughter appeared and beckoned her mother to follow her. There, there she would find rest for her feet. She began to float in a car, shouting with all her might to her daughter to stand still for a moment, for without her she would lose her bearings among so many shirts and stockings. While she was floating, the car disappeared from under her and she fell down on a metal trunk that had been thrown outdoors, 'the trunk of books'. A hanging skull wailed behind her—it was the skull of the magician who sang *Kol Nidrei* out of a box and whose voice evoked horror as if predicting dire and ominous tidings.

She would awaken in the middle of such dreams in the dead of night and lie awake in fear. Then she would perceive with shocking clarity the awesome distance separating her from her far-away townlet. Then, too, she would feel the fear of the void which stretched before her in the twilight of her life.

One cloudy morning her smooth-shaven son came to her room and announced that his friend's father had died and that the neighbours planned a magnificent funeral. Twelve limousines had been rented. And since Mrs Robbins could not bear such occasions, he invited her to join him in his car to go to the funeral. Firstly, she would be performing a sacred duty, for the deceased was a pious Jew. It was rumoured that from the time he arrived in America he ate only bread and onions. Secondly, he would like to honour her at least once with a drive in his car. And, by the way, she would see

for an English translation see *High Holyday Prayer Book*, Birnbaum (trans.), p. 490. See, too, Agnon, *Days of Awe*, pp. 203–15.

what an American cemetery was like. 'A Jewish burial ground?' the old woman asked, astonished to find that since her arrival she had not given any thought to this most sacred matter. She had avoided the most basic facts of existence.

'They call it a *cemetery*,' her son explained. 'It's worth your while to see the monuments American Jews have erected on their graves! You'll find monuments as beautiful as houses. Without exaggeration they cost tens of thousands of dollars!'

The old woman put on her wide dress, covered her head with the black shawl and cautiously followed her son. While they were sitting in the car on the way to the funeral, Mr Robbins said to his mother, 'Don't worry, Mother! Trust me, there'll be no accidents. I've become a professional coachman, thank God!'

In front of the chapel there stood a long line of black limousines. On the wide porch and in the open hallway groups of people were chatting, laughing and smoking thick cigars. Mr Robbins greeted his friends heartily, slapping each one on the back. The old woman cringed near the door and the *mezuzah*,[6] and looked at the complacent people with self-satisfied faces who were milling about. The women were dressed as though they were going to a banquet. The deceased's son was leaning against the wall, calmly conducting a long conversation on the telephone. No tears, no sobs, no signs of mourning—a grotesque funeral!

'Hello, Marcus!'—Mr Robbins greeted the deceased's son with a slap on the back. 'Your old man is really dead, eh? I'm very sorry, on my word . . . Nevertheless, as the saying goes: may no-one die younger than he did . . . Listen, Marcus, maybe you would like a comfortable seat in a brand-new car —I'll take you and Mrs Marcus with me. The car's empty, there's only my mother and me.'

'Do you want to bury him along with his father today? Leave him alone, he's still too young,' one of the men joked and everyone burst out laughing. The deceased's son grinned and displayed his gold teeth. But then he remembered that it was improper for him to laugh and assumed a solemn expression.

The adjacent room was opened. In it stood a long wide casket wrapped in black and covered by an old faded velvet cloth with a

6. *Mezuzzah*, see page 69, note 8.

white star of David embroidered on it. A yellowish-bearded gentleman with a hard top hat that rested on his ears put his head through the door and remarked in a hoarse authoritative voice,

'Well? What are you waiting for, eh? Where's the son? Let them bring him the *tallit*, the *tallit*!'[7]

The funeral was short and hurried. The cars sped along empty streets and vacant fields, like a band of black devils pursuing the dead man who was fleeing from them. The old woman shuddered in her son's car, and looked out of the window at strange buildings, steel bridges that floated in the hazy air as if suspended over a void, and factory smokestacks pouring black soot into the fog. Then the procession passed through deserted lanes between decrepit houses, and came upon long rows of big wagons laden with coal, construction lumber, and waste paper. The cars slowed down as they drove jerkily over the cobblestones of a torn-up road. Here and there Jewish and non-Jewish monuments with bright gilt lettering stood on display. Finally they reached the bare fields, bald hills and dales, and the forlorn trees standing mournfully over their fallen leaves.

The procession stopped. The mourners left their cars and walked slowly behind the pall-bearers through an iron gate that was opened for them. Monuments with English inscriptions lined both sides of the path, which was covered with fine gravel. Here and there stood magnificent mausoleums.

'Do you see what's going on here?' Mr Robbins said to his mother, holding her hand as though he were leading her on a tour of his domain. 'Not bad at all.' A light rain began to fall and the people hurried to finish their task. Two gravediggers stood near the open grave with spades in their hands. Their shaven jaws bespoke disdain for all these odd ceremonies.

'Grab the head, Eugene!' one of them angrily called to his friend, pointing to the top of the casket with his spade.

Quickly they refilled the grave with dirt. The yellowish-bearded man with the top hat chanted the service in a harsh voice, using a tune which sounded as if it had been borrowed from *Akdamut*[8]

7. See *A Barbarian*, note 2.
8. *Akdamut* (Preludes). An acrostic poem composed by Rabbi Meir ben Isaac of the eleventh century and chanted on *Shavuot*, the spring harvest

recited on *Shavuot*. Then he faced the group which had crowded around the fresh dirt mound and shouted, 'Where's the son, *Kaddish! Kaddish!*'[9]

The rain became a downpour. Through the mist which enveloped the empty fields, the monuments looked like reminders of another world. The people rushed to their cars. Mr Robbins invited some of his acquaintances to join him and opened the door with his wet face wreathed in smiles. Again the car rattled as it travelled over the bumpy road now covered with rain. The old woman sat crouched between two strange men. She closed her eyes and fell into a deep reverie. She saw a large, black wagon laden with coal, an empty field at the edge of the horizon, strange shining monuments in the autumn rain, and felt herself alone in the blackness of a pit, cut off from God and the memories of a family that had vanished into a great abyss.

Upon returning home from the funeral, Mr Robbins invited his friends to have a snack. In honour of her guests and because of the inclement weather Mrs Robbins served a strong cherry liqueur. The guests discussed the funeral and joked about the son's inability to recite the *Kaddish*. In the middle of the conversation Mr Robbins recalled that his mother had not had time to prepare her kosher meal that morning and had now gone to her room. When he came to the door, he seemed to hear odd sounds emerging from it, almost like the sounds of an infant's crying. Mr Robbins slowly opened the door.

His mother was sitting in an odd position on the trunk of books. She was bent over, shaking her head between her hands, and moaning softly to herself. She was helpless and hopeless as a wretched young orphan, deserted by man and God.

festival. An English rendering and commentary can be found in *Daily Prayer Book*, P. Birnbaum (trans.), (New York, 1949), pp. 648–54.

9. *Kaddish* (Sanctification), a doxology composed in Aramaic. Though it contains no reference to death or the dead, one form of the *kaddish* has become the prayer recited by mourners. For a brief history of the various types of *Kaddish*, see *The Jewish Encyclopedia*, Vol. VII, pp. 402–3.

Excerpt from
Menahem Mendel in Eretz Yisrael

Letter No. 8

Menahem Mendel's meeting with his son in the Valley of Jezreel

From Menahem Mendel in the Valley of Jezreel to his wife Shayne-Sheindl in Brownsville, New York.[1]

To my dear, chaste, wise wife Mrs Shayne-Sheindl, God bless her and keep her. With greetings to all my family, may they all be blessed.

First let me inform you that, thank God, I am in good health. God grant that we hear only good tidings from each other from now to eternity—Amen.

Second, you ought to know that, as I suspected, after I arrived safely in the Emek, our son, Moshe Hershl, known here as Moshe Tzevi[2] the *halutz*, this son of mine—this barbarian, gave me such a warm welcome that I could have buried myself alive—he practically threw me out. To tell you the truth, he did throw me out, may it not be held against him; and I was just about to turn around and return to Tel-Aviv when an angel of God in the shape of a *halutzah* appeared to console me. Not only did she reconcile father and son, but she gave me the opportunity of meeting a good and pleasant young lady. I imagine all this sounds like *Targum Onkelos*,[3] and

1. Brownsville. N.Y.—a once predominantly Jewish residential section of Brooklyn, in which I. D. Berkowitz's parents lived.
2. Moshe Hershl, or Moshe Tzevi. *Hersh* in Yiddish has the Hebrew equivalent, *Tzevi*. Both mean 'deer'.
3. *Targum Onkelos*. An Aramaic translation of the Pentateuch said by some to have been translated by the proselyte Aquila. The *Targum Onkelos* is the oldest of the *Targumim*. The other two are *Targum Jonathan*, *Targum Yerushalmi*.

most probably you don't know what I'm talking about—so let me tell you the story in its proper sequence—first things first and last things last, so that you may realize that our Lord is a merciful Father, and that even wayward sons always remain sons.

In short, from my last letter you know that my partner Avraham Schwarzapple and I decided to go to the Emek to see our sons in order to beg forgiveness for our sins—he from his youngest son, and I from my eldest son. We hoped to set out at the beginning of the week, but since we were still struggling in the slough of our 'Menahem Mendeliah'[4] from which we could not easily extricate ourselves, we were delayed and couldn't leave till this morning, a Friday morning. We hoped to arrive at the kibbutz before the lighting of the Sabbath candles. We travelled with several other Jews in a Jewish bus which was so magnificent it could be run in New York—even on Fifth Avenue. But I'll never forget the road. If I attempted to describe everything I saw and felt during our four-hour trip—I couldn't. *Man's pen is powerless*—to quote our *melammed* when he was teaching us to write the holy letters in *heder*.[5] Suffice it to say that we travelled the same road that Joseph walked when he went looking for his brothers. That's where he met his downfall too, for they sold him into slavery in Egypt. That's what Avram'l Schwarzapple told me, and you can always rely on him because he is as much an expert in the geography of *Eretz Yisrael* as a Jew is in *Ashrei*.[6] He claims to have measured the length and breadth of the land, from Dan to Beer Sheba, without exaggeration, eighteen times. I sat next to the window with him and watched our bus climb up and up, zigzagging around the ancient, barren rocky mountains—as old and

4. *Menahem Mendeliah.* A term used to deride shoddy and speculative adventures of a commercial nature. It was to be a 'colony' named after Menahem Mendel.

5. *Ḥeder* (a room)—a one-room schoolhouse usually quartered in the *melammed's* home. For details see Zborowski and Herzog, *Life Is With People*, pp. 88–97.

6. *Ashrei* (Happy are those . . .)—a prayer recited three times daily and therefore very well known. It is composed of Psalm 145 and two introductory verses; Psalms 84:5 'Happy are those who dwell in thy house' (hence the title) and Psalms 144:15.

desolate as our exile. Over the peaks of those mountains hovers a strange silence and a wonderful splendour—yet it enshrines a certain sadness too, as if the Holy-One-Praised-Be-He in his majesty were looking down from the heights of his blue heavens through the great burning sun and silently mourning the destruction of his land. I began to think: 'This must be the real destruction of *Eretz Yisrael* for which we weep and lament in the *Tisha BeAv*[7] lamentations. Who would have believed that I would see it with my own eyes?' Avram'l Schwarzapple, who is sitting next to me, prods me and asks, 'Do you know what mountains you are looking at? Those are the mountains of Samaria where the ten tribes used to dwell. Have you any idea of the wealth buried in those mountains? Billions, untold treasures, all kinds of metals and minerals, as sure as it's Friday today the world over! Do you see that tall mountain with the ruined tower on top? That's where the city of Samaria once stood, when it was the capital of the Israelite kings; now nothing is left but the remains of desolate ruins where the Bedouin graze their flocks. But don't despair, it is still ours, purchased with our money: we have a cast-iron contract. Our Book of Kings explicitly states: "And he bought the hill of Samaria of Shemer for two talents of silver."[8] That is, Omri, king of Israel, purchased the mountain from a Gentile called Shemer for two bars of silver. I admit it was a bargain, dirt cheap really, for in those days, we didn't know about the plague called "speculation". But what's bought is bought. No one in the world can deny that. If only our Zionists, he says, weren't "undesirables", we could take the British to court and force them to give up: Now, you English always boast that the Bible is Holy Writ— well, if so, he says, make your choice, either/or: either return the mountain which our ancestors purchased for cash, or scratch the deed from the Bible, and then see what happens. . . .'

While we were still talking and marvelling at the desolate beauty of our sacred land, we were slowly approaching the Emek. I had thought that the Emek was just a steep narrow valley—that's the way our teacher in *ḥeder* translated it—so I was amazed when I heard

7. *Tisha BeAv* (Ninth of Av). A day-long fast commemorating the destruction of the Temple, on which various dirges are recited.

8. The reference is to I Kings 16:25.

that pioneers were able to live there. But a tremendous, spectacular expanse unfolded before our eyes, a little world of its own spreading far and wide with green, yellow, and greyish fields. It was like a multi-coloured carpet surrounded on all sides by mountain ranges gleaming in the light of heaven and dotted with dozens of Jewish settlements which sparkle amid green woods, the white houses with their red roofs shimmering in the hot sun! Our first stop was at the nice little Jewish town of Afula—which seemed, with its scattered gardens, houses, and synagogues standing in a field, to be somehow set in the middle of nowhere, as if someone had just left it at the crossroads and then gone off and forgotten about it. 'We'll return to that town, God willing. I suspect we'll find important business there,' Avram'l Schwarzapple informed me. In the meantime we were hurrying to reach our sons, for it was Sabbath Eve. Since the Tel-Aviv bus went no further, we rented a ramshackle car which sapped the last ounce of our energy but soon brought us to the *kibbutzim*.[9] First Avram'l was conveyed to the *kibbutz* of the younger *halutzim* where his son lived, and then I was delivered to the *kibbutz* of the older *halutzim*, to our Moshe Hershl. And that's where the story begins.

When I arrived at the large *kibbutz* it was already dusk. In front of me I saw a spacious yard, around which were clustered long, white houses, newly built, and stables, granaries, and silos. Here and there one could see green furrows, young saplings, and other plants. And further on, like a watchman, stood a mountain, its peak shining in the glowing sun while the evening shadows crept up its sides. In the yard, I saw peculiar people running about—Jews who looked like farmers, like peasants from our hometown. The men were wearing large straw hats with wide brims, the girls were dressed in shorts which exposed their sunburned thighs. Everyone was working: one was carrying a spade and ploughshare on his shoulder, another was bringing in a wagon-load of potatoes, a third was working on the flower beds, a fourth was just about to wash down a horse or a mule in honour of the Sabbath. So these, then, were our famous *halutzim* whom the journals are always praising! . . . I stood dumbstruck and stared at each *halutz* that passed by. My heart began to pound—

9. *Kibbutz* (plural *kibbutzim*)—a collective settlement.

perhaps this one was Moshe Hershl? Would I recognize him or not?
... Thirteen years ago when we left Kasrilevka[10] and went to
America, he insisted on going off to *Eretz Yisrael* with a group of
young friends. He was still a young lad then and had only just begun to
shave—how does he look now? I recall how he looked when I came
home for Passover and tested him on a chapter of Pentateuch and
Rashi.[11] I also recall an incident that occurred when he was an infant.
How upset I was, when you wrote in one of your letters that Moshe
Hershl had swallowed a *kopeka* and pointing to his mouth cried,
'Mommy, a "topeta", Mommy!' He was my pride and joy, the
most beloved of all my children, and I mean that sincerely. He was
always honest and forthright, he loved justice and righteousness
passionately, and he was devoted to the poor. I even admired those
sharp, biting comments he made about me when we parted—that
he would never follow in my footsteps—he would not become a
Menahem Mendel like his father!

I was standing alone with my thoughts when one of the *ḥalutzim*,
a young boy in shorts, came up to me and asked me in a very friendly
manner who it was I wanted, perhaps he could help. I told him,
'I'm looking for comrade Moshe Tzevi.' He replied, 'We have
three members with the name Moshe Tzevi; do you mean Moshe
Tzevi, Menahem's son?' Hearing this I was overjoyed and answered,
'Right you are, I'm that Menahem.' He looked at me and smiled
'Menahem Mendel?' I replied, 'Menahem Mendel!' He led me to
the silos in the far corner of the yard and pointed to a tall wagon
loaded with hay, on top of which a man was standing dressed in a
dusty shirt and busy with a huge hay-fork. He said: 'That's your
son!' I'm sure you want to know what our son said to me? May we
never come to harm any more than I could make him out! That is,
I understood him well enough and what he meant, for his remarks
pierced me to the quick, like red-hot nails. First of all, he asked me

10. Kasrilevka—The fictional village through which Sholom Aleichem
    humorously depicted the life and people of the small Jewish town in
    Eastern Europe, and which, ultimately, as explained in this letter,
    became a by-word and a slogan. See *Kitvei Sholom Aleichem*, trans. I. D.
    Berkowitz, vol. 5 (Tel-Aviv, 1956), pp. 9-223.

11. See *A Barbarian*, note 4.

bluntly, why had I come to *Eretz Yisrael*. Who invited me? Who
needed me here? . . . He has been running away from me for years
now, he doesn't want to know me, he's afraid of my shadow . . . he
says, his coming to live here was only a way to save himself and
cleanse himself of my ruinous legacy, to eradicate me from his heart
. . . all these years he has toiled here doing back-breaking work,
broiled in the sun, drenched in sweat; but he was content, he says,
to sacrifice his youth for the sake of these fields, because he felt that
with every drop of sweat he was ridding himself of another drop of
Menahem Mendel, another bit of his despised father's bequest; with
each day of physical work, he was becoming more and more cleansed,
of more benefit to the world—an honest labourer! Moreover, he
claims he purged me from his body by suffering a deadly malaria! . . .
now I come and make a mockery of all his labours. He sows and I
trample on it; he plants and I uproot, I transform everything into
'plots', and 'Menahem Mendeliahs' for easy profit—the despicable
and ugly practice of all who eat without working for it. He claims
that I am defiling the land for our children and our children's
children, bringing it into rack and ruin—total destruction!

He unleashed these remarks with hatred and in one short breath.
When he finished, he turned his back on me, and quickly walked
away and disappeared. Like a man who has been shamed and
slapped across the face, I stood there trembling. I wanted to run after
him, but my knees turned to jelly. I stumbled to the nearest tree,
buried my face, and why should I hide anything from you, my dear
wife?—I wept as bitterly as a child. I don't know what came over
me—either because my nerves were upset or because of the profound silence all around me and the mountain bathed in soft light
staring down at me with compassion—but a sort of tremor took
hold of me and gripped me by the throat. A stream of bitter tears
flowed from my eyes over my face and beard. Who knows how
long I would have stood crying in that lonely spot had I not suddenly felt a soft hand and heard a woman's voice speaking gently to
me. 'Are you Moshe Tzevi's father? . . . Please, stop crying, I beg
you. I'm Moshe Tzevi's wife . . .' I opened my eyes with difficulty
—and standing in front of me was a pretty, dark *halutzah* wearing
trousers and looking at me with a pleasant, sympathetic smile. I

never dreamed that our Moshe Tzevi had married on the *kibbutz*, for that rascal never wrote us a word. I wanted to say something, but I couldn't because the tears still choked me. Without ceremony, she placed her hand casually under my arm and said, 'Come with me. Moshe Tzevi must have been even more stupid than usual. He must have read you a sermon. You're right,' she said, 'when you refer to him in your letters as a "rascal". You can rest assured,' she said, 'that he'll get his deserts from me!' She brought me to her home—only one room—and there I found Moshe Hershl, all sad and depressed, sitting with his face in his hands. She said to him, 'Moshe Tzevi, you're a fine one! Is this how you fulfil the commandment of honouring your father—by bringing him to tears? Shame upon you!' Moshe Hershl arose, looked at me strangely with kindness and compassion like a prodigal son, and gave me his hand. I hugged him and began to cry again. Then he said to me, 'Father, you've grown old, Father!' I replied, 'Eh, that's an old story! But I'd better congratulate you and wish you *Mazal Tov.*' 'What's the *Mazal Tov* for?' 'What do you mean? You've got married.' They both burst out laughing and said, 'Now, that's an old story—over seven years already!'

In short, what shall I tell you, my dear wife? The-Holy-One-Praised-Be-He has granted us a daughter-in-law, a beautiful ḥalutzah, of whom we can be justly proud. Besides the fact that she is a lovely, charming, and intelligent young woman, she comes from a famous family of rabbis. She has only one fault—she's a Lithuanian and speaks with 'esses.'[12] However, since the common language here is Hebrew you'd never know it . . . She brought me back to life with her good sense and her kind heart. In half an hour I recovered my spirits and quickly forgot all the pain I had endured. Besides, ḥalutzim began to come out to greet me. 'Your name, Menahem Mendel,' they say, 'we've known for a long time; a whole literature has grown up round you!' 'I imagine that you ḥalutzim don't set great store by my name!' I commented. 'On the contrary,' they replied, 'you're the person who inspired us to leave the exile and come to *Eretz Yisrael* and till its land. Your image frightened us so that we had no choice . . .' Now, how do you like that for a compliment? Nevertheless, it was pleasant to hear it. What was it your mother,

12. Lithunanian Jews pronounced the 'sh' sound as 's'.

may she rest in peace, always used to say, 'You may call me half-baked as long as you give me a cake . . .!' Since I'm still very excited and it's already growing dark, I'll be brief. In my next letter, God willing, I'll write you in more detail. For the time being, may the Holy-One-Praised-Be-He grant us blessing and success in all we do. Keep well and give my regards to the children, bless them, and best wishes to everyone

From me, your husband, Menahem Mendel.

P.S. I forgot the most important fact. My dear wife, I send you a second *Mazal Tov.* Not only have we a daughter-in-law here but two grandchildren as well—a boy and a girl. The boy's name is Gideon, and he is named after the famous biblical Gideon who lived in this same Emek and judged Israel.[13] And the girl they have given another strange name, Ayelet ha-Shahar (Morning Star) taken from the Book of Psalms.[14] I suppose it's the custom here. And you should see what this Ayelet ha-Shahar'l is like! She's the elder, a dear, lovable child, full of goodness and just like her Lithuanian mother. Since the moment she heard I'm her grandfather she's clung to me and hasn't left me alone. She took me to see the rows of vegetables she had planted, which are growing under her care, may they come to no harm! Gideon, on the other hand, the younger child, is like his grandmother, that is, he looks like your family: he has red hair and a freckled face. I met him playing with the other children in a large play-pen in the corner of the yard. His tiny face was smeared and dirty, but his eyes shone with wisdom. I took out my handkerchief and said to him in my pidgin Hebrew, 'Put your nose here, Gideonchik, your nose, your nose!' But he refused, and gazing at me with his shrewd eyes, the eyes of a rascal, he said to me very calmly, 'You're no good!' That is, I'm a bad man. I replied, 'And you?' He hesitated for a minute and said with a knowing smile, 'I'm no good, either!' That means, he isn't all that pleasant either . . . What do you say to such a brilliant child? At last, we have been fortunate enough to get some pleasure out of that rascal, Moshe Hershl.

M.M.

13. See Judges 6–8.   14. See Psalms 22:1.

BIBLIOGRAPHY

Abrahams, I., *Jewish Life in the Middle Ages*, Philadelphia, 1961.

Agnon, S. J. *Days of Awe*, New York, 1948.

Arestad, S., 'Ibsen's Concept of Tragedy,' *Publication of the Modern Language Association*, vol. 74, June 1959, pp. 258–97.

Auerbach, E., *Mimesis*, trans. by W. Trask, Princeton, 1953.

Avinery, Y., *I. D. Berkowitz Oman ha-Signon*, in *Gilyonot*, vol. 18, 1945, pp. 192–3.

Avinor, G., *Yemot ha-Mashiaḥ be-Einei I. D. Berkowitz*, in *Moznayim*, vol. 11, Nov. 1960, pp. 438–41.

Baron, S. W., 'The Modern Age,' in L. W. Schwarz, ed., *Great Ages and Ideas of the Jewish People*, New York, 1956, pp. 315–484.

The Russian Jew under Tsars and Soviets, New York, 1964.

The Jewish Community, Philadelphia, 1942.

Modern Nationalism and Religion, New York, 1960.

Bates, H. E., *The Modern Short Story: A Critical Survey*, London, 1941.

Bendavid, A., *Leshon Mikra u-Leshon Ḥakhamim*, vol. 1 Tel-Aviv 1967.

Ben-Or, A., *Toledot ha-Sifrut ha-Ivrit ha-Ḥadashah*, vol. 3, Tel-Aviv, 1963.

Bentley, E., *The Playwright as Thinker*, New York, 1946.

Berkowitz, I. D., *Gesammelte Schriften* (Yiddish), Warsaw, 1910.

(trans.) *Die Letzte Masken*, a One-Act Play by Arthur Schnitzler, *Zukunft*, vol. 13, 1908, pp. 617–25.

(trans.) '*Yaldut*' a short story by Lev Tolstoy in *Kitvei L. N. Tolstoy*, Vilna, 1911, vol. I, pp. 105–107.

Sippurim, Crakow, 1910.

Sippurim, Odessa, 1918.

Sippurim, New York, 1919.

(ed.) *Mikraot Ketanot*, 1922. (includes *Mishak Purim, Mahazeh Hittulim, El ha-Dod ba-Amerika, Ha-Aharon.*)

Sippurim, Jerusalem, 1922.

Sippurim, Berlin, 1923.

Mahazot, 1928.

Aharonim: Kovetz Sippurim, Tel-Aviv, 1929.

Menahem Mendel be-Eretz Yisrael, Tel-Aviv, 1936.

Yemot ha-Mashiah, Roman, Tel-Aviv, 1937.

Ha-Rishonim Kivnei Adam. Sippurei Zikhronot al Sholom Aleichem u-Venei Doro, Tel Aviv, 1938–43 (5 vols).

Kitvei I. D. Berkowitz (revised ed.), Tel-Aviv, 1951 (10 vols.).

(ed.) *Dos Sholom Aleichem Buch*, New York 1926, 1958.

Kitvei I. D. Berkowitz (I. D. Berkowitz–Writings) vol. I, *Sippurim u-Mahazot, Menahem Mendel be-Eretz Yisrael, Mahazot* and *Yemot ha-Mashiah*, Tel-Aviv, 1959. Vol. II. *Ha-Rishonim Kivnei Adam* and *Yom Etmol*, Tel-Aviv, 1963.

Yom Etmol Ki Avar, Tel-Aviv, 1962.

Pirkei Yaldut, Tel-Aviv, 1965.

Unzere Rishonim: Zikhronos un Derzehlungen Vegen Sholom Aleichem un zein Dor, Tel-Aviv, 1966

(trans.) *Kitvei Sholom Aleichem*, revised ed. 15 vols, Tel-Aviv, 1966, *Baginen: Roman*, Tel-Aviv, 1968 (Yiddish version of *Yemot ha-Mashiah*).

Bialik, H. N., *Kol Kitvei*, Tel-Aviv, 1953.

Complete Poetic Works (I. Efros, ed.), New York, 1948.

Birnbaum, P., *Daily Prayer Book*, New York, 1949

High Holyday Prayer Book, New York, 1951.

Bogard, T. and Oliver, W. I., eds., *Modern Drama: Essays in Criticism*, New York, 1965.

Booth, W. C., *The Rhetoric of Fiction*, Chicago–London, 1961.

Brooks, C., ed., *Tragic Themes in Western Literature*, New Haven, 1955.

Brooks, C. and Warren, R. P., *Understanding Fiction*, New York, 1959.

Brown, M. G., 'All, All Alone, the Hebrew Press in America 1914–1924,' *American Jewish Historical Quarterly*, vol. 59, no. 2 Dec. 1969, pp. 139–78.

Bull, F., *Ibsen the Man and the Dramatist*, Oxford, 1959.

Chekhov, A., *Ward Six and Other Stories*, trans. by A. Dunnigan, New York, 1965.

Chinitz, N. and Nachman, Sh., eds., *Pinkas Slutzk u-Venoteihah*, New York–Tel-Aviv, 1962 (Eng. title, *Slutzk and Vicinity: Memorial Book*).

Chinitz, N., *Misihotai im I. D. Berkowitz, Hadoar*, vol. 49, 1969, no. 10, pp. 151–2; no. 17, p. 268; no. 19, p. 300; no. 24, p. 389.

Crews, F .C., 'Literature and Psychology' in J. Thorpe, ed., *Relations of Literary Study*, New York, 1967, pp. 73–87.

Daiches, D., *A Study of Literature for Readers and Critics*, New York, 1964.

Davidson, I., *Parody in Jewish Literature*, New York, 1907.

Dawidowicz, L. S., *The Golden Tradition: Jewish Life and Thought in Eastern Europe*, London 1967.

Dubnow, S. M., *History of the Jews in Russia and Poland From the Earliest Times Until the Present Day*, trans. by I. Friedlander, Philadelphia, 1916–20.

Edel, L., *The Modern Psychological Novel*, New York, 1955.

Eden, New York, 1925.

Elbogen, I., *A Century of Jewish Life*, trans. by M. Hadas, Philadelphia, 1944.

Epstein, A., *Soferim*, New York, 1935.

   I. D. Berkowitz, Bi-Devarav ha-Hadashim, in *Hadoar*, vol. 15, Dec. 27, 1935, pp. 141–3.

   Soferim Ivrim ba-Amerikah, Tel-Aviv, 1952.

Falstein, L., *The Man Who Loved to Laugh: The Story of Sholom Aleichem*, Philadelphia, 1968.

Fenson, H. and Kritzer, H., *Reading, Understanding, and Writing about Short Stories*, New York, 1966.

Fermor, U. E., *The Frontiers of Drama*, London, 1945.

Fichman, Y., *Kitvei*, Tel-Aviv, 1960.

Forster, E. M., *Aspects of the Novel*, London, 1927.

Freud, S., *On Dreams*, trans. by J. Strachey, New York, 1952.

Friedman, D. A., *I. D. Berkowitz; Sippurim*, in *Ha-Tekufah*, vol. 17, 1920, pp. 511–12.

Fromm, E., *The Art of Loving*, New York, 1956.

Frye, N., *Anatomy of Criticism*, New York, 1966.

Gartner, L., *The Jewish Immigrant in England, 1870–1914*, London, 1960.

Gil, M., *Sippurei ha-Ayarah shel I. D. Berkowitz*, in *Gilyonot*, vol. 18, 1945, pp. 186–92.

    Sholom Aleichem u-Venei Doro ba-Aspaklariah shel Berkowitz, in *Moznayim*, vol. 11, Nov. 1960, pp. 441–6.

Gilboa, Y. (Glauberman), *Ha-Ayarah be-Sippurei I. D. Berkowitz*, in *Bitzaron*, vol. 28, July, 1953, pp. 152–7.

Gore, N. C., *Tzenah U'Reenah: A Jewish Commentary on the Book of Exodus*, New York, 1965.

Greenberg, L., *The Jews in Russia*, New Haven, 1944, 1951.

Hagan, J., 'Chekhov's Fiction and the Ideal of Objectivity,' *Publication of the Modern Language Association*, vol. 81, Oct. 1966, pp. 409–17.

Halkin, S., *I. D. Berkowitz ha-Mesapper*, in *Gilyonot*, vol. 3, Sept.–Oct. 1935, pp. 368–72.

    Arai Va-Keva, New York, 1942.

    Modern Hebrew Literature: Trends and Values, First edition, New York, 1950.

    Mavo la-Sipporet ha-Ivrit (mimeographed notes compiled by S. Hillel based on Prof. Halkin's lectures, 1952), Jerusalem, 1958.

    Bein Talush li-Meḥubbar, in *Moznayim*, April–May, 1969, pp. 331–5

    Derakhim ve-Tzeddei Derakhim ha-Sifrut; Jerusalem, 1969, vol. i, pp. 211–18, vol. ii. pp. 168–83.

Ha-Olam, Vilna.

Ha-Toren, New York.

Ha-Tzofeh, Vilna.

Ha-Zeman, St Petersburg and Vilna.

Hershon, P. I., *Rabbinical Commentary on Genesis*, London 1885.

Hogan, R. and Molin, S. E., *Drama, The Major Genres*, New York, 1967.

Holtz, A., *Ha-Doktor Winik ke-Gibbor Moderni*, in *Bitzaron*, vol. 57, March–April, 1968, pp. 221–6.

Hurgin, Y., *Devarim al I. D. Berkowitz*, in *Moznayim*, vol. 25, 1956–7, pp. 207–16.

James, H., *The Art of Fiction*, New York, 1948.

Janowsky, O. I., *The American Jew: A Composite Portrait*, New York–London, 1942.

Kabak, A. A., *I. D. Berkowitz*, in *Ha-Tekufah*, vol. 29, 1936, pp. 321–326.

Kaplan, H., *The Passive Voice: An Approach to Modern Fiction*, Ohio, 1966.

Karu, B., *I. D. Berkowitz ha-Metargem*, in *Moznayim*, vol. 25, June 1967, pp. 12–15.

Katznelson, G., *Ha-Bayit ha-Shokea be-Sippurei I. D. Berkowitz*, in *Gilyonot*, vol. 30, no. 5, 1954, pp. 239–43.

Al ha-Novelah le-Berkowitz, in *Ha-Aretz*, Aug. 22, 1952, p. 5.

Keniston, K., *The Uncommitted: Alienated Youth in American Society*, New York, 1960.

Keshet, Y., *Bedor Oleh*, Tel-Aviv, 1950.

Kimhi, D., *Soferim*, Tel-Aviv, 1953.

Klausner, Y., *Historiah shel ha-Sifrut ha-Ivrit ha-Hadashah*, 6 vols., Jerusalem, 1953–8.

Komem (Kominkovski), A., *Le-Inyan ha-Realism shel I. D. Berkowitz*, in *Measef*, vol. 4, 1964, pp. 243–53.

Kremer, S., *I. D. Berkowitz be-Sippurav ha-Ketzarim*, in *Moznayim*, vol. 11, Nov. 1960, pp. 422–7.

Ha-Realism u-Shevirato, Ramat Gan, 1968.

Kressel, G., *Shetei Teudot*, in *Moznayim*, vol. 25, June 1967, pp. 20–24.

Krieger, M., *The Tragic Vision: Variations on a Theme in Literary Interpretation*, Chicago, 1966.

Lachover, F., *Toledot ha-Sifrut ha-Ivrit ha-Hadashah*, 4 vols., Tel-Aviv, 1963.

Lander, P., *Sippurav shel I. D. Berkowitz*, in *Moznayim*, vol. 21, 1946, pp. 300–2.

Leavis, F. R., *The Great Tradition*, London, 1948.

Lermontov, M., *The Demon*, trans. by R. Burness, Edinburgh, 1918 and by G. Shelley, London, 1930.

Lever, K., *The Novel and the Reader: A Primer for Critics*, New York, 1961.

Levin, J. L., *Kishron Ha-Maaseh*, Vienna, 1877.

Lisitzky, E., *Eleh Toledot Adam*, Jerusalem, 1949.

Lowenthal, W., 'Literature and Sociology,' in J. Thorpe, ed. *Relations of Literary Study*, New York, 1967, pp. 73–110.

Malachi, A. R., *Berkowitz ha-Orekh*, in *Hadoar*, vol. 15, Dec. 27, 1935, p. 144.

Meyer, M., *Henrik Ibsen, The Making of a Dramatist, 1828–1863*, London, 1967.

Meyerhoff, H., *Time in Literature*, Los Angeles, 1960.

Miklat, New York.

Mortensen, B. M. and Dorons, B. W., *Strindberg, An Introduction to his Life and Works*, Cambridge, 1965.

Niger, S. (Charney, S.), *Vegen Yiddishe Schreiber: Kritishe Artiklen* (Yiddish), Warsaw, 1913.

　I. D. Berkowitz, Sofer Du-Leshoni, in *Hadoar*, vol. 15, Dec. 27, 1935, pp. 143–4.

O'Connor, F., *The Lonely Voice: A Study of the Short Story*, New York, 1965.

O'Faolain, S., *The Short Story*, New York, 1964.

Ovadiah, M., *Me-Aharonei ha-Rishonim*, in *Moznayim*, vol. 25, June 1967, pp. 9–12.

Papirna, A. I., *Kol ha-Ketavim*, ed. by I. Zemorah, Tel-Aviv, 1952.

Patterson, D., *Hebrew Literature: The Art of the Translator*, London, 1958.

　The Hebrew Novel in Czarist Russia, Edinburgh, 1964.

　'Hebrew Drama,' *Bulletin of the John Rylands Library*, vol. 43, Sept. 1960, no. 1, pp. 88–108.

　Abraham Mapu, London, 1964.

Pearl, C., *Rashi*, New York, 1970.

Penueli, S. I., *I. D. Berkowitz*, *Moznayim*, vol. 21, 1946, pp. 298–300.

　Demuyot be-Sifruteinu ha-Hadashah, Tel-Aviv, 1946.

　Ha-Realism shel Berkowitz, *Moznayim*, vol. 11, Nov. 1960, pp. 427–30.

　Massah al ha-Yafeh she-be-Omanut ha-Sifrut, Tel-Aviv, 1964.

Persky, D., *Keddaber Ish el Reieihu*, in *Hadoar*, vol. 15, Dec. 27, 1935, pp. 140–2.

Philips, A. T., *Prayer Book for the Day of Atonement*, New York, 1931.

Rabbi, Y., *Min ha-Hekeifim el ha-Merkaz*, in *Al ha-Mishmar*, Nov. 5, 1965, pp. 5–6.

Rabin, H., *Olelot le-Toledot ha-Dramah ba-Haskalah ha-Germanit*, in *Melilah*, vol. 5, 1955, pp. 201–21.

Rabinovich, I., *Major Trends in Modern Hebrew Fiction*, trans. by M. Roston, Chicago, London, 1968, English version of *Ha-Sipporet ha-Ivrit Mehappeset Gibbor*, Tel-Aviv, 1967.

Rabinowitz, S. J. (Sholom Aleichem), *Alle Verk fun Sholom Aleichem*, New York, 1923.

Raisin, J. S., *The Haskalah Movement in Russia*, Philadelphia, 1913.

Revusky, A., *Jews in Palestine*, New York, 1945.

Ribalow, M., *I. D. Berkowitz bi-Melot lo Hamishim Shanah*, in *Hadoar*, vol. 15, Dec. 27, 1935, pp. 137–9 included in *Soferim ve-Ishim*, New York, 1936.

Roth, C., *The Jews in the Renaissance*, Philadelphia, 1959.

Ruppin, A., *Ha-Sotziologia shel ha-Yehudim*, Tel-Aviv, 1931. (English version as follows).

The Jews in the Modern World, London, 1934.

Sachar, H. M., *The Course of Modern Jewish History*, New York, 1958.

Samuel, M., *The World of Sholom Aleichem*, New York, 1943.

Sdan, D., *Avnei Bohan*, Tel-Aviv, 1951.

Seger, Z., *Ha-Hevrah ha-Yehudit be-Sippurei I. D. Berkowitz*, in *Niv ha-Kevutzot*, Oct. 1964, pp. 636–51.

Shaanan, A., *Ha-Sifrut ha-Ivrit li-Zerameihah*, 4 vols., Tel-Aviv, 1962–7.

Shaked, G., *Ha-Telishut ha-Hadashah*, in *Moznayim*, vol. 11, 1960, pp. 431–8.

Al Arbaah Sippurim, Jerusalem, 1963.

Motiv Yom ha-Kippurim be-Sippur: Al Sheloshah Sippurim u-Mahazeh shel I. D. Berkowitz, in *Mahanayim*, Rosh Hashanah, 1961, pp. 130–5.

Oto ve-et Beno shel I. D. Berkowitz u-Massoret ha-Mahazeh ha-Realisti, in *Yerushalayim*, vol. 2, 1966, pp. 197–210, included in: *Al Sheloshah Mahazot: Perakim bisodot ha-Mahazeh*, Jerusalem, 1968, pp. 11–40.

Shaked, M., *Al Shenei Sippurim shel I. D. Berkowitz*, Jerusalem, 1969.

Sholom Aleichem. See Rabinowitz, S. J.

Shestov, L., *Chekhov and Other Essays*, Ann Arbor, 1966.

Shinn, R. L., *The Existentialist Posture*, New York, 1959.

Shipley, J. T., *Dictionary of World Literature*, London, 1945.

Shtreit, S., *Penei ha-Sifrut*, Tel-Aviv, 1939.

Simmons, J. E., *Introduction to Russian Realism*, Bloomington, 1965.

Slonim, M., *Modern Russian Literature: From Chekhov to the Present*, New York, 1953.

Sommo, L. J., *Tzaḥut Bediḥutah de-Kiddushin*, 2nd ed. Jerusalem, 1965.

Szajkowski, Z., 'How the Mass Migration to America Began,' in *Jewish Social Studies*, vol. 4, no. 4, Oct. 1942, pp. 291–310.

Thorpe, J., ed., *Relations of Literary Study: Essays on Interdisciplinary Contributions*, New York, 1967.

Toren, H., *Sholom Aleichem ve-I. D. Berkowitz*, in *Moznayim*, vol. 19, 1945, pp. 56–9.

Trask, G., and Burkhart, C., eds., *Storytellers and their Art*, New York, 1963.

Turov, N., *Roeh ve-Eino Nireh*, in *Hadoar*, vol. 15, Dec. 27, 1935, pp. 140–1.

Tversky, Y., *I. D. Berkowitz ve-Sifruteinu ba-Amerikah*, in *Moznayim*, vol. 11, Nov. 1960, pp. 446–7.

Ungerfeld, M., *I. D. Berkowitz*, in *Gazit*, vol. 8, March–April 1940, pp. 53–6.

Bein H. N. Bialik le-vein I. D. Berkowitz, in *Moznayim*, vol. 25, June 1967, pp. 15–20.

Valency, M., *The Flower and the Castle*, New York, 1963.

The Breaking String: The Plays of Anton Chekhov, New York, 1966.

Van Ghent, D., *The English Novel: Form and Function*, New York, 1953.

Waxman, M., *A History of Jewish Literature*, 5 vols., New York, 1936–61.

Waife-Goldberg, M., *My Father Sholom Aleichem*, New York, 1968.

Wellek, R. and Warren, A., *Theory of Literature*, London, 1961.

Wellek, R., *Concepts of Criticism*, New Haven, 1963.

Wilson, E., *Axel's Castle*, New York, 1931.

Yaari, A., *Ha-Maḥazeh ha-Ivri*, Jerusalem, 1956.

Yaffe, A. B. *Bein Shetei Reshuyot*, in *Moznayim*, vol. 25,

Yardeni, G., *Tet-Zayin Siḥot im Soferim*, Tel.-Aviv, 1965.

Zborowski, M. and Herzog, E., *Life Is With People*, New York, 1952.

BIBLIOGRAPHICAL NOTE

There is, to date, no critical edition of Berkowitz's works containing the various versions which so many of his short stories and novellas went through. However, the following table attempts to indicate to the student where the various versions of Berkowitz's short stories are to be found. In a few instances the author has been unable to trace the original place and date of publication of a story. Where this is the case, a blank has been left.

Even a cursory comparison of the 1951 edition with the earlier works shows that no work was spared a thorough revision. Sometimes the revision was very considerable and affected the overall structure of a story. On other occasions the revision was not so complete. In every case, however, the language of the 1951 edition shows the attempts Berkowitz made to modernize his early works in the light of the developments of contemporary Hebrew—for example the original Russian slang was replaced by contemporary Hebrew expressions.

Title in 1951 edition [translated title as used in this volume]	Original date and place of publication	Page no. in Cracow: Fisher edition (1910)	Page no. in New York Kadimah edition (1919)	Page no. in Tel Aviv edition (1959)
Be-Erev Yom ha-Kippurim. (Yom Kippur Eve)	*Ha-Tzofeh*, I, Sept. 1903, no. 216: pp. 921-2. Completely re-written for the 1951, 1959 editions.			5-9
Mishael	Originally appeared as 'Yeḥiel' in *Ha-Tzofeh*, I, Sept. 1903, no. 223, pp. 958-9.	as 'Mishael' 142-8		10-13

Title in 1951 edition [translated title as used in this volume]	Original date and place of publication	Page no. in Cracow: Fisher edition (1910)	Page no. in New York Kadimah edition (1919)	Page no. in Tel Aviv edition (1959)
Malkot (Lashes)	Ha-Tzofeh, I, Oct., 1903, no. 241, pp. 1035-6	178–183		14–17
*Baal Simḥa (A Proud Father)	Ha-Tzofeh, I, Nov. 1903, no. 251, pp. 1077–8, no. 252 p. 1081. [Totally revised for the 1951 edition etc.]		56–68	18–21
Ben Zakhar (A Male Child)	Ha-Shiloaḥ, XIII, Jan. 1904, pp. 112–20. [Sequence of events and the entire structure of the story radically revised for 1951 ed.]	154–64		22–8
Lifnei-ha-Shulḥan (At the Table)	Ha-Tzofeh, II, March, 1904, no. 354, pp. 229–30 [Considerably expanded for 1910 ed. and revised further for 1951 ed.]	149–153		29–30
Be-Yad ha-Lashon (The Power of Speech)	Ha-Tzofeh, II, Sept. 1904, no. 497, pp. 843–4. [Chief character's name is changed from Peṣah Zalman to Bentzil for 1951 ed. Major stylistic revision]	190–4		31–3

Title in 1951 edition [translated title as used in this volume]	Original date and place of publication	Page no. in Cracow: Fisher edition (1910)	Page no. in New York Kadimah edition (1919)	Page no. in Tel Aviv edition (1959)
Ushpizin (Guests)	Appeared as 'Eliose' in *Ha-Tzofeh*, II, Sept., 1904, no. 511, pp. 915–16. [Radically revised and expanded for 1951 ed.]	Appeared as 'Koaḥ ha-Dimyon': 184–9		34–36
*Talush (Severed)	*Ha-Shiloaḥ*, XIII–XIV, 1904, pp. 209–21 (erroneously not listed in index to this volume). [Minor revisions for 1910 ed., basic alteration for 1951 ed.]	1–18		37–45
*Pere Adam (A Barbarian)	*Ha-Shiloaḥ*, XV, 1905, pp. 29–37. [Stylistic revision for 1951 ed.]	131–41		46–50
Maftir (Maftir)	*Ha-Tzofeh*, II, Oct. 1904, no. 527, pp. 983–4. [Changed slightly for 1910 ed: considerable stylistic revision for 1951 ed.]	195–9		51–3
Pega Ra (A Plague)	Appeared in Yiddish as 'Der Mushlam' in *Die Zukunft* XIII, 1908, pp. 294–300.	169–77		54–8

Title in 1951 edition [translated title as used in this volume]	Original date and place of publication	Page no. in Cracow: Fisher edition (1910)	Page no. in New York Kadimah edition (1919)	Page no. in Tel Aviv edition (1959)
Pega Ra (A Plague)—contd.	The Yiddish version has the protagonist's name as Perelmutter. In the 1910 ed. his name is Leifmanovitz, in the 1951 ed. his name is Schainin. In each edition there are slight stylistic changes.			
Nekhed (Grandchild)		112–21		59–63
Mariashka (Mariashka)		Entitled 'Bikhfar' 19–35		64–72
Banekhar (In a Foreign Place)		87–96		73–8
Melafefonim (Cucumbers)	Appeared first as 'Yerakot' in Ha-Olam, III, 1909, Feb. 9th, pp. 2–4 Feb. 24th, pp. 2–4, March 17th, pp. 2–4, April 2nd, pp. 3–4, June 29th, pp. 3–4, July 13th, pp. 2–6, August 24th, pp. 2–4, August 31st, pp. 2–4. This is the basic text for the 1910 ed.	Entitled 'Yerakot' pp. 45–78		79–93

Title in 1951 edition [translated title as used in this volume]	Original date and place of publication	Page no. in Cracow: Fisher edition (1910)	Page no. in New York Kadimah edition (1919)	Page no. in Tel Aviv edition (1959)
Melafefonim (Cucumbers) —contd.	The 1951 ed. was revised considerably.			
Viddui (Confession)	Appeared first in Yiddish in Die Zukunft, XIII, 1908, pp. 49–54. [Same text as the 1910 ed. The 1951 ed. considerably revised.]	79–86		94–8
Moshkele Ḥazir (Moshkele Pig)	Ha-Tzofeh, II, Jan. 1904, no. 297, pp. 1293–5. [Major changes in 1951 ed.]	122–30		99–104
Pelitim (Refugees)	First appeared in Yiddish as 'In Hekdesh' in Die Zukunft, XIII, 1908 pp. 357–62. [Basically, the same text as 1951 ed.]			105–9
Ruḥot Raot (Evil Spirits)	The basic elements of this story can be found in 'Im Ha-Aviv', Ha-Tzofeh II April, 1904, nos 386 and 387, pp. 373 and 377. In its present form it first appeared as 'Nidaḥim'.		as 'Nidaḥim' 71–108	110–18

Title in 1951 edition [translated title as used in this volume]	Original date and place of publication	Page no. in Cracow: Fisher edition (1910)	Page no. in New York Kadimah edition (1919)	Page no. in Tel Aviv edition (1959)
Ruḥot Raot (Evil Spirits) —contd.	Ha-Toren, IV, 38, Dec. 7th, 1917, pp. 7–8; 39, Dec. 14th, 1917, pp. 10–11; 42, Jan. 4th, 1918, pp. 5–6; 43, Jan. 11th, 1918, pp. 9–11; 44, Jan. 18th, 1918, pp. 6–7; 45, Jan. 25th, 1918, pp. 5–7.			
*Yom ha-Din Shel Faivke (Faivke's Judgement Day)	First appeared as 'Benei-Khefar' in Ha-Olam, V, 1911, Oct. 26th, pp. 7–9, Nov. 5th, pp. 9–11, Nov. 13th, pp. 7–9. This is the basic text for the 1919 ed. Many revisions for the 1951 ed. The name of the village in 1919 ed. is Koslov in the 1951 ed. Starodubov.		as Benei-Khefar pp. 23–32	119–25
Klei-Zemer (Minstrels)	First appeared as 'Shakhne Pandra' in Ha-Toren, New York, IV, 1917, May 11th, pp. 12–14, May 18th, pp. 8–10,			126–30

Title in 1951 edition [translated title as used in this volume]	Original date and place of publication	Page no. in Cracow: Fisher edition (1910)	Page no. in New York Kadimah edition (1919)	Page no. in Tel Aviv edition (1959)
Klei-Zemer (Minstrels) —contd.	May 25th, pp. 10–11. [The 1951 ed. has slight changes.]			
Ha-Mikhtav (The Letter)	Ha-Toren, IV, 1917, July 13th, pp. 11–13, July 20th, pp. 9–11. [The 1951 ed. has a few minor revisions.]			131–4
Klei-Zekhukhit (Glass)	Ha-Olam (weekly), IV, March 17th, 1910, no. 9, pp. 19–22. [This is the basic text for 1910 ed. and 1951 ed.]		7–20	135–7
Mi-Merḥakim (From Distant Lands)	Luaḥ Aḥiasaf, 1904 vol. XII (no page nos). [Slightly revised for 1910 ed. and major revision for 1951 ed.]	36–44		138–43
Yarok (Green-horn)	Ha-Am, I, 1908 (New York) Appeared as Ha-yerukim vehatzehubim: mimonologei Sander Hatzartuni.	Appeared as 'Me-Ever la-Okianus: Yarok' 105–11. Minor revisions		144–6

Title in 1951 edition [translated title as used in this volume]	Original date and place of publication	Page no. in Cracow: Fisher edition (1910)	Page no. in New York Kadimah edition (1919)	Page no. in Tel Aviv edition (1959)
Shetar Ra-Mazzal (An Unlucky Bill)				147–9
Oreah mi-Koslov (A Guest from Koslov)	Ha-Toren, III, May 5th, 1916, pp. 8–11; May 12th pp. 6–9. [Very slight revisions for 1951 ed.]			150–6
Ezrah (Citizen)	Ha-Toren, III, March 10th, 1916, pp. 7–9. [Changed slightly for 1951 ed.]			157–9
Kol-Bo (Jack of All Trades)				160–1
Doktor le-Philosofia				162–3
*Karet (Twilight)	Miklat (New York), I, 1919, pp. 114–25. [Slight changes for 1951 ed.]			164–9
Yemot ha-Mashiah (Messianic Days)	Ha-Toren, IV, April 20th, 1917, pp. 6–8: May 4th, 1917, pp. 8–10. [Minor syntactical changes for 1951 ed.]			170–4
El ha-Dod ba-Amerikah (To an Uncle in America)	Mikraot Ketanot, IV, 1922. [Slight revisions for 1951 ed.]			175–7

Title in 1951 edition [translated title as used in this volume]	Original date and place of publication	Page no. in Cracow: Fisher edition (1910)	Page no. in New York Kadimah edition (1919)	Page no. in Tel Aviv edition (1959)
Be-Veit ha-Ḥolim Shel Bubot (In the Dolls' Hospital)	*Eden*, II, 1925, no. 1, pp. 6–10. (Very slight revision for 1951 ed.)			178–80
Amerika Olah le-Eretz Yisrael (America comes to Eretz Yisrael)				181–98
Ha-Nehag (The Chauffeur)	*Moznayim*, I, March 15th, 1929, pp. 5–9. [Several changes in the 1951 ed.]			199–209
Baal Akhsaniah be-Tel-Aviv (An Innkeeper in Tel-Aviv)	*Moznayim*, II, May 21st, 1921, pp. 3–5. [Slight changes for the 1951 ed.]			204–6
Ha-Senuniot ha-Rishonot (The First Swallows)				207–9
Ha-Aḥaron (The Last)	*Mikraot Ketanot*, 1922, vol. 8. [Slight variations for 1951 ed.]			210–14

NEVER INCLUDED IN A COLLECTION OF HIS WORKS

Title	Original date and place of publication	Page no. in Cracow: Fisher edition (1910)	Page no. in New York Kadimah edition (1919)	Page no. in Tel Aviv edition (1959)
Baal Melakhah (Artisan)	*Ha-Tzofeh*, I, Dec. 1903, no. 279, p. 2.			

Title in 1951 edition [translated title as used in this volume]	Original date and place of publication	Page no. in Cracow: Fisher edition (1910)	Page no. in New York Kadimah edition (1919)	Page no. in Tel Aviv edition (1959)
Sekhar Limmud (Tuition)	*Ha-Tzofeh*, II, April, 1904, no. 368, pp. 297–8.			
Im ha-Aviv (With the Spring)	*Ha-Tzofeh*, II, April, 1904, nos 386, 7, pp. 373, 377.			
Mi-Tokh Kaas (Out of Anger)	*Ha-Tzofeh*, II, May, 1904 (Literary Supplement to no. 405—pagination unclear)			
Yishuv Eretz Yisrael (The Settlement of Eretz Yisrael)	*Ha-Tzofeh*, II, July, 1904, no. 457, p. 681 (The 1910 ed. included a story 'Nedavot' based on this)			
Im Shemesh (With the Sun)	*Ha-Toren*, III, 1917, no. 9, pp. 15–16.			
Al Kiddush ha-Ḥayyim (On the Sanctification of Life)	*Ha-Toren*, IV, 1917, 20, July 27, pp. 8–9; 21, Aug. 3, pp. 10–11; 22, Aug. 10, pp. 7–8; 23, Aug. 17th, pp. 7–9; 26, Sept. 17th, pp. 10–12; 27, Sept. 14th, pp. 10–11.			

Title in 1951 edition [translated title as used in this volume]	Original date and place of publication	Page no. in Cracow: Fisher edition (1910)	Page no. in New York Kadimah edition (1919)	Page no. in Tel Aviv edition (1959)
Orḥei-Laylah (Night Visitors)	*Ha-Toren*, V, Feb. 21, 1919, pp. 7–8; Feb. 28, 1919, pp. 7–8; March 7th, 1919, pp. 8–9.			
Ba-Aratzot ha-Reḥokot (In Distant Lands)	*Ha-Toren*, VI, 1920, 6, pp. 449–67			

INCLUDED IN 1910 EDITION BUT NOT IN 1951 EDITION

Eretz Moladeti (My Birth-place)		97–104		
Nedavot (Contributions)		165–8		

*Works translated in this volume

BERKOWITZ IN ENGLISH

The translations included in Part Two were prepared by the author of this volume exclusively for this series. The following is a list of I. D. Berkowitz's works previously available in English translation, based on Y. Goell, *Bibliography of Modern Hebrew Literature in English Translation* (Jerusalem. 1968), p. 63, nos. 1972–86.

1. *Contributions*, tr.: Yisrael Ben Ari. (In: *World Jewry: Universal Press Review*, v. 2 no. 84, Dec. 13, 1935, pp. 20–1.)

2. *Country Folk*, tr.: Helena Frank. (In: Frank, H., ed., *Yiddish Tales* ([Philadelphia, The Jewish Publication Society of America, 1912], pp. 533–65.) Translated from the Yiddish version.

3. *Glass* (In: *Reflex*, v. 1, no. 4, Oct. 1927, pp. 18–22. Also in: *The Canadian Jewish Chronicle*, v. 20, no. 23, Oct. 21, 1932, pp. 6, 15. Also in: Schwarz, L. W., ed., *A Golden Treasury of Jewish Literature* [New York, Farrar & Rinehart, 1937], pp. 254–60.)

4. *The Greenhorn* (In: *The American Jewish Chronicle*, v. 2, no. 9, Mar. 16, 1917, pp. 591–3). Translated from the Yiddish version.

5. *The Heart of a Chauffeur*, tr.: Tamara Kahana. (In: *Commentary*, v. 15, no. 2, Feb., 1953, pp. 159–65.)

6. *Landsleit* (In Bessie F. White, *Nine One-Act Plays from the Yiddish* [Boston, 1932], pp. 141–72.)

7. *The Last of Them*, tr.: Helena Frank. (In: Frank, H., ed., *Yiddish Tales*, pp. 566–77.) Translated from the Yiddish version.

8. *The Last One*, tr.: Curt Leviant. (In: *The Jewish Spectator*, v. 27, no. 5, May, 1962, pp. 17–19.)

9. *The Last One*, tr.: Tamara Kahana. (In: Penueli, S. Y. and Ukhmani, A., ed., *Hebrew Short Stories* [Tel-Aviv, Institute for the Translation of Hebrew Literature & Megiddo Pub. Co., 1965], v. 1, pp. 192–9.)

10. *The Last Rabbi*, tr.: I. Reuven. (In: *The Jewish Standard*, v. 7, no. 2, Feb., 1936, pp. 5, 10, 14.)

11. *The Letter*, tr.: Samuel P. Rudens. (In: *East and West* [New York], v. 1, no. 10, Jan., 1916, pp. 297–300.) Translated from the Yiddish version. (Also in: *Reflex*, v. 3, no. 3, Sept. 1928, pp. 75–80. Also in: *The Canadian Jewish Chronicle*, v. 20, no. 19, Sept. 23, 1932, pp. 7–8, 16.)

12. *Menahem Mendel Helps to Build the Homeland.* (In: *The South African Menorah*, v. 17, no. 5, May, 1944, pp. 9, 18; v. 17, no. 6, June, 1944, pp. 17–18. Also in: *Binyan*, v. 5, no. 6, Dec. 1947, p. 11. Also in: *Furrows*, v. 6, no. 2, Feb. 1948 pp. 26–9.)

13. *The Outcast*, tr.: I. Reuven. (In: *The Jewish Standard*, v. 7, no. 4, April 1936, pp. 5, 33–8, 42.)

14. *Press and Literature in New York*, tr.: Tamara Kahana. (In *Israel Argosy*, no. 6, 1958, pp. 139–60.) An extract from *Ha-Rishonim Kivnei Adam*.

15. *Purim Play*, tr.: Tamara Kahana. (In: Haezrahi, Y. ed., *Presenting Purim*, (Jerusalem, 1950), pp. 50–9.)

16. *The Road to Jerusalem*, tr.: I. M. Lask. (In: *Palestine Review*, v. 2, 1937–8, p. 852.) An extract from Yemot ha-Mashiah.

17. *Sabbath in Tel Aviv.* (In *New Palestine*, v. 18, no. 9 March 7, 1930, pp. 143–5.) Extract from *Yom Etmol*.

18. *Severed*, tr.: Tamara Kahana. (In *Israel Argosy*, no. 4, 1956, pp. 59–79.)

19. *Sholom Aleichem as the People's Editor.* (In *The Canadian Jewish Chronicle*, v. 18, no. 43, March 13, 1931, pp. 417.)

20. *Thursday with Peretz.* (In *The Canadian Jewish Chronicle*, v. 18, no. 42, March 6, 1931, pp. 4, 23.)

21. *To Uncle in America*, tr.: Tamara Battavi. (In: *The B'nei Brit Magazine*, v. 44, no. 9, June 1930, pp. 363–5. Also in: *The Canadian Jewish Chronicle*, v. 18, no. 7, July 4, 1930, pp. 13, 16.)

22. *The Uncle in America*, tr.: T. W.–R. (Trude Weiss Rosmarin). (In: *The Jewish Spectator*, v. 17, no. 10, Nov. 1952, pp. 22–4.)

INDEX

The works of I. D. Berkowitz discussed or quoted in the text are printed here in small capitals. For a fuller list of his writings see the tables on pages 224–34

History of Jewish Literature (Wax-
man), 17 n. 6
History of the Jews (Graetz), 89
Holocaust, the European, 3 n. 3, 26
Ḥumash (Pentateuch), 162 n. 4

Ibsen, 37, 40
Israel Government Prize, 26
Israel, State of, 3 n. 2
IN A FOREIGN PLACE, 10 n. 16, 12
n. 20, 52, 57, 86, 88, 227
IN DISTANT LANDS, 41–3, 47, 48, 59,
230
INNKEEPER IN TEL-AVIV, AN, 92, 97,
232

Jacob b. Ḥabib of Zamora, 142 n. 13
Jerusalem, B. in, 100–1

Ka-Tzetnik, 26
Kaddish, 207 n. 9
Kahana, Tamara, 54 n. 5, 92 n. 2
KARET see TWILIGHT
Katznelson, Yitzhak, 18
Keniston, Kenneth, 51
Kevurat Ḥamor (A Donkey's Burial),
89, 160 n. 1
kibbutzim, 101
Kiev, 7
Kishinev pogrom, 5
Kishron ha-Maaseh (Levin), 66
Klausner, J., 18
KLEI-ZEMER see MINSTRELS
Koren, Pesah, 16
Krylov, 89

Lachover, P., 32 n. 10
Lament, The (Chekhov), 17
LASHES, 9, 18, 72, 225
Lermontov, 17 n. 5, 89, 136 n. 9

LETTER, THE, 55, 79
Letze Masken (Final Masks), 17 n. 5
Levin, J. L., 66 n. 3
Levin, Dr Shemarya, 24
Levinsky, A. L., 18
LIFNEI HA-SHULḤAN see AT THE TABLE
Linetzky, Yitzhak Yoel, 37
Lithuania, 7
Little Shimon (Sholom Aleichem), 28
Litvak, B., pseudonym of B, 19
Lodz, 17
London, B.'s visit to, 21

MAFTIR, 58, 72, 86 n. 5, 226
Maimonides, 89
Makhpelah, Cave of, 100
MALE CHILD, A, 5, 86 n. 5, 225
MALKOT see LASHES
Mapu, 16
MARIASHKA, 56, 58, 61, 96, 227
Marx, 89
Maskilim, 54
Meir ben Isaac, Rabbi, 206 n. 8
MELAFEFONIM see CUCUMBERS
Melamed, Dr S. M., 24
melammed, 9, 15, 165 n. 6
MENAHEM MENDEL IN ERETZ YISRAEL,
13, 25, 92, 101–5, 208–15
Mendele Mokher Seforim, 20, 37,
65, 86 n. 7
Meshiah's Zeiten, 25
Messianic Days, 3 n. 1, 25, 106–19,
231
MI NAVI VE-YEDA see WHO CAN FORE-
TELL
Migrations of Jews, 4–5
Mikraot Ketanot, 24
MINSTRELS, 55, 75 n. 15, 79, 229–30
MIRAH, 41, 45–7, 48
MISHAEL, 17, 18, 70, 79